The Art of Public Speaking

TWELFTH EDITION

Stephen E. Lucas
University of Wisconsin—Madison

CST 100
Principles of Public Speaking
Special Edition for Thomas Nelson Community College
Compiled by the Thomas Nelson Community College
Communication Department

McGraw Hill Education

McGraw Hill Education

1 2 3 4 5 6 7 8 9 0 QVS QVS 17 16 15 14

ISBN-13: 978-1-30-850639-5
ISBN-10: 1-30-850639-2

Learning Solutions Consultant: Valerie Walo
Project Manager: Jenny Bartell
Cover Photo Credits: Public Speaking_front_cmyk2.tif © Photodisc/PunchStock

Brief Contents

Contents

Selected Materials from **Introducing Communication Theory Analysis and Application**, Fifth Edition, by Richard West, Lynn H. Turner

Selected Materials from **The Art of Public Speaking**, Twelfth Edition, by Stephen E. Lucas

VARIETIES OF PUBLIC SPEAKING

Chapter 5 Speaking to Inform 82

Selected Materials from **Read, Reason, Write An Argument Text And Reader**, Eleventh Edition, by Dorothy U. Seyler

Chapter 6 UNDERSTANDING THE BASICS OF ARGUMENT 104

Selected Materials from **The Art of Public Speaking**, Twelfth Edition, by Stephen E. Lucas

VARIETIES OF PUBLIC SPEAKING

Chapter 8 **Methods of Persuasion** 158

Selected Materials from **Between One and Many The Art and Science of Public Speaking**, Seventh Edition, by Steven R. Brydon, Michael D. Scott

Chapter 9 Speaking Beyond the Classroom 187

Selected Materials from **The Art of Public Speaking**, Twelfth Edition, by Stephen E. Lucas

PRESENTING THE SPEECH

Appendix Speeches for Analysis and Discussion A1

CHAPTER 1

The *Rhetoric*

Based on the writings of ***Aristotle***

Camille Ramirez

Camille Ramirez knew that she would have to take a public speaking course for her major. Although she had been active in high school—serving as treasurer for the student council and playing on the lacrosse team—she had never done any public speaking. Now that she was in her second semester, she wanted to get the required course out of the way, so she had enrolled in Public Speaking 101.

The class seemed to be going quite well. She felt fairly confident about her speaking abilities; she had received two As and one B on her speeches so far. The final speech, however, would be her most challenging. It was a persuasive speech, and she decided that she would speak on the dangers of drinking and driving. The topic was a personal one for Camille because she would talk about her Uncle Jake, a wonderful man who had died last year in an accident with a drunk driver. As she prepared for the speech, she thought that she would blend both emotion and logic into her presentation. Camille also thought that she would have to identify both sides of the drinking issue—the desire to let loose and the need to be responsible.

On the day of her speech, Camille took several deep breaths before the class started; it was a strategy that had worked before her previous speeches. As she approached the lectern, she could feel the butterflies well up in her stomach. She reminded herself about the topic and its personal meaning. So, as planned, she began with a short story about her favorite time with Uncle Jake—the time they went to Philadelphia to see the Liberty Bell. Camille then talked about the night—two weeks after her trip—that her uncle died; he was driving home from his daughter's soccer game, and a drunk driver slammed his car from behind, forcing Jake to the embankment. His car then slid into a pond where he drowned.

The room was silent as Camille finished the story. She proceeded to identify why she was speaking on the topic. She told the group that considering their classroom was filled with people under the age of 25, it was important that they understand how fragile life is. Her words resonated with the group. For the next five minutes, Camille mentioned her Uncle Jake several times as she repeated the importance of not drinking and getting behind the wheel of a car.

Camille felt relieved as she finished her speech. She thought that she had done a decent job with her assignment, and she also felt that it helped her to be able to talk about her uncle again. After class, several of Camille's classmates came up and congratulated her. Many of them posted words of sympathy on her Facebook page. They told her that it took a lot of guts to talk about such a personal subject in front of so many people. A few of them also commented that they felt her topic was perfect for the audience; in fact, one of her classmates said that he wanted Camille to give the same speech to his fraternity brothers. As Camille walked to her dorm, she couldn't help but think that she had made a difference and that the speech was both a personal and a professional success.

Contemporary life provides us scores of opportunities to speak in front of others. Politicians, spiritual leaders, physicians, custodian supervisors, and investment brokers are examplars of the types of people who spend much of their time speaking to others—in both formal and informal ways. Especially as members of the academy, and whether by choice or by accident, we find ourselves speaking in the classroom, in our organizations, with our professors, on our dorm floors, among many other locations.

Studying public speaking and communication in general is important in U.S. society for several reasons. First, for over a decade now, the National Association of Colleges and Employers (naceweb.org/so12082010/college_skills/) has identified "communication skills" as paramount to securing and maintaining a job. Second, public speaking, by definition, suggests that as a society we are receptive to listening to views of others, even views that may conflict with our own. Deliberation and debate in the United States are hallmarks of a democracy (West, 2012). Third, when one speaks before a group, the information resonates beyond that group of people. For instance, when a politician speaks to a small group of constituents in southwest Missouri, what she says frequently gets told and retold to others. When a minister consoles his congregation after a fatal shooting at a local middle school, the words reverberate even into the living rooms of those who were not present at the service. Finally, effective communication is identified as paramount in communication among individuals from various parts of the globe (Holliday, 2013); it is not just a topic that resonates solely in the United States. Clearly, effective public speaking has the ability to affect individuals beyond the listening audience, and it is a critical skill for us as citizens of a democratic society.

Despite the importance of public speaking in our lives, it remains a dreaded activity. In fact, some opinion polls state that people fear public speaking more than they fear death! Comedian Jerry Seinfeld reflects on this dilemma: "According to most studies, people's number one fear is public speaking. Number two is death. Death is number two. Does that seem right? This means to the average person, if you have to go to a funeral, you're better off in the casket than doing the eulogy" (youtube.com/watch?v=kL7fTLjFzAg).

Public speaking is not so funny to people like Camille Ramirez. She must work through not only her anxiety about speaking before a group, but also her anxiety about discussing a very personal topic. For Camille, having a sense of what to speak about and what strategies to adopt are foremost in her mind. Based on her classmates' reactions, her speech remains effective. Camille may not know that the reasons for her success may lie in the writings of Aristotle, published more than 25 centuries ago.

Aristotle is generally credited with explaining the dynamics of public speaking. *The Rhetoric* consists of three books: one primarily concerned with public speakers, the second focusing on the audience, and the third attending to the speech itself. His *Rhetoric* is considered by historians, philosophers, and communication experts to be one of the most influential pieces of writing in the Western world. In addition, many still consider Aristotle's works to be the most significant writing on speech preparation and speech making. In a sense, Aristotle was the first to provide the "how to" for public speaking. Lane

> ***Theory at a Glance*** • *The* Rhetoric
>
> Rhetorical Theory centers on the notion of rhetoric, which Aristotle calls the available means of persuasion. That is, a speaker who is interested in persuading his or her audience should consider three rhetorical proofs: logic (logos), emotion (pathos), and ethics/credibility (ethos). Audiences are key to effective persuasiveness, and rhetorical syllogisms, requiring audiences to supply missing pieces of a speech, are used in persuasion.

Cooper (1932) agrees. More than 80 years ago, Cooper observed that "the rhetoric of Aristotle is a practical psychology, and the most helpful book extant for writers of prose and for speakers of every sort" (p. vi). According to Cooper, people in all walks of life—attorneys, legislators, clergy, teachers, and media writers—can benefit in some way when they read Aristotle's writings. That is some accolade for a man who has been dead for over 2,500 years!

To understand the power behind Aristotle's words, it's important first to understand the nature of the *Rhetoric*. In doing so, we will be able to present the simple eloquence of rhetorical theory. First, in order for you to understand the historical context of the theory, we present a brief history of life in Aristotle's day followed by a discussion of his definition of rhetoric.

The Rhetorical Tradition

The son of a physician, Aristotle was encouraged to be a thinker about the world around him. He went to study with his mentor, Plato, at the age of 17. Aristotle and Plato had conflicting worldviews; therefore, their philosophies differed as well. Plato was always in search of absolute truths about the world. He didn't care much whether these truths had practical value. Plato felt that as long as people could agree on matters of importance, society would survive. Aristotle, however, was more interested in dealing with the here and now. He wasn't as interested in achieving absolute truth as he was in attaining a logical, realistic, and rational view of society. In other words, we could argue that Aristotle was much more grounded than Plato, trying to understand the various types of people in Athenian society.

Because he taught diverse groups of people in Greek society, Aristotle became known as a man committed to helping the ordinary citizen—at the time, a land-owning male. During the day, common citizens (men) were asked to judge murder trials, oversee city boundaries, travel as emissaries, and defend their property against would-be land collectors (Golden, Berquist, Coleman, & Sproule, 2011). Because there were no professional attorneys at that time, many citizens hired **Sophists**, teachers of public speaking, to instruct them in basic principles of persuasion. These teachers established small schools where they

Sophists
teachers of public speaking (rhetoric) in ancient Greece

taught students about the public speaking process and where they produced public speaking handbooks discussing practical ways to become more effective public speakers. Aristotle, however, believed that many of these handbooks were problematic in that they focused on the judicial system to the neglect of other contexts. Also, he thought that authors spent too much time on ways to arouse judges and juries: "It is not right to pervert the judge by moving him to anger or envy or pity—one might as well warp a carpenter's rule before using it," Aristotle observes (cited in Rhys & Bywater, 1954, p. 20). Aristotle reminds speakers not to forget the importance of logic in their presentations.

The *Rhetoric* could be considered Aristotle's way of responding to the problems he saw in these handbooks. Although he challenges a number of prevailing assumptions about what constitutes an effective presentation, what remains especially important is Aristotle's definition of rhetoric: the available means of persuasion. For Aristotle, however, availing oneself of all means of persuasion does not translate into bribery or torture, common practices in ancient Greece, where slavery was institutionalized. What Aristotle envisions and recommends is for speakers to work beyond their first instincts when they want to persuade others. They need to consider all aspects of speech making, including their audience members. When Camille prepared for her speech by assessing both her words and her audience's needs, she was adhering to Aristotle's suggestions for successful speaking.

For some of you, interpreting rhetoric in this way may be unfamiliar. After all, the word has been tossed around by so many different types of people that it may have lost Aristotle's original intent. For instance, Jasper Neel (1994) comments that "the term *rhetoric* has taken on such warm and cuddly connotations in the postmodern era" (p. 15) that we tend to forget that its meaning is very specific. For people like Neel, we must return to Aristotle's interpretation of rhetoric or we will miss the essence of his theory. Politicians often indict their opponents by stating that their "rhetoric is empty" or that they're all "rhetoric, with little action." These sorts of criticisms only trivialize the active and dynamic process of rhetoric and its role in the public speaking process. Indeed, rhetoric is an "art of using language" (Cuddon, 2013, p. 606) and therefore, simply because someone talks or chats aimlessly does not mean that person is using rhetorical discourse. Consider this important caveat as you review this chapter.

Assumptions of the *Rhetoric*

To this end, let's examine two primary assumptions of Rhetorical Theory as proposed by Aristotle. You should be aware that Rhetorical Theory covers a wide range of thinking in the communication field, and so it is nearly impossible to capture all of the beliefs associated with the theory. Nonetheless, Aristotelian theory is guided by the following two assumptions:

- Effective public speakers must consider their audience.
- Effective public speakers employ a number of proofs in their presentations.

The first assumption underscores the interpretation of communication that we presented in Chapter 1: Communication is a transactional process. Within a public speaking context, Aristotle suggests that the speaker–audience relationship must be acknowledged and even primary in the speaking process. Speakers should not construct or deliver their speeches without considering their audiences. Speakers need to be audience centered. They should think about the audience as a group of individuals with motivations, decisions, and choices and not as some undifferentiated mass of homogeneous people. The effectiveness of Camille's speech on drinking and driving derived from her ability to understand her audience. She knew that students, primarily under the age of 25, rarely think about death, and, therefore, her speech prompted them to think about something that they normally would not consider. Camille, like many other public speakers, engaged in **audience analysis**, which is the process of evaluating an audience and its background (e.g., age, sex, educational level, etc.) and tailoring one's speech so that listeners respond as the speaker hopes they will.

audience analysis
an assessment and evaluation of listeners

Aristotle believed that audiences are crucial to a speaker's ultimate effectiveness. He observes, "Of the three elements in speech-making—speaker, subject, and person addressed—it is the last one, the hearer, that determines the speech's end and object" (rhetoric.eserver.org/aristotle/rhet1-3.html). Each listener, however, is unique, and what works with one listener may fail with another. Expanding on this notion, Carnes Lord (1994) observes that audiences are not always open to rational argument. Consider Camille's speech on drinking and driving. Her speech may have worked wonderfully in the public speaking classroom, but she might have different results with a group of alcohol distributors. As you can see, understanding the audience is critical before a speaker begins constructing his or her speech.

The second assumption underlying Aristotle's theory pertains to what speakers do in their speech preparation and their speech making. Aristotle's proofs refer to the means of persuasion, and, for Aristotle, three proofs exist: ethos, pathos, and logos. **Ethos** refers to the perceived character, intelligence, and goodwill of a speaker as they become revealed through his or her speech. Eugene Ryan (1984) notes that ethos is a broad term that refers to the mutual influence that speakers and listeners have on each other. Ryan contends that Aristotle believed that the speaker can be influenced by the audience in much the same way that audiences can be influenced by the speaker. Interviewing Kenneth Andersen, a communication ethicist, Pat Arneson (2007) relates Andersen's thoughts about Aristotle and ethos. Ethos, according to Andersen, is "something you create on the occasion" (p. 131). To that end, a speaker's ethos is not simply something that is brought into a speaking experience; it is the speaking experience. Melissa Waresh (2012) contends that ethos must necessarily take into consideration the relationship between speaker and audience. She states: "Ethos is character. Character implicates trust. Trust is based on relationship. Relationship persuades" (p. 229).

ethos
the perceived character, intelligence, and goodwill of a speaker

Aristotle felt that a speech by a trustworthy individual was more persuasive than a speech by an individual whose trust was in question. Michael Hyde

(2004) contends that Aristotle felt that ethos is part of the virtue of another and, therefore, "can be trained and made habitual" (p. xvi). **Logos** is the logical proof that speakers employ—their arguments and rationalizations. For Aristotle, logos involves using a number of practices, including using logical claims and clear language. To speak in poetic phrases results in a lack of clarity and naturalness. **Pathos** pertains to the emotions that are drawn out of listeners. Aristotle argues that listeners become the instruments of proof when emotion is stirred in them; listeners judge differently when they are influenced by joy, pain, hatred, or fear. Let's return to our example of Camille to illustrate these three Aristotelian proofs.

logos
logical proof; the use of arguments and evidence in a speech

pathos
emotional proof; emotions drawn from audience members

The ethos that Camille evokes during her presentation is important. Relating a personal account of her relationship with her Uncle Jake and describing his subsequent death at the hands of a drunk driver bolster perceptions of her credibility. Undoubtedly, her audience feels that she is a credible speaker by virtue of her relationship with Jake and her knowledge of the consequences of drinking and driving. Logos is evident in Camille's speech when she decides to logically argue that although drinking is a part of recreation, mixing it with driving can be deadly. Using examples to support her claims underscores Camille's use of logical proof. The pathos inherent in the speech should be apparent from the subject matter. She chooses a topic that appeals to her college listeners. They most likely will feel for Camille and reflect on how many times they or their friends have gotten behind the wheel after having a few drinks. The proofs of Aristotelian theory, therefore, guide Camille's effectiveness.

Each of these three—ethos, logos, and pathos—is critical to speech effectiveness. But each, alone, may not be sufficient. Keep in mind Kenneth Burke's belief that according to Aristotle, "an audience's confidence in the speaker is the most convincing proof of all" (Burke, 2007, p. 335).

For Aristotle, logos is much more than offering evidence in a speech. He delineates this proof in more detail in his writings. In his discussion, he notes that speakers who consider logos must necessarily consider syllogisms. We now turn our attention to this critical Aristotelian principle.

Syllogisms: A Three-Tiered Argument

We noted that logos is one of the three proofs that, according to Aristotle, create a more effective message. Nestled in these logical proofs is something called syllogisms. The term requires clarification because there is some debate among scholars on its precise meaning.

Communication scholars have studied the *Rhetoric* and its meaning for years and have attempted to untangle some of Aristotle's words. We look here at the term syllogism, defined as a set of propositions that are related to one another and draw a conclusion from the major and minor premises. Typically, syllogisms contain two premises and a conclusion. A **syllogism** is nothing more than a deductive argument, a group of statements (premises) that lead to

syllogism
a set of propositions that are related to one another and draw a conclusion from the major and minor premises

another group of statements (conclusions). In other words, premises are starting points or beginners used by speakers. They establish justification for a conclusion. In a syllogism, both major and minor premises exist. Symbolically, a syllogism looks like this:

$$A \rightarrow B$$

$$B \rightarrow C$$

$$\text{Therefore, } A \rightarrow C$$

Consider this classic example of a syllogism:

Major Premise:	All people are mortal.
Minor Premise:	Aristotle is a person.
Conclusion:	Therefore, Aristotle is mortal.

Let's use the beginning story about Camille and construct a syllogism that she might employ in her speech:

Major Premise:	Drunk driving can kill people.
Minor Premise:	College students drink and drive.
Conclusion:	Therefore, college students can kill others (by drinking and driving).

As a speaker, you might (unwittingly) incorporate syllogisms to persuade your audience. However, in an often complex and convoluted society, drawing such a clear conclusion from preliminary premises may not be appropriate. Syllogistic reasoning may undercut a point you're making. For example, it is usually difficult to draw a clear conclusion when dealing with the behaviors of close friends or family members. Personality, relational history, and timing all intersect to make drawing a simple conclusion quite difficult. Further, syllogistic reasoning is, like many issues in this book, impacted by culture. Audience members do not always share a speaker's logical progression of ideas. Therefore, speakers need to be cautious in expecting audience members to draw conclusions in similar ways.

Syllogisms are a critical part of the speaking process for Aristotle. Speakers use them to enhance effectiveness in their speeches. In addition, speakers also incorporate other techniques that are labeled *canons*.

Canons of *Rhetoric*

Aristotle was convinced that, for a persuasive speech to be effective, speakers must follow certain guidelines or principles, which he called *canons*. These are recommendations for making a speech more compelling. Classical rhetoricians have maintained Aristotle's observations, and to this day, most writers of public speaking texts in communication follow canons for effective speaking that early Greeks and Romans advocated.

Table 18.1 Aristotle's Canons of *Rhetoric*

CANON	DEFINITION	DESCRIPTION
Invention	Integration of reasoning and arguments in speech	Using logic and evidence in speech makes a speech more powerful and more persuasive.
Arrangement	Organization of speech	Maintaining a speech structure—Introduction, Body, Conclusion—bolsters speaker credibility, enhances persuasiveness, and reduces listener frustration.
Style	Use of language in speech	Incorporating style ensures that a speech is memorable and that a speaker's ideas are clarified.
Delivery	Presentation of speech	Delivering an effective speech complements a speaker's words and helps to reduce speaker anxiety.
Memory	Storing information in speaker's mind	Knowing what to say and when to say it eases speaker anxiety and allows a speaker to respond to unanticipated events.

Although his writings in the *Rhetoric* focused on persuasion, these canons have been applied in a number of speaking situations. Five prescriptions for effective oratory exist and we now discuss these canons, which are highlighted in Table 18.1.

Invention

The first canon is invention. This term can be confusing because invention of a speech does not mean invention in a scientific sense. **Invention** is defined as the construction or development of an argument that is relevant to the purpose of a speech. Invention is discovering all the proofs a speaker plans to use. Invention is broadly interpreted as the body of information and knowledge that a speaker brings to the speaking situation. This stockpile of information can help a speaker in his or her persuasive approaches.

invention
a canon of rhetoric that pertains to the construction or development of an argument related to a particular speech

Suppose, for instance, you are presenting a speech on DNA testing. Invention associated with this speech would include appeals woven throughout your speech (e.g., "DNA helps living organisms pass along information to their offspring," "DNA is the fundamental blueprint for all life," or "DNA testing has proven to be instrumental in capturing rapists"). In constructing your arguments, you may draw on all these examples.

Aids to invention are identified as topics. **Topics,** in this sense, refer to the lines of argument or modes of reasoning a speaker uses in a speech. Speakers may draw on these invention aids as they decide which speaking strategy

topics
an aid to invention that refers to the arguments a speaker uses

will persuade their audiences. Topics, therefore, help speakers enhance their persuasiveness.

civic spaces
a metaphor suggesting that speakers have "locations" where the opportunity to persuade others exists

Speakers look to what are called **civic spaces**, or the metaphorical locations where rhetoric has the opportunity to effect change, "where a speaker can look for 'available means of persuasion'" (Kennedy, 1991, p. 45). Recall, for instance, Camille's decision to talk about drinking and driving in her public speaking class. As she speaks, she defines her terms, looks at opposing arguments, and considers ideas similar to her own. That is, she identifies a "location" in her speech where she is able to adapt to an audience that may be losing attention. Camille does whatever it takes to ensure that she has the chance to persuade her audience.

Arrangement

arrangement
a canon of rhetoric that pertains to a speaker's ability to organize a speech

A second canon identified by Aristotle is called arrangement. **Arrangement** pertains to a speaker's ability to organize a speech. Aristotle felt that speakers should seek out organizational patterns for their speeches to enhance the speech's effectiveness. Artistic unity among different thoughts should be foremost in a speaker's mind. Simplicity should also be a priority because Aristotle believed that there are essentially two parts to a speech: stating the subject and finding the proof, or what he calls "demonstrating it" (Kennedy, 1991, p. 258). At the time, he felt that speakers were organizing their speeches haphazardly, making them less-effective speakers.

introduction
part of an organizational strategy in a speech that includes gaining the audience's attention, connecting with the audience, and providing an overview of the speaker's purpose

Aristotle, however, is very clear in his organizational strategy. Speeches should generally follow a threefold approach: introduction, body, and conclusion. The **introduction** should first gain the audience's attention, then suggest a connection with the audience, and finally provide an overview of the speech's purpose.

Introductions can be quite effective in speeches that are intended to arouse emotionally. Gaining attention by incorporating emotional wording is an effective persuasive technique. Consider Camille's introductory words. She obviously captures the audience's attention by personalizing a very difficult subject. She then suggests her relationship with the topic, followed by an overview of her speaking purpose:

> Jake McCain was killed by someone he didn't know. Jake was a wonderful man and the person who killed him never knew that. Yet, Jake's death could have been prevented. You see, he was killed by someone who was drunk. The driver may have a future, but Jake will never have a chance to see his grandchild grow up or see his sister get married. I know about Jake McCain: He's my uncle. Today, I wish to discuss the dangers of drunk driving and identify how you can avoid becoming one of the many thousands who get behind a wheel after drinking too much.

body
part of an organizational strategy in a speech that includes arguments, examples, and important details to make a point

Arrangement also includes the body and conclusion of the speech. The **body** includes all of the arguments, supporting details, and necessary examples to make a point. In addition to the entire speech being organized, the body of the speech also follows some sort of organizational structure. Aristotle states that audiences need to be led from one point to another.

Finally, the **conclusion** or epilogue of a speech is aimed at summarizing the speaker's points and arousing emotions in the audience. Conclusions should be arrived at logically and should also attempt to reconnect with listeners. Camille's conclusion clearly demonstrates her desire to leave her listeners with a message:

> So I leave you today after examining the prevalence of drunk driving, the current laws associated with this behavior, and what you and I can personally do to help rid our society of this terrible and overlooked part of being a college student. The next time you go and have a drink, don't forget to give your keys to a friend. Or get a cab. I'm sure your family will thank you. Do it for me. Do it for my Uncle Jake.

We can feel Camille's passion for a topic that is both personal and personally difficult.

conclusion
part of an organizational strategy in a speech that is aimed at summarizing a speaker's main points and arousing emotions in an audience

Style

The use of language to express ideas in a certain manner is called **style**. In his discussion of style, Aristotle includes word choice, word imagery, and word appropriateness. He believes that each type of rhetoric has its own style, yet style is often overlooked. He notes that strange words or **glosses** (e.g., antiquated words and phrases, such as "colored person" or "girl Friday") should be avoided. Speaking in terms that are too simplistic will also turn off an audience. To bridge this gap between the unfamiliar and the too familiar, Aristotle introduces the notion of **metaphor**, or a figure of speech that helps to make the unclear more understandable. Metaphors are critical devices to employ in speeches, according to Aristotle, because they have the capacity to change the perceptions and the minds of listeners (Moran, 1996).

Style can be better understood through an example from Camille's speech on drunk driving. If Camille were concentrating on style, her speech would have the following passage:

> Drinking is often viewed as a means to release. After a very long day at work or at school, there may be nothing better than having a cold beer. So they say. Yet, too often, one beer turns into two, which by the end of a few hours, has turned into a six-pack. And the result can be tragic: How many times have you watched your friend or family member get into a car after a six-pack? This person can be as dangerous as a bullet, unleashed from a gun that is randomly pointed at someone. If you must drink, it's not only your business; but, it's my business, too.

Camille's words evoke some strong imagery; mentally, we can recreate the scene that she has laid out. Her word choice is unmistakable in that she uses familiar words. Finally, she uses the compelling metaphor of a bullet.

style
a canon of rhetoric that includes the use of language to express ideas in a speech

glosses
outdated words in a speech

metaphor
a figure of speech that helps to make the unclear more understandable

Memory

Storing invention, arrangement, and style in a speaker's mind is **memory**. In contrast to the previous four canons, Aristotle does not spend significant time delineating the importance of memory in speech presentation. Rather, he alludes

memory
a canon of rhetoric that refers to a speaker's effort in storing information for a speech

Theory in Popular Press • *Excellent Public Speeches*

Writer Helen Coster tackles, in *Forbes* magazine (a business-anchored publication), one of the most ubiquitous of all topics in the corporate world: How to prepare and deliver public speeches. Coster begins her essay by invoking commencement speakers and their ability to present messages that engage audiences. She presents some simple, but important, recommendations that adhere to Aristotle's thinking. In particular, Coster notes: "Forget fancy PowerPoint presentations and loads of data. Instead, keep your speech simple, with a clear beginning, middle and end." Further, in what amounts to a clear nod to Aristotle's speaking values, Coster states: "Be relevant to your audience." Indeed, audience analysis is identified as critical to being an effective public speaker. The essayist encourages speakers to use stories and to be atune to one's body language as both can convey credibility, one of the principle proofs of Aristotle. In sum, Coster encourages public speakers to "try to enjoy the experience."

Source: Coster, H. (2010, August 16). How to give a great speech, forbes.com/2010/08/16/public-speaking-speeches-communication-leadership-careers-advice.html.

to memory in his writings. Throughout the *Rhetoric*, for instance, Aristotle reminds us to consider a number of issues prior to the presentation (e.g., examples, signs, metaphors, delivery techniques, etc.). He further notes that to speak persuasively, a speaker has to have a basic understanding of many of these devices when constructing and presenting a speech. In other words, speakers need to have memorized a great deal before getting up to speak.

Today, people interpret memory in speech-making differently from Aristotle. Memorizing a speech often means having a basic understanding of material and techniques. Although other rhetoricians like Quintilian made specific recommendations on memorizing, Aristotle felt that familiarizing oneself with the speech's content was understood. When Camille presents her speech on drinking and driving, for example, she has some parts of her speech committed to memory and other parts overviewed on notes.

Student Voices

Vlad

I know that I'm probably oversimplifying a great theory, but a lot of the *Rhetoric* is something that I remember from my public speaking class. I was always told to keep my speeches organized and to persuade people by getting to them emotionally. I did my persuasive speech on organ donation because my sister was waiting for a kidney. I know my delivery was pretty smooth because I believed in what I was saying. That probably also improved my ethos.

Delivery

Thus far we have concentrated on how a speech is constructed. Aristotle, however, was also interested in how a speech is delivered. In this case, **delivery** refers to the nonverbal presentation of a speaker's ideas. Delivery normally includes a host of behaviors, including eye contact, vocal cues, pronunciation, enunciation, dialect, body movement, and physical appearance. For Aristotle, delivery specifically pertains to the manipulation of the voice. He especially encouraged speakers to use appropriate levels of pitch, rhythm, volume, and emotion. He believed that the way in which something is said affects its intelligibility.

delivery
a canon of rhetoric that refers to the nonverbal presentation of a speaker's ideas

Aristotle believed that delivery could not be easily taught, yet it is crucial for a speaker to consider. He also taught that speakers should strive to be natural in their delivery. Speakers should not use any vocal techniques that may detract from the words and should strive to capture a comfortable presence in front of an audience. In other words, speakers should avoid being "gimmicky" in their presentations and strive for authenticity.

The canons of rhetoric are incorporated into a number of different persuasive speeches. Our exploration of Aristotle's Rhetorical Theory concludes with a discussion of the three types of rhetoric.

Types of Rhetoric

You will recall that during Aristotle's time citizens were asked to take part in a number of speaking activities—from judge to attorney to legislator. It was in this spirit that Aristotle identified different speaking situations for citizens to consider when conversing on trade, finance, national defense, and war. He denoted three types of rhetoric, or what he called three types of oratory: forensic, epideictic, and deliberative. **Forensic rhetoric** pertains to establishing a fact; at the core of forensic rhetoric is justice. **Epideictic rhetoric** is discourse related to praise or blame. **Deliberative rhetoric** concerns speakers who must determine a course of action—something should or should not be done. The three types refer to three different time periods: forensic to the past, epideictic to the present, and deliberative to the future. We discuss these three rhetorical types next and illustrate them in Figure 18.1.

forensic rhetoric
a type of rhetoric that pertains to speakers prompting feelings of guilt or innocence from an audience

epideictic rhetoric
a type of rhetoric that pertains to praising or blaming

deliberative rhetoric
a type of rhetoric that determines an audience's course of action

Forensic oratory, or judicial rhetoric, specifically refers to speaking in courtrooms. Its intent is to establish guilt or innocence; in Aristotle's day, forensic speakers directed their presentation to courtroom judges. Aristotle examined forensic rhetoric within a legal framework, and thus many of his beliefs on the law are found in the *Rhetoric*. Amelie Rorty (1996) notes that forensic speaking requires focusing on arguments that tap into judges' psyches, including their beliefs about why certain criminals act the way they do and which types of circumstances tempt people to break the law. Because past actions are frequently indicative of a person's current behavior, forensics orators rely on previous behaviors.

Aristotle recognized that a person's character is critical in forensic rhetoric. He interprets character as both status (i.e., whether a person is young or old, rich

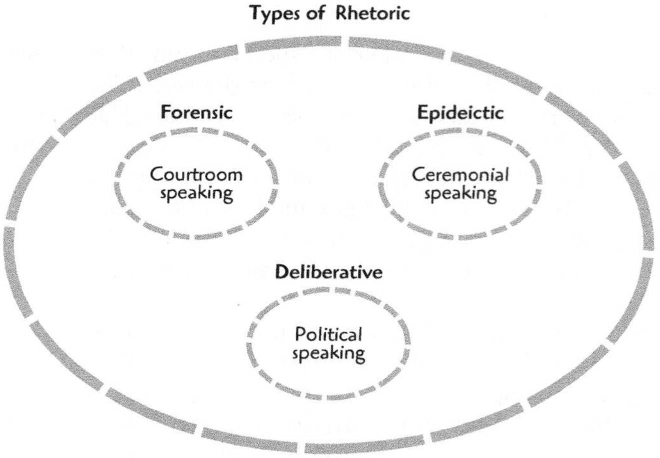

Figure 18.1
Types of Rhetoric

or poor, fortunate or unfortunate) and morality (i.e., whether a person is just or unjust, reasonable or unreasonable). If people act voluntarily, Aristotle argued, the choices they make have consequences. To establish guilt, the forensic speaker needs to establish motivation for doing wrong. In speaking before an audience, then, speakers will invoke what Aristotle called the "moral habits" of a person.

Examples of forensic rhetoric abound in our society. Forensic speakers have played prominent roles in U.S. courtrooms. Attorneys, in particular, have effectively and persuasively used their forensic rhetoric over the years. One of the most memorable forensic presentations in history took place in the closely watched trial of football legend O. J. Simpson. Prosecutors tried to implicate Simpson's morals by playing a tape recording of a 911 call in which Simpson could be heard yelling at his wife and by showing pictures of her beaten body to the jury. More recent forensic efforts by prosecutors include the legal proceedings of corruption charges by former Illinois governor, Rod Blagojevich, the Bernie Madoff investment scandal, and the trial of home décor guru Martha Stewart, who was found guilty of lying to government agents about stock trading. In all these cases, forensic speaking was used to undercut the moral integrity of the defendant and to establish guilt (Stewart, 2012).

The second type of rhetoric, epideictic, is also called ceremonial speaking. Speeches during Aristotle's time were given in public arenas with the goal of praising, honoring, blaming, or shaming. Epideictic rhetors include people, events, organizations, or nations in their speeches. These speeches usually focus on social issues because, according to Aristotle, people are interested in the here and now. Epideictic speaking cannot be separated from ethos, Aristotle stated. He believed that by understanding the need to praise or blame, epideictic speakers understand the importance of their own character. For instance, a speech criticizing prison conditions may not resonate deeply with an audience if the speaker is on death row for rape and murder.

At times, there are speeches that simply are generic in nature and yet, the target of blame is implied. In 2012, for instance, the Sandy Hook Elementary

School killings of more than 20 school children and staff resulted in many epideictic speeches about the need for stricter gun laws and the lax oversight of semiautomatic weapons. While many speeches did not name the National Rifle Association by name, it was clear that many speakers were blaming this organization for its influence on restricting gun legislation.

Epideictic speaking is greatly informed by the study of virtues or values—a theme that Aristotle borrowed from Plato. The epideictic speaker must be able to relate the virtues of the topic to a diverse audience. Aristotle felt that courage and justice ranked above all virtues, but virtue is defined according to the law of the land.

Epideictic rhetoric is exemplified in funeral practices in our country. Eulogies, which are commonplace at many funerals, usually laud the life of the deceased. Commenting on contemporary values, the epideictic speaker at a funeral frequently compares the virtues of the dead person with those of society. For instance, after the death of his grandmother, one of your authors was asked to give the eulogy at the funeral. During his speech, he talked about his grandmother's uplifting spirit and how she rarely complained about her ailments or about her financial situation. He evoked images of contemporary society in his speech, noting how unusual it is today for someone to refrain from self-centered complaining. His speech centered on a prevailing virtue of his grandmother—her selflessness—and also commented on society as a whole.

The third type is deliberative rhetoric, also called political rhetoric, and it was the focus of much of Aristotle's comments on rhetorical discourse. As we mentioned earlier, deliberative rhetoric is associated with the future—what an audience will do or think as a result of a speaker's efforts. Deliberative speaking, then, requires the speaker to be adept at understanding how his or her thoughts are aligned with those of the audience. The deliberative speaker should be prepared to consider subjects that are relevant to the audience and to which the speaker can personally relate. Aristotle identified five subjects on which people deliberated in his day: revenue, war and peace, the defense of the country, commerce, and legislation (san.beck.org/EC22-Aristotle.html). Today's list of deliberative topics might include health insurance, taxes, relationships, education, and civil rights. Deliberative speakers might try to raise interest in these topics, and once interest is piqued, they might find that listeners are more prone to being persuaded.

Larry Arnhart (1981) comments that the deliberative rhetorician needs to know not only the actual subject of deliberation but also the elements of human nature that influence deliberation. There are a number of topics, therefore, which are suited for deliberation and others that are not. Aristotle focused on what deliberative speakers can say to an assembly (a body of legislators, for example), and today this deliberative oratory continues. Consider the following example. When asked to give a short presentation to her state's legislative committee on health insurance, Beverly, a 64-year-old mother of four, spoke about the health insurance of elderly people. As the caretaker of her 90-year-old mother-in-law, a patient in a local nursing home, Beverly knew precisely the kinds of persuasive strategies to use with the group of politicians. Her speech focused on the difficulties of being old and how these problems are amplified by not having enough insurance. She asked the legislators to consider their own aging parents in their discussions. She outlined five points of action for the committee to follow. Three of the points could be undertaken immediately: establishing a task force, interviewing elderly citizens, and setting up a toll-free number to solicit citizen concerns and complaints. The remaining two required funding from the legislature. At the conclusion of her brief speech, Beverly was satisfied that her suggestions would not be ignored.

Aristotle would have approved of Beverly's rhetoric. Her recommendations were doable (the committee enacted three of the five), and she made her experiences relevant to her audience by asking the group to think about their own parents. This approach elicited personal identification, which is an important tactic in deliberative speaking. By eliciting these feelings, Beverly knew that she would be able to get her audience to agree with her thinking.

Integration, Critique, and Closing

Aristotle's *Rhetoric* remains an influential theoretical foundation in communication studies. You can pick up any public speaking text and find discussions on delivery, organization, and style. Students of public speaking have benefited greatly from the words and values of Aristotle, and for this reason the theory will resonate deeply for years to come. The evaluative criteria for communication we wish to discuss center on three primary areas: logical consistency, heurism, and test of time.

Integration

Communication Tradition	**Rhetorical** | Semiotic | Phenomenological | Cybernetic | Socio-Psychological | Socio-Cultural | Critical
Communication Context	Intrapersonal | Interpersonal | Small Group | Organizational | **Public/Rhetorical** | Mass/Media | Cultural
Approach to Knowing	Positivistic/Empirical | **Interpretive/Hermeneutic** | **Critical**

Critique

Evaluation Criteria	Scope | **Logical Consistency** | Parsimony | Utility | Testability | **Heurism** | **Test of Time**

Logical Consistency

Critics of Aristotle's theory have taken issue with some tenets of the theory. For instance, Aristotle has been criticized for contradiction and incoherence. Charles Marsh (2006), for instance, reports on one critic who undercut the notion of ethos as proposed by Aristotle: "In a society so small, where everyone knew one another, how could [Aristotle] think—was he really that dumb—that a person of bad character could hoodwink the other leaders of society?" (p. 339). Lord (1994) contends that in developing his theory, Aristotle blasts his contemporaries for focusing too much on the audience's emotions. Although Aristotle encourages speakers to avoid focusing on emotions while making their points, he proceeds to do just that when he stresses the importance of presenting emotions and invoking audience passions (pathos) during a speech. This makes the theory somewhat inconsistent.

John Cooper (1996) challenges Lord's critique. He argues that Aristotle was simply responding to the Sophists' messages of the day. Because most of the speeches in ancient Greece were directed to judges and rulers, Aristotle indicated that speakers should try to elicit feelings of pity in the courtroom. To do that, Aristotle felt that speakers should try to view judges in congenial ways.

Further criticism of the logical consistency of the theory has been offered. First, scholars agree that the *Rhetoric* is a rather unorganized undertaking; in fact, the theory is assembled from Aristotle's lecture notes (Neel, 2013). It is not surprising, then, that Aristotle seems to discuss topics in a random and arbitrary manner. At times, Aristotle introduces a topic and then drops it, only to return to it later. His terminology is especially problematic for some scholars. You may not find this too earth-shattering, but recall that researchers need clear foundations of terms before they can embark upon testing or clarifying theory. Larry Arnhart (1991) concludes that Aristotle defined his terms in less than precise ways so that audiences (readers) would have a broader understanding of his words and ideas. Arnhart believes that this conscious decision to remain unclear does not mean that Aristotle's thoughts should be discarded.

Finally, the logical consistency is further challenged by an examination of how Aristotle views the audience. Critics charge Aristotle with ignoring the critical nature of listeners. For instance, Jasper Neel (1994) states, "Aristotle makes clear that the introduction [of a speech] has nothing to do with the 'speech itself.' It exists only because of the hearer's weak-minded tendency to listen to what is beside the point" (p. 156). Eugene Ryan (1984) is more blunt: "Aristotle is thinking of listeners who have some difficulty keeping their minds on the speaker's business, are easily distracted, tend to forget what has gone on before, [and] are not absorbed with abstract ideas" (p. 47). From these writers, we get the impression that Aristotle perceived audiences to be incapable of being discriminating listeners or critical thinkers. It's important to note, though, that Aristotle was writing at a time when people were rather passive listeners; they did not watch the evening news and did not have access to information about world events. Furthermore, when one considers that the *Rhetoric* is based on lecture notes and that students back then were not accustomed to openly challenging their mentors, Aristotle's view of the audience is not so implausible.

Heurism

Few would argue that Aristotle's *Rhetoric* is one of the most heuristic theories found in communication. Scholars in political science, medicine, English

Student Voices

Ned

When I gave my first speech in public speaking, I was pretty amazed that the three proofs of Aristotle worked so well. I gave my speech on physician-assisted suicide. My aunt wanted her doctor to help her commit suicide, and my whole family was against it. I was, too. So I was trying to persuade the class that we should never allow this to happen anywhere. I had credibility because it was right in my family (ethos), I used emotion and caused emotion in my speech (pathos), and I offered some statistics on how many people try to get their doctors to help in suicides (logos). I had a lot of students come up to me after the speech and tell me how effective my speech was. And all of that was thanks to Aristotle!

composition, and philosophy have studied Rhetorical Theory and incorporated Aristotelian thinking in their research. The theory has spawned a number of subareas in the communication discipline, such as communication apprehension, and has generated research. In fact, much of the writing in public speaking is based on the writings of Aristotle. Some interesting research has discussed the deliberative rhetoric of an African American activist (McClish, 2007). Much of the discussion related to preaching in churches can be directly attributed to Aristotle's thinking (Broadus, 2012). Aristotelian proofs have been employed to student umbilical cord blood banking (White, 2006), and in the analyses of environmental reports (Higgins & Walker, 2012). Aristotle's theory will continue to resonate with scholars across disciplines and in a variety of contexts.

Test of Time

No other theory in the communication discipline has withstood the test of time as well as Aristotle's *Rhetoric*. With more than 2,000 years behind it and public speaking textbooks, teachers, and researchers communicating Aristotelian principles, it's hard to believe that any other theory in the field of communication will ever achieve such longevity!

As the twenty-first-century continues, we are in an informed position to reflect on some of the greatest written works of all time. The *Rhetoric* is clearly such a work. Aristotle's words continue to resonate in a society that is far different from his day. Some people may reject his thoughts as outdated in an age in which multiple ways of knowing are embraced. Particularly given the technology that pervades nearly every culture across the globe, Aristotle's theory may be viewed by some as irrelevant. Still, a theory focusing on how speakers use and engender emotions, logic, and trustworthiness cannot be ignored. And, it's fair to say that despite Facebook, Skype, or other technologies, public speaking will continue to be instrumental across cultures.

Discussion Starters

TECH QUEST: Aristotle never could envision social media as he was discussing public speaking. Considering the vast availability of various social media platforms such as LinkedIn and Instagram, discuss how public speeches can be both enhanced and undermined by social media.

1. In the chapter-opening scene, Camille Ramirez relied on Aristotle's view of public speaking. Do you believe that she could have been more effective? In what way? Use examples in your response.

2. Aristotle's critics have focused on the fact that his theory is simply a collection of lecture notes that are contradictory, vague, and often narrow. Do you agree or disagree, based on the information in this chapter? What examples can you point to for support?

3. Employ syllogistic reasoning for and against each of the following topics: physician-assisted suicide, same-sex marriage, and medicinal marijuana use.

4. Discuss what canon of rhetoric is most important when politicians speak to their constituents. Use examples to defend your view.

5. If Aristotle were alive today and you were his student, what additional suggestions would you offer him for a new edition of the *Rhetoric*? Why do you believe your suggestions are important to address in public speaking? Incorporate examples in your response.

6. Aristotle spent a great deal of time discussing the role of the audience. If you were giving a speech on safety to a group of convenience store employees, what sort of audience analysis would you undertake?

7. Explain how principles from the *Rhetoric* relate to job interviews.

Online Learning Center www. mhhe.com/west5e

Visit the Online Learning Center at www.mhhe.com/west5e for chapter-specific resources, such as story-into-theory and multiple-choice quizzes, as well as theory summaries and theory-connection questions.

ed."

2

Speaking in Public

- The Power of Public Speaking
- The Tradition of Public Speaking
- Similarities Between Public Speaking and Conversation
- Differences Between Public Speaking and Conversation
- Developing Confidence: Your Speech Class
- Public Speaking and Critical Thinking
- The Speech Communication Process
- Public Speaking in a Multicultural World

Growing up in the mountain town of Mingora, Pakistan, Malala Yousafzai had no idea how far her voice would travel. A bright and outspoken student, she dreamed of being a doctor. But her passion for education flew in the face of the Taliban regime that controlled her town. When Malala was 15 years old, two armed gunmen boarded her school bus and shot her at close range in the head and neck.

Miraculously, Malala survived. Since that time, she has become a symbol of the struggle for the rights of girls and women across the globe. She has established her own nonprofit organization, has met with leaders from many nations, and has turned her story of survival into a lesson on the importance of education. At age 16, she became the youngest person ever nominated for a Nobel Peace Prize.

How has Malala achieved all this? Partly through her bravery, partly through her commitment to education, and partly through her unyielding hope for a better world. But also important is her ability to communicate with people through public speaking, which has become a primary medium for spreading her message.

Best known is the speech Malala gave to the United Nations General Assembly on July 12, 2013, her 16th birthday. In addition to describing the attack on her school bus and the compassion she now felt for her attackers, she made her experience part of a larger struggle for human rights. "I speak not for myself," she told world leaders, "but so those without a voice can be heard."

If you had asked Malala several years ago, "Do you see yourself as an important international speaker?" she would probably have laughed at the idea. Yet today she gives at least one presentation in almost every city she visits. In addition to speaking at the United Nations, she has addressed Amnesty International, the World Bank, and the European Parliament. Her speeches have captivated audiences the world over.

The Power of Public Speaking

Throughout history people have used public speaking as a vital means of communication. What the Greek leader Pericles said more than 2,500 years ago is still true today: "One who forms a judgment on any point but cannot explain" it clearly "might as well never have thought at all on the subject."[1] Public speaking, as its name implies, is a way of making your ideas public—of sharing them with other people and of influencing other people.

During modern times, many women and men around the globe have spread their ideas and influence through public speaking. In the United States, the list includes Franklin Roosevelt, Billy Graham, Cesar Chavez, Barbara Jordan, Martin Luther King, Ronald Reagan, Hillary Clinton, and Barack Obama. In other countries, we have seen the power of public speaking employed by people such as Margaret Thatcher, Nelson Mandela, and Aung San Suu Kyi.

As you read these names, you may think to yourself, "That's fine. Good for them. But what does that have to do with me? I don't plan to be a president or a preacher or a crusader for any cause." Nevertheless, the need for public speaking will almost certainly touch you sometime in your life—maybe tomorrow, maybe not for five years. Can you imagine yourself in any of these situations?

> You are one of seven management trainees in a large corporation. One of you will get the lower-management job that has just opened. There is to be a large staff meeting at which each of the trainees will discuss the project he or she has been developing. One by one your colleagues make their presentations. They have no experience in public speaking and are intimidated by the higher-ranking managers present. Their speeches are stumbling and awkward. You, however, call upon all the skills you learned in your public speaking course. You deliver an informative talk that is clear, well reasoned, and articulate. You get the job.
>
> One of your children has a learning disability. You hear that your local school board has decided, for budget reasons, to eliminate the special teacher who has been helping your child. At an open meeting of the school board, you stand up and deliver a thoughtful, compelling speech on the necessity for keeping the special teacher. The school board changes its mind.
>
> You are the assistant manager in a branch office of a national company. Your immediate superior, the branch manager, is about to retire, and there will be a

retirement dinner. All the executives from the home office will attend. As his close working associate, you are asked to give a farewell toast at the party. You prepare and deliver a speech that is both witty and touching—a perfect tribute to your boss. After the speech, everyone applauds enthusiastically, and a few people have tears in their eyes. The following week you are named branch manager.

Fantasies? Not really. Any of these situations could occur. In a recent survey of more than 300 employers, 93 percent stated that the ability to think critically and communicate clearly is more important for career success than is a job candidate's undergraduate major. In another survey, the American Management Association asked 768 executives and managers to rank the skills most essential to today's workplace. What was at the top of their list? Communication skills.[2]

The importance of such skills is true across the board—for accountants and architects, teachers and technicians, scientists and stockbrokers. Even in highly specialized fields such as civil and mechanical engineering, employers consistently rank the ability to communicate above technical knowledge when deciding whom to hire and whom to promote.

Businesses are also asking people to give more speeches in the early stages of their careers, and many young professionals are using public speaking as a way to stand out in today's highly competitive job market.[3] In fact, the ability to speak effectively is so prized that college graduates are increasingly being asked to give a presentation as part of their job interview.

Nor has the growth of the Internet and other new technologies reduced the need for public speaking. In this age of Instagram and Twitter, businesses are concerned that college graduates are losing the ability to talk in a professional way. As career expert Lindsey Pollak states, "It's so rare to find somebody who has that combination of really good technical skills and really good verbal communication skills. You will be head and shoulders above your colleagues if you can combine those two."[4]

The same is true in community life. Public speaking is a vital means of civic engagement. It is a way to express your ideas and to have an impact on issues that matter in society. As a form of empowerment, it can—and often does—make a difference in things people care about very much. The key phrase here is "make a difference." This is what most of us want to do in life—to make a difference, to change the world in some small way. Public speaking offers you an opportunity to make a difference in something you care about very much.

The Tradition of Public Speaking

Given the importance of public speaking, it's not surprising that it has been taught and studied around the globe for thousands of years. Almost all cultures have an equivalent of the English word "orator" to designate someone with special skills in public speaking. The oldest known handbook on effective speech was written on papyrus in Egypt some 4,500 years ago. Eloquence was highly prized in ancient India, Africa, and China, as well as among the Aztecs and other pre-European cultures of North and South America.[5]

In classical Greece and Rome, public speaking played a central role in education and civic life. It was also studied extensively. Aristotle's *Rhetoric,* composed during the third century B.C., is still considered the most important work on its subject, and many of its principles are followed by speakers (and writers) today. The great Roman leader Cicero used his speeches to defend liberty and wrote several works about oratory in general.

Over the centuries, many other notable thinkers have dealt with issues of rhetoric, speech, and language—including the Roman educator Quintilian, the Christian preacher St. Augustine, the medieval writer Christine de Pizan, the British philosopher Francis Bacon, and the American critic Kenneth Burke. In recent years, communication researchers have provided an increasingly scientific basis for understanding the methods and strategies of effective speech.

Your immediate objective is to apply those methods and strategies in your classroom speeches. What you learn, however, will be applicable long after you leave college. The principles of public speaking are derived from a long tradition and have been confirmed by a substantial body of research. The more you know about those principles, the more effective you will be in your own speeches—and the more effective you will be in listening to the speeches of other people.

Similarities Between Public Speaking and Conversation

How much time do you spend each day talking to other people? The average adult spends about 30 percent of her or his waking hours in conversation. By the time you read this book, you will have spent much of your life perfecting the art of conversation. You may not realize it, but you already employ a wide range of skills when talking to people. These skills include the following:

1. *Organizing your thoughts logically.* Suppose you were giving someone directions to get to your house. You wouldn't do it this way:

> When you turn off the highway, you'll see a big diner on the left. But before that, stay on the highway to Exit 67. Usually a couple of the neighbors' dogs are in the street, so go slow after you turn at the blinking light. Coming from your house you get on the highway through Maple Street. If you pass the taco stand, you've gone too far. The house is blue.

Instead, you would take your listener systematically, step by step, from his or her house to your house. You would organize your message.

2. *Tailoring your message to your audience.* You are a geology major. Two people ask you how pearls are formed. One is your roommate; the other is your nine-year-old niece. You answer as follows:

> To your roommate: "When any irritant, say a grain of sand, gets inside the oyster's shell, the oyster automatically secretes a substance called nacre, which is principally calcium carbonate and is the same material that lines the oyster's shell. The nacre accumulates in layers around the irritant core to form the pearl."
>
> To your niece: "Imagine you're an oyster on the ocean floor. A grain of sand gets inside your shell and makes you uncomfortable. So you decide to cover it up. You cover it with a material called mother-of-pearl. The covering builds up around the grain of sand to make a pearl."

Many skills used in conversation also apply in public speaking. As you learn to speak more effectively, you may also learn to communicate more effectively in other situations.

3. *Telling a story for maximum impact.* Suppose you are telling a friend about a funny incident at last week's football game. You don't begin with the punch line ("Keisha fell out of the stands right onto the field. Here's how it started. . . ."). Instead, you carefully build up your story, adjusting your words and tone of voice to get the best effect.

4. *Adapting to listener feedback.* Whenever you talk with someone, you are aware of that person's verbal, facial, and physical reactions. For example:

> You are explaining an interesting point that came up in biology class. Your listener begins to look confused, puts up a hand as though to stop you, and says "Huh?" You go back and explain more clearly.
>
> A friend has asked you to listen while she practices a speech. At the end you tell her, "There's just one part I really don't like—that quotation from the attorney general." Your friend looks very hurt and says, "That was my favorite part!" So you say, "But if you just worked the quotation in a little differently, it would be wonderful."

Each day, in casual conversation, you do all these things many times without thinking about them. You already possess these communication skills. And these are among the most important skills you will need for public speaking.

To illustrate, let's return briefly to one of the hypothetical situations at the beginning of this chapter. When addressing the school board about the need for a special teacher:

- You *organize* your ideas to present them in the most persuasive manner. You steadily build up a compelling case about how the teacher benefits the school.
- You *tailor your message* to your audience. This is no time to launch an impassioned defense of special education in the United States. You must show how the issue is important to the people in that very room—to their children and to the school.

- You *tell your story* for maximum impact. Perhaps you relate an anecdote to demonstrate how much your child has improved. You also have statistics to show how many other children have been helped.
- You *adapt to listener feedback.* When you mention the cost of the special teacher, you notice sour looks on the faces of the school board members. So you patiently explain how small that cost is in relation to the overall school budget.

In many ways, then, public speaking requires the same skills used in ordinary conversation. Most people who communicate well in daily talk can learn to communicate just as well in public speaking. By the same token, training in public speaking can make you a more adept communicator in a variety of situations, such as conversations, classroom discussions, business meetings, and interviews.

Differences Between Public Speaking and Conversation

Despite their similarities, public speaking and everyday conversation are not identical. Imagine that you are telling a story to a friend. Then imagine yourself telling the story to a group of seven or eight friends. Now imagine telling the same story to 20 or 30 people. As the size of your audience grows, you will find yourself adapting to three major differences between conversation and public speaking:

1. *Public speaking is more highly structured.* It usually imposes strict time limitations on the speaker. In most cases, the situation does not allow listeners to interrupt with questions or commentary. The speaker must accomplish her or his purpose in the speech itself. In preparing the speech, the speaker must anticipate questions that might arise in the minds of listeners and answer them. Consequently, public speaking demands much more detailed planning and preparation than ordinary conversation.

2. *Public speaking requires more formal language.* Slang, jargon, and bad grammar have little place in public speeches. When Malala Yousafzai addressed the United Nations, she didn't say, "We've got to stop Taliban creeps from going after innocent people." Listeners usually react negatively to speakers who do not elevate and polish their language when addressing an audience. A speech should be "special."

3. *Public speaking requires a different method of delivery.* When conversing informally, most people talk quietly, interject stock phrases such as "like" and "you know," adopt a casual posture, and use what are called vocalized pauses ("uh," "er," "um"). Effective public speakers, however, adjust their voices to be heard clearly throughout the audience. They assume a more erect posture. They avoid distracting mannerisms and verbal habits.

With study and practice, you will be able to master these differences and expand your conversational skills into speechmaking. Your speech class will provide the opportunity for this study and practice.

Developing Confidence: Your Speech Class

One of the major concerns of students in any speech class is stage fright. We may as well face the issue squarely. Many people who converse easily in all kinds of everyday situations become frightened at the idea of standing up before a group to make a speech.

If you are worried about stage fright, you may feel better knowing that you are not alone. A 2001 Gallup Poll asked Americans to list their greatest fears. Forty percent identified speaking before a group as their top fear, exceeded only by the 51 percent who said they were afraid of snakes. A 2005 survey produced similar results, with 42 percent of respondents being terrified by the prospect of speaking in public. In comparison, only 28 percent said they were afraid of dying.[6]

stage fright

Anxiety over the prospect of giving a speech in front of an audience.

In a different study, researchers concentrated on social situations and, again, asked their subjects to list their greatest fears. More than 9,000 people were interviewed. Here is the ranking of their answers:[7]

Greatest Fear

Public speaking

Speaking up in a meeting or class

Meeting new people

Talking to people in authority

Important examination or interview

Going to parties

Talking with strangers

Again, speechmaking is at the top in provoking anxiety.

NERVOUSNESS IS NORMAL

If you feel nervous about giving a speech, you are in very good company. Some of the greatest public speakers in history have suffered from stage fright, including Abraham Lincoln, Margaret Sanger, and Winston Churchill. The famous Roman orator Cicero said, "I turn pale at the outset of a speech and quake in every limb and in my soul."[8]

Jennifer Lawrence, Conan O'Brien, and Oprah Winfrey all report being anxious about speaking in public. Early in his career, Leonardo DiCaprio was so nervous about giving an acceptance speech that he hoped he would not win the Academy Award for which he had been nominated. Eighty-one percent of business executives say public speaking is the most nerve-wracking experience they face.[9] What comedian Jerry Seinfeld said in jest sometimes seems literally true: "Given a choice, at a funeral most of us would rather be the one in the coffin than the one giving the eulogy."

Actually, most people tend to be anxious before doing something important in public. Actors are nervous before a play, politicians are nervous before a campaign speech, athletes are nervous before a big game. The ones who succeed have learned to use their nervousness to their advantage. Listen to tennis star Andy Murray speaking after his 2013 Wimbledon title match against Novak Djokovic: "If I'm feeling butterflies in the stomach, I know I'm ready, focused on what I'm going to try and accomplish. If you aren't nervous before playing on Centre Court at Wimbledon, maybe you're doing the wrong job." Putting his butterflies to good use, Murray beat Djokovic in straight sets to become the first British man to capture Wimbledon in 77 years.

Much the same thing happens in speechmaking. Most experienced speakers have stage fright before taking the floor, but their nervousness is a healthy sign that they are getting "psyched up" for a good effort. Novelist and lecturer I. A. R. Wylie once said: "I rarely rise to my feet without a throat constricted with terror and a furiously thumping heart. When, for some reason, I *am* cool and self-assured, the speech is always a failure."

adrenaline

A hormone released into the bloodstream in response to physical or mental stress.

In other words, it is perfectly normal—even desirable—to be nervous at the start of a speech. Your body is responding as it would to any stressful situation—by producing extra *adrenaline.*

This sudden shot of adrenaline is what makes your heart race, your hands shake, your knees knock, and your skin perspire. Every public speaker experiences all these reactions to some extent. The question is: How can you control your nervousness and make it work for you rather than against you?

DEALING WITH NERVOUSNESS

positive nervousness

Controlled nervousness that helps energize a speaker for her or his presentation.

Rather than trying to eliminate every trace of stage fright, you should aim at transforming it from a negative force into what one expert calls *positive nervousness*—"a zesty, enthusiastic, lively feeling with a slight edge to it. . . . It's still nervousness, but it feels different. You're no longer victimized by it; instead, you're vitalized by it. You're in control of it."[10]

Don't think of yourself as having stage fright. Instead, think of it as "stage excitement" or "stage enthusiasm."[11] It can help you get focused and energized in the same way that it helps athletes, musicians, and others get primed for a game or a concert. Actress Jane Lynch, talking about her gig hosting *Saturday Night Live*, said that she got through it with "that perfect cocktail of nervousness and excitement." Think of that cocktail as a normal part of giving a successful speech.

Here are six time-tested ways you can turn your nervousness from a negative force into a positive one.

Acquire Speaking Experience

You have already taken the first step. You are enrolled in a public speaking course, where you will learn about speechmaking and gain speaking experience. Think back to your first day at kindergarten, your first date, your first day at a new job. You were probably nervous in each situation because you were facing something new and unknown. Once you became accustomed to the situation, it was no longer threatening. So it is with public speaking. For most students, the biggest part of stage fright is fear of the unknown. The more you learn about public speaking and the more speeches you give, the less threatening speechmaking will become.

Of course, the road to confidence will sometimes be bumpy. Learning to give a speech is not much different from learning any other skill—it proceeds by trial and error. The purpose of your speech class is to shorten the process, to minimize the errors, to give you a nonthreatening arena—a sort of laboratory—in which to undertake the "trial."

The need for public speaking arises in many situations. Here United Nations Commissioner Pierre Krähenbühl speaks at a news conference in Gaza City.

Your instructor recognizes that you are a novice and is trained to give the kind of guidance you need to get started. In your fellow students you have a highly sympathetic audience who will provide valuable feedback to help you improve your speaking skills. As the class goes on, your fears about public speaking will gradually recede until they are replaced by only a healthy nervousness before you rise to speak.[12]

Prepare, Prepare, Prepare

Another key to gaining confidence is to pick speech topics you truly care about—and then to prepare your speeches so thoroughly that you cannot help but be successful. Here's how one student combined enthusiasm for his topic with thorough preparation to score a triumph in speech class:

> Jesse Young was concerned about taking a speech class. Not having any experience as a public speaker, he got butterflies in his stomach just thinking about talking in front of an audience. But when the time came for Jesse's first speech, he was determined to make it a success.
>
> Jesse chose Habitat for Humanity as the topic for his speech. He had been a volunteer for three years, and he believed deeply in the organization and its mission. The purpose of his speech was to explain the origins, philosophy, and activities of Habitat for Humanity.
>
> As Jesse spoke, it became clear that he was enthusiastic about his subject and genuinely wanted his classmates to share his enthusiasm. Because he was intent on communicating with his audience, he forgot to be nervous. He spoke clearly, fluently, and dynamically. Soon the entire class was engrossed in his speech.
>
> Afterward, Jesse admitted that he had surprised even himself. "It was amazing," he said. "Once I passed the first minute or so, all I thought about were those people out there listening. I could tell that I was really getting through to them."

How much time should you devote to preparing your speeches? A standard rule of thumb is that each minute of speaking time requires one to two hours of preparation time—perhaps more, depending on the amount of research needed for the speech. This may seem like a lot of time, but the rewards are well worth it. One professional speech consultant estimates that proper preparation can reduce stage fright by up to 75 percent.[13]

If you follow the techniques suggested by your instructor and in the rest of this book, you will stand up for every speech fully prepared. Imagine that the day for your first speech has arrived. You have studied your audience and selected a topic you know will interest them. You have researched the speech thoroughly and practiced it several times until it feels absolutely comfortable. You have even tried it out before two or three trusted friends. How can you help but be confident of success?

Think Positively

Confidence is mostly the well-known power of positive thinking. If you think you can do it, you usually can. On the other hand, if you predict disaster and doom, that is almost always what you will get. This is especially true when it comes to public speaking. Speakers who think negatively about themselves and the speech experience are much more likely to be overcome by stage fright than are speakers who think positively. Here are some ways you can transform negative thoughts into positive ones as you work on your speeches:

Negative Thought	Positive Thought
I wish I didn't have to give this speech.	This speech is a chance for me to share my ideas and gain experience as a speaker.
I'm not a great public speaker.	No one's perfect, but I'm getting better with each speech I give.
I'm always nervous when I give a speech.	Everyone's nervous. If other people can handle it, I can too.
No one will be interested in what I have to say.	I have a good topic and I'm fully prepared. Of course they'll be interested.

Many psychologists believe that the ratio of positive to negative thoughts in regard to stressful activities such as speechmaking should be at least five to one. That is, for each negative thought, you should counter with a minimum of five positive ones. Doing so will not make your nerves go away completely, but it will help keep them under control so you can concentrate on communicating your ideas rather than on brooding about your fears and anxieties.

Use the Power of Visualization

Visualization is closely related to positive thinking. It is used by athletes, musicians, actors, speakers, and others to enhance their performance in stressful situations. How does it work? Listen to Jamie Anderson, who, during the 2014 Winter Olympics, won the first-ever gold medal in the women's Slopestyle event. Afterward, she talked about how she used visualization to settle her nerves before the winning ride:

> There was so much anticipation leading up to this event, I just had to calm my mind and have the trust and faith that I was capable of doing what I really

> wanted to do. At the top of the course, I took a moment, took a deep breath, and saw everything I wanted to see happen. . . . I was visualizing it, seeing it to the end, and knowing that I was going to land everything perfectly with as much style as possible.

Of course, visualization doesn't mean that Anderson wins every competition she enters. But research has shown that the kind of mental imaging she describes can significantly increase athletic performance.[14] It has also shown that visualization can help speakers control their stage fright.[15]

visualization

Mental imaging in which a speaker vividly pictures himself or herself giving a successful presentation.

The key to visualization is creating a vivid mental blueprint in which you see yourself succeeding in your speech. Picture yourself in your classroom rising to speak. See yourself at the lectern, poised and self-assured, making eye contact with your audience and delivering your introduction in a firm, clear voice. Feel your confidence growing as your listeners get more and more caught up in what you are saying. Imagine your sense of achievement as you conclude the speech knowing you have done your very best.

As you create these images in your mind's eye, be realistic but stay focused on the positive aspects of your speech. Don't allow negative images to eclipse the positive ones. Acknowledge your nervousness, but picture yourself overcoming it to give a vibrant, articulate presentation. If one part of the speech always seems to give you trouble, visualize yourself getting through it without any hitches. And be specific. The more lucid your mental pictures, the more successful you are likely to be.

As with your physical rehearsal of the speech, this kind of mental rehearsal should be repeated several times in the days before you speak. It doesn't guarantee that every speech will turn out exactly the way you envision it—and it certainly is no substitute for thorough preparation. But used in conjunction with the other methods of combating stage fright, it is a proven way to help control your nerves and to craft a successful presentation.

Know That Most Nervousness Is Not Visible

Many novice speakers are worried about appearing nervous to the audience. It's hard to speak with poise and assurance if you think you look tense and insecure. One of the most valuable lessons you will learn as your speech class proceeds is that only a fraction of the turmoil you feel inside is visible on the outside. "Your nervous system may be giving you a thousand shocks," says one experienced speaker, "but the viewer can see only a few of them."[16]

Even though your palms are sweating and your heart is pounding, your listeners probably won't realize how tense you are—especially if you do your best to act cool and confident on the outside. Most of the time when students confess after a speech, "I was so nervous I thought I was going to die," their classmates are surprised. To them the speaker looked calm and assured.

Knowing this should make it easier for you to face your listeners with confidence. As one student stated after watching a videotape of her first classroom speech, "I was amazed at how calm I looked. I assumed everyone would be able to see how scared I was, but now that I know they can't, I won't be nearly so nervous in the future. It really helps to know that you look in control even though you may not feel that way."

Don't Expect Perfection

It may also help to know that there is no such thing as a perfect speech. At some point in every presentation, every speaker says or does something that

Like many well-known public figures, Jennifer Lawrence often experiences stage fright before a speech. Most speakers report that their nervousness drops significantly after the first 30 to 60 seconds of a presentation.

does not come across exactly as he or she had planned. Fortunately, such moments are usually not evident to the audience. Why? Because the audience does not know what the speaker *plans* to say. It hears only what the speaker *does* say. If you momentarily lose your place, reverse the order of a couple of statements, or forget to pause at a certain spot, no one need be the wiser. When such moments occur, just proceed as if nothing happened.

Even if you do make an obvious mistake during a speech, that is no catastrophe. If you have ever listened to Martin Luther King's "I Have a Dream," you may recall that he stumbles twice during the speech. Most likely, however, you don't remember. Why? Because you were focusing on King's message, rather than on the fine points of his delivery.

One of the biggest reasons people are concerned about making a mistake in a speech is that they view speechmaking as a performance rather than an act of communication. They feel the audience is judging them against a scale of absolute perfection in which every misstated word or awkward gesture will count against them. But speech audiences are not like judges in a violin recital or an ice-skating contest. They are not looking for a virtuoso performance, but for a well-thought-out address that communicates the speaker's ideas clearly and directly. Sometimes an error or two can actually enhance a speaker's appeal by making her or him seem more human.[17]

As you work on your speeches, make sure you prepare thoroughly and do all you can to get your message across to your listeners. But don't panic about being perfect or about what will happen if you make a mistake. Once you free your mind of these burdens, you will find it much easier to approach your speeches with confidence and even with enthusiasm.

Besides stressing the six points just discussed, your instructor will probably give you several tips for dealing with nervousness in your first speeches. They may include:

- Be at your best physically and mentally. It's not a good idea to stay up until 3:00 A.M. partying with friends or cramming for an exam the night before your speech. A good night's sleep will serve you better.
- As you are waiting to speak, quietly tighten and relax your leg muscles, or squeeze your hands together and then release them. Such actions help reduce tension by providing an outlet for your extra adrenaline.
- Take a couple of slow, deep breaths before you start to speak. When they are tense, most people take short, shallow breaths, which only reinforces their anxiety. Deep breathing breaks this cycle of tension and helps calm your nerves.
- Work especially hard on your introduction. Research has shown that a speaker's anxiety level begins to drop significantly after the first 30 to 60 seconds of a presentation.[18] Once you get through the introduction, you should find smoother sailing the rest of the way.
- Make eye contact with members of your audience. Remember that they are individual people, not a blur of faces. And they are your friends.
- Concentrate on communicating with your audience rather than on worrying about your stage fright. If you get caught up in your speech, your audience will too.
- Use visual aids. They create interest, draw attention away from you, and make you feel less self-conscious.

checklist

Speaking with Confidence

YES	NO	
☐	☐	1. Am I enthusiastic about my speech topic?
☐	☐	2. Have I thoroughly developed the content of my speech?
☐	☐	3. Have I worked on the introduction so my speech will get off to a good start?
☐	☐	4. Have I worked on the conclusion so my speech will end on a strong note?
☐	☐	5. Have I rehearsed my speech orally until I am confident about its delivery?
☐	☐	6. Have I worked on turning negative thoughts about my speech into positive ones?
☐	☐	7. Do I realize that nervousness is normal, even among experienced speakers?
☐	☐	8. Do I understand that most nervousness is not visible to the audience?
☐	☐	9. Am I focused on communicating with my audience, rather than on worrying about my nerves?
☐	☐	10. Have I visualized myself speaking confidently and getting a positive response from the audience?

If you are like most students, you will find your speech class to be a very positive experience. As one student wrote on her course evaluation at the end of the class:

> I was really dreading this class. The idea of giving all those speeches scared me half to death. But I'm glad now that I stuck with it. It's a small class, and I got to know a lot of the students. Besides, this is one class in which I got to express *my* ideas, instead of spending the whole time listening to the teacher talk. I even came to enjoy giving the speeches. I could tell at times that the audience was really with me, and that's a great feeling.

Over the years, thousands of students have developed confidence in their speechmaking abilities. As your confidence grows, you will be better able to stand before other people and tell them what you think and feel and know—and to make them think and feel and know those same things. The best part about confidence is that it nurtures itself. After you score your first triumph, you will be that much more confident the next time. And as you become a more confident public speaker, you will likely become more confident in other areas of your life as well.

Public Speaking and Critical Thinking

> That guy at the party last night really owned me when we were talking about the economy. I know my information is right, and I'm sure his argument didn't make sense, but I can't put my finger on the problem.
>
> I worked really hard on my term paper, but it's just not right. It doesn't seem to hang together, and I can't figure out what's wrong.
>
> Political speeches are so one-sided. The candidates sound good, but they all talk in slogans and generalities. It's really hard to decide who has the best stands on the issues.

critical thinking

Focused, organized thinking about such things as the logical relationships among ideas, the soundness of evidence, and the differences between fact and opinion.

Have you ever found yourself in similar situations? If so, you may find help in your speech class. Besides building confidence, a course in public speaking can develop your skills as a critical thinker. Those skills can make the difference between the articulate debater and the pushover, the A student and the C student, the thoughtful voter and the coin tosser.

What is critical thinking? To some extent, it's a matter of logic—of being able to spot weaknesses in other people's arguments and to avoid them in your own. It also involves related skills such as distinguishing fact from opinion, judging the credibility of statements, and assessing the soundness of evidence. In the broadest sense, critical thinking is focused, organized thinking—the ability to see clearly the relationships among ideas.[19]

If you are wondering what this has to do with your public speaking class, the answer is quite a lot. As the class proceeds, you will probably spend a good deal of time organizing your speeches. While this may seem like a purely mechanical exercise, it is closely interwoven with critical thinking. If the structure of your speech is disjointed and confused, odds are that your thinking is also disjointed and confused. If, on the other hand, the structure is clear and cohesive, there is a good chance your thinking is too. Organizing a speech is not just a matter of arranging the ideas you already have. Rather, it is an important part of shaping the ideas themselves.

What is true of organization is true of many aspects of public speaking. The skills you learn in your speech class can help you become a more effective thinker in a number of ways. As you work on expressing your ideas in clear, accurate language, you will enhance your ability to think clearly and accurately. As you study the role of evidence and reasoning in speechmaking, you will see how they can be used in other forms of communication as well. As you learn to listen critically to speeches in class, you will be better able to assess the ideas of speakers (and writers) in a variety of situations.

To return to the examples at the beginning of this section:

> The guy at the party last night—would well-honed critical thinking skills help you find the holes in his argument?
>
> The term paper—would better organization and a clear outline help pull it together?
>
> Political speeches—once you get past the slogans, are the candidates drawing valid conclusions from sound evidence?

If you take full advantage of your speech class, you will be able to enhance your skills as a critical thinker in many circumstances. This is one reason public speaking has been regarded as a vital part of education since the days of ancient Greece.

Using public speaking in your CAREER

It's been three years since you graduated from college, and one year since you and your friends launched a mobile app development company. The app, a note-taking and collaboration tool for college students, has taken a while to create, but now you're ready to unveil it at a regional technology conference. Although you have given a few brief talks since your speech class in college, the conference will be your first major presentation to a large audience.

The closer you get to the day of the speech, the harder it is to control the butterflies in your stomach. There will be approximately 200 people in your audience, including potential investors, rival development companies, and members of the press. All eyes will be on you. It's important that you come across as confident and well informed, but you're afraid your stage fright will send the opposite message. What strategies will you use to control your nerves and make them work for you?

The Speech Communication Process

As you begin your first speeches, you may find it helpful to understand what goes on when one person talks to another. Regardless of the kind of speech communication involved, there are seven elements—speaker, message, channel, listener, feedback, interference, and situation. Here we focus on how these elements interact when a public speaker addresses an audience.

SPEAKER

speaker

The person who is presenting an oral message to a listener.

Speech communication begins with a speaker. If you pick up the telephone and call a friend, you are acting as a speaker. (Of course, you will also act as a listener when your friend is talking.) In public speaking, you will usually present your entire speech without interruption.

Your success as a speaker depends on *you*—on your personal credibility, your knowledge of the subject, your preparation of the speech, your manner of speaking, your sensitivity to the audience and the occasion. But successful speaking also requires enthusiasm.

You can't expect people to be interested in what you say unless you are interested yourself. If you are truly excited about your subject, your audience is almost sure to get excited along with you. You can learn all the techniques of effective speechmaking, but before they can be of much use, you must first have something to say—something that sparks your own enthusiasm.

MESSAGE

message

Whatever a speaker communicates to someone else.

The message is whatever a speaker communicates to someone else. If you are calling a friend, you might say, "I'll be a little late picking you up tonight." That is the message. But it may not be the only message. Perhaps there is a certain tone in your voice that suggests reluctance, hesitation. The underlying message might be "I really don't want to go to that party. You talked me into it, but I'm going to put it off as long as I can."

Your goal in public speaking is to have your *intended* message be the message that is *actually* communicated. Achieving this depends both on what you say (the verbal message) and on how you say it (the nonverbal message).

Getting the verbal message just right requires work. You must narrow your topic down to something you can discuss adequately in the time allowed for the speech. You must do research and choose supporting details to make your ideas clear and convincing. You must organize your ideas so listeners can follow them without getting lost. And you must express your message in words that are accurate, clear, vivid, and appropriate.

Besides the message you send with words, you send a message with your tone of voice, appearance, gestures, facial expression, and eye contact. Imagine that one of your classmates gets up to speak about student loans. Throughout her speech she slumps behind the lectern, takes long pauses to remember what she wants to say, stares at the ceiling, and fumbles with her visual aids.

Her intended message is "We must make more money available for student loans." But the message she actually communicates is "I haven't

The powers of critical thinking you develop in researching and organizing your speeches can be applied in many forms of communication, including meetings and group projects.

prepared very well for this speech." One of your jobs as a speaker is to make sure your nonverbal message does not distract from your verbal message.

CHANNEL

The channel is the means by which a message is communicated. When you pick up the phone to call a friend, the telephone is the channel. Public speakers may use one or more of several channels, each of which will affect the message received by the audience.

channel

The means by which a message is communicated.

Consider a speech to Congress by the President of the United States. The speech is carried to the nation by the channels of radio and television. For the radio audience the message is conveyed entirely by the President's voice. For the television audience the message is conveyed by both the President's voice and the televised image. The people in Congress have a more direct channel. They not only hear the President's voice as amplified through a microphone, but they also see him and the setting firsthand.

In a public speaking class, your channel is the most direct of all. Your classmates will see you and hear you without any electronic intervention.

LISTENER

The listener is the person who receives the communicated message. Without a listener, there is no communication. When you talk to a friend on the phone, you have one listener. In public speaking you will have many listeners.

listener

The person who receives the speaker's message.

Everything a speaker says is filtered through a listener's *frame of reference*—the total of his or her knowledge, experience, goals, values, and attitudes. Because a speaker and a listener are different people, they can never have

frame of reference

The sum of a person's knowledge, experience, goals, values, and attitudes. No two people can have exactly the same frame of reference.

exactly the same frame of reference. And because a listener's frame of reference can never be exactly the same as a speaker's, the meaning of a message will never be exactly the same to a listener as to a speaker.

You can easily test the impact of different frames of reference. Ask each of your classmates to describe a chair. If you have 20 classmates, you'll probably get 20 different descriptions. One student might picture a large, overstuffed easy chair, another an elegant straight-backed chair, yet another an office chair, a fourth a rocking chair, and so on.

Even if two or more envision the same general type—say, a rocking chair—their mental images of the chair could still be different. One might be thinking of an early American rocker, another of a modern Scandinavian rocker—the possibilities are unlimited. And "chair" is a fairly simple concept. What about "patriotism" or "freedom"?

Because people have different frames of reference, a public speaker must take great care to adapt the message to the particular audience being addressed. To be an effective speaker, you must be *audience-centered.* You will quickly lose your listeners' attention if your presentation is either too basic or too sophisticated. You will also lose your audience if you do not relate to their experience, interests, knowledge, and values. When you make a speech that causes listeners to say "That is important to *me,*" you will almost always be successful.

FEEDBACK

feedback

The messages, usually nonverbal, sent from a listener to a speaker.

When the President addresses the nation on television, he is engaged in one-way communication. You can talk back to the television set, but the President won't hear you. Most situations, however, involve *two-way* communication. Your listeners don't simply absorb your message like human sponges. They send back messages of their own. These messages are called feedback.

In public speaking there is plenty of feedback to let you know how your message is being received. Do your listeners lean forward in their seats, as if paying close attention? Do they have quizzical looks on their faces? Do they shuffle their feet and gaze at the clock? The message sent by these reactions could be "I am fascinated," "I am bored," "I agree with you," "I don't agree with you," or any number of others. As a speaker, you need to be alert to these reactions and adjust your message accordingly.

Like any kind of communication, feedback is affected by one's frame of reference. How would you feel if, immediately after your speech, all your classmates started to rap their knuckles on the desks? Would you run out of the room in despair? Not if you were in a European university. In many parts of Europe, students rap their knuckles on their desks to show admiration for a classroom lecture. You must understand the feedback to be able to deal with it.

INTERFERENCE

Interference is anything that impedes the communication of a message. When you talk on the telephone, sometimes there is static, or wires get crossed so that two different conversations are going on at once. That is a kind of interference.

In public speaking there are two kinds of interference. One, like the static or crossed wires in a phone conversation, is *external* to the audience. Many classrooms are subject to this kind of interference—from traffic outside the building, the clatter of a radiator, students conversing in the hall, a room that is stifling hot or freezing cold. Any of these can distract listeners from what you are saying.

A second kind of interference is *internal* and comes from within your audience. Perhaps one of your listeners has a toothache. She may be so distracted by the pain that she doesn't pay attention to your speech. Another listener could be worrying about a test in the next class period. Yet another could be brooding about an argument with his girlfriend.

As a speaker, you must try to hold your listeners' attention despite these various kinds of interference. In the chapters that follow you will find many ways to do this.

interference

Anything that impedes the communication of a message. Interference can be external or internal to listeners.

SITUATION

The situation is the time and place in which speech communication occurs. Conversation always takes place in a certain situation. Sometimes the situation helps—as when you propose marriage over an intimate candlelight dinner. Other times it may hurt—as when you try to speak words of love in competition with blaring music. When you have to talk with someone about a touchy issue, you usually wait until the situation is just right.

Public speakers must also be alert to the situation. Certain occasions—funerals, church services, graduation ceremonies—require certain kinds of speeches. Physical setting is also important. It makes a great deal of difference whether a speech is presented indoors or out, in a small classroom or in a gymnasium, to a densely packed crowd or to a handful of scattered souls. When you adjust to the situation of a public speech, you are only doing on a larger scale what you do every day in conversation.

For a complete model of the speech communication process, see Figure 1.1 below.[20]

situation

The time and place in which speech communication occurs.

FIGURE 1.1

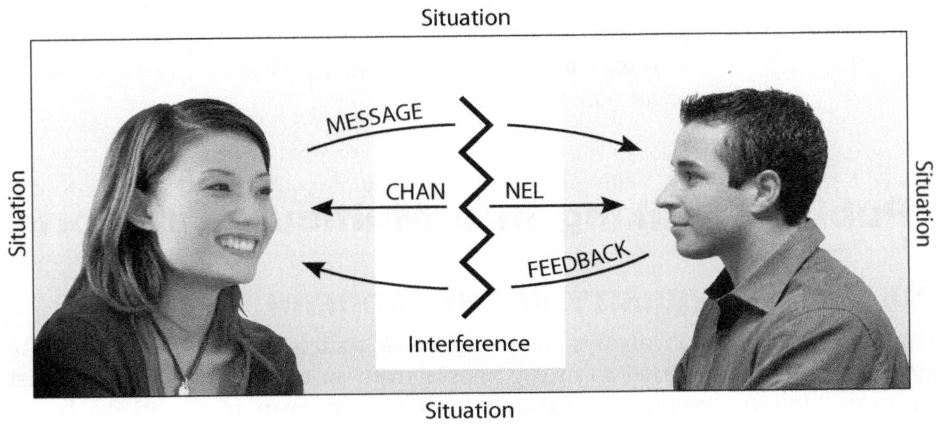

THE SPEECH COMMUNICATION PROCESS: EXAMPLE WITH COMMENTARY

The following example shows how the various components of the speech communication process interact:

Situation	It was 5:15 P.M., and the Midwest Food Festival and Expo had been going on all day. Gourmet food vendors from across the Great Lakes region were presenting their products to distributors and restaurant owners, but the presentations had taken much longer than expected.
Speaker	Jason Cruz, owner and operator of a gourmet salsa company, was worried. As the last speaker of the day, he knew he faced a tough situation. He had been allotted 30 minutes, but the festival was scheduled to end in 15 minutes, and the success of his products depended in large part on his presentation.
Channel	Jason stepped to the microphone and began to speak. He could see members of the audience looking at their watches, and he knew they were eager to get to dinner after a long day of meetings.
Adapting to Interference	"Good afternoon," Jason said, "and thanks for your attention. I know everyone is ready to relax after a long day—I certainly am. I was given 30 minutes to tell you about my salsa, but I'll do my best to finish in 15. I think you'll find the time well worth your while, because your customers are going to love my products." Jason was relieved to see people smiling as they settled back in their seats.
Message	Now that he had the audience's attention, Jason presented each of his products as briefly as he could. He streamlined his planned remarks to emphasize the salsas that would be most appealing to grocery shoppers and restaurant diners. He ended by handing out samples of two new salsas that had won awards in recent food shows.
Feedback	As promised, Jason finished in 15 minutes. "So, that's it!" he concluded. "Thanks for your attention after such a long day." The festival organizer came up to Jason after his presentation. "Great stuff—both the talk and the salsa," she said. "Next year I think we'll try to make all the presentations as concise and efficient as yours."

Public Speaking in a Multicultural World

CULTURAL DIVERSITY IN THE MODERN WORLD

The United States has always been a diverse society. By the middle of the 19th century, it contained so many people from so many lands that novelist Herman Melville exclaimed, "You cannot spill a drop of American blood without spilling the blood of the whole world."[21]

One can only imagine what Melville would say today! The United States is the most diverse society on earth. That diversity can be seen in cities and towns, schools and businesses, community groups, and houses of worship all across the land.

Globally, we live in an age of international multiculturalism. The Internet allows for instant communication. CNN is broadcast to more than 1 billion people around the world. Social media connect people across ancient boundaries. Despite political, social, and religious differences, all nations are becoming part of a vast global network. For example:

- There are 82,000 transnational corporations around the world, and they account for one-third of the world's economic output.
- McDonald's sells twice as many hamburgers and French fries abroad than it does in the United States; Nike makes 63 percent of its sales through exports.
- France has more Muslims than practicing Catholics; radio CHIN in Toronto, Canada, broadcasts in over 30 languages.

CULTURAL DIVERSITY AND PUBLIC SPEAKING

Speechmaking becomes more complex as cultural diversity increases. Part of the complexity stems from the differences in language from culture to culture. Nothing separates one culture from another more than language. Language and culture are so closely bound that "we communicate the way we do because we are raised in a particular culture and learn its language, rules, and norms."[22]

The meanings attached to gestures, facial expressions, and other nonverbal signals also vary from culture to culture. Even the gestures for such basic messages as "hello" and "goodbye" are culturally based. The North American

Public speaking is a vital mode of communication in cultures around the world. Indian President Narendra Modi addresses an audience at the Gujarat Training Academy in Ahmedabad.

"goodbye" wave is interpreted in many parts of Europe and South America as the motion for "no," while the Italian and Greek gesture for "goodbye" is the same as the U.S. signal for "come here."[23]

Many stories have been told about the fate of public speakers who fail to take into account cultural differences between themselves and their audiences. Consider the following scenario:[24]

> The sales manager of a U.S. electronics firm is in Brazil to negotiate a large purchase of computers by a South American corporation. After three days of negotiations, the sales manager holds a gala reception for all the major executives to build goodwill between the companies.
>
> As is the custom on such occasions, time is set aside during the reception for an exchange of toasts. When it is the sales manager's turn to speak, he praises the Brazilian firm for its many achievements and talks eloquently of his respect for its president and other executives. The words are perfect, and the sales manager can see his audience smiling in approval.
>
> And then—disaster. As the sales manager closes his speech, he raises his hand and flashes the classic U.S. "OK" sign to signal his pleasure at the progress of the negotiations. Instantly the festive mood is replaced with stony silence; smiles turn to icy stares. The sales manager has given his Brazilian audience a gesture with roughly the same meaning as an extended middle finger in the United States.
>
> The next day, the Brazilian firm announces that it will buy its computers from another company.

As this story illustrates, public speakers can ill afford to overlook their listeners' cultural values and customs. The methods of effective speech explained throughout this book will be helpful to you when addressing culturally diverse audiences. Here we need to stress the importance of avoiding the ethnocentrism that often blocks communication between speakers and listeners of different cultural backgrounds.

AVOIDING ETHNOCENTRISM

ethnocentrism

The belief that one's own group or culture is superior to all other groups or cultures.

Ethnocentrism is the belief that our own group or culture—whatever it may be—is superior to all other groups or cultures. Because of ethnocentrism, we identify with our group or culture and see its values, beliefs, and customs as "right" or "natural"—in comparison to the values, beliefs, and customs of other groups or cultures, which we tend to think of as "wrong" or "unnatural."[25]

Ethnocentrism is part of every culture, and it can play a positive role in creating group pride and loyalty. But it can also lead to prejudice and hostility toward different racial, ethnic, religious, or cultural groups. To be an effective public speaker in a multicultural world, you need to keep in mind that all people have their special beliefs and customs.

Avoiding ethnocentrism does not mean that you must agree with the values and practices of all groups and cultures. At times you might try to convince people of different cultures to change their traditional ways of doing things—as speakers from the United Nations seek to persuade farmers in Africa to adopt more productive methods of agriculture, or as delegates from the United States and China attempt to influence the other country's trade policies.

If such speakers are to be successful, however, they must show respect for the cultures of the people they address. They need to adapt their messages to the values and expectations of their listeners.

When you work on your speeches, be alert to how cultural factors might affect how listeners respond. Try to put yourself in their place and to hear your message through their ears. If there is a language difference, avoid words or phrases that might cause misunderstanding. When researching the speech, keep an eye out for visual aids and other materials that will relate to a wide range of listeners. When delivering the speech, be alert to feedback that might indicate the audience is having trouble grasping your ideas.

It is also important to avoid ethnocentrism when listening to speeches. When you listen to a speaker from a different cultural background, be on guard against the temptation to judge the speaker on the basis of his or her appearance or manner of delivery. No matter what the cultural background of the speaker, you should listen to her or him as attentively as you would want your audience to listen to you.[26]

Summary

Public speaking has been a vital means of personal empowerment and civic engagement throughout history. The need for effective public speaking will almost certainly touch you sometime in your life. Your speech class will give you training in researching topics, organizing your ideas, and presenting yourself skillfully. This training is invaluable for every type of communication.

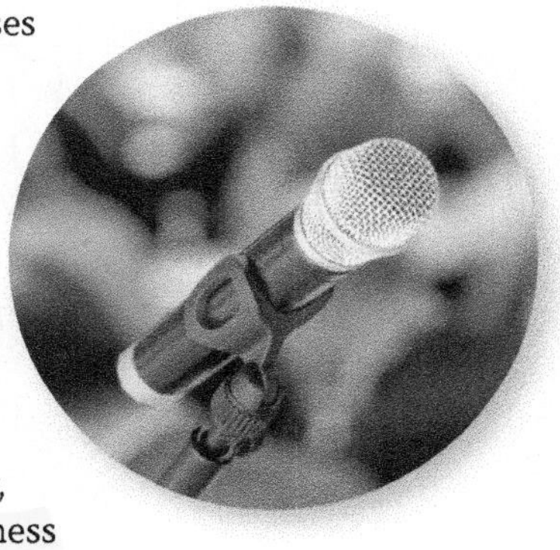

There are many similarities between public speaking and daily conversation, but public speaking is also different from conversation. First, it usually imposes strict time limitations and requires more detailed preparation than does ordinary conversation. Second, it requires more formal language. Listeners react negatively to speeches loaded with slang, jargon, and bad grammar. Third, public speaking demands a different method of delivery. Effective speakers adjust their voices to the larger audience and work at avoiding distracting physical mannerisms and verbal habits.

One of the major concerns of students in any speech class is stage fright. Your class will give you an opportunity to gain confidence and make your nervousness work for you rather than against you. You will take a big step toward overcoming stage fright if you think positively, prepare thoroughly, visualize yourself giving a successful speech, keep in mind that most nervousness is not visible to the audience, and think of your speech as communication rather than as a performance in which you must do everything perfectly.

A course in public speaking can also help develop your skills as a critical thinker. Critical thinking helps you organize your ideas, spot weaknesses in other people's reasoning, and avoid them in your own.

The speech communication process includes seven elements—speaker, message, channel, listener, feedback, interference, and situation. The speaker is the person who initiates a speech transaction. Whatever the speaker communicates is the message, which is sent by means of a particular channel. The listener receives the communicated message and provides feedback to the speaker. Interference is anything that impedes the communication of a message, and the situation is the time and place in which speech communication occurs. The interaction of these seven elements determines the outcome in any instance of speech communication.

Because of the diversity of modern life, many—perhaps most—of the audiences you address will include people of different cultural backgrounds. When you work on your speeches, be alert to how such factors might affect the responses of your listeners and adapt your message accordingly. Above all, avoid the ethnocentric belief that your own culture or group is superior to all others. Also keep in mind the importance of avoiding ethnocentrism when listening to speeches. Accord every speaker the same courtesy and attentiveness you would want from your listeners.

Key Terms

stage fright (9)
adrenaline (10)
positive nervousness (10)
visualization (13)
critical thinking (16)
speaker (18)
message (18)
channel (19)
listener (19)
frame of reference (20)
feedback (20)
interference (21)
situation (21)
ethnocentrism (24)

Review Questions

After reading this chapter, you should be able to answer the following questions:

1. In what ways is public speaking likely to make a difference in your life?
2. How is public speaking similar to everyday conversation?
3. How is public speaking different from everyday conversation?
4. Why is it normal—even desirable—to be nervous at the start of a speech?
5. How can you control your nervousness and make it work for you in your speeches?
6. What are the seven elements of the speech communication process? How do they interact to determine the success or failure of a speech?
7. What is ethnocentrism? Why do public speakers need to avoid ethnocentrism when addressing audiences with diverse cultural, racial, or ethnic backgrounds?

connect

For further review, go to the LearnSmart study module for this chapter.

Exercises for Critical Thinking

1. Think back on an important conversation you had recently in which you wanted to achieve a particular result. (*Examples:* asking your employer to change your work schedule; explaining to a friend how to change the oil and filter in a car; attempting to talk your spouse or partner into buying the computer you like rather than the one he or she prefers.) Work up a brief analysis of the conversation.

   In your analysis, explain the following: (1) your purpose in the conversation and the message strategy you chose to achieve your purpose; (2) the communication channels used during the conversation and how they affected the outcome; (3) the interference—internal or external—you encountered during the conversation; (4) the steps you took to adjust to feedback; (5) the strategic changes you would make in preparing for and carrying out the conversation if you had it to do over again.

2. Divide a sheet of paper into two columns. Label one column "Characteristics of an Effective Public Speaker." Label the other column "Characteristics of an Ineffective Public Speaker." In the columns, list and briefly explain what you believe to be the five most important characteristics of effective and ineffective speakers. Be prepared to discuss your ideas in class.
3. On the basis of the lists you developed for Exercise 2, candidly evaluate your own strengths and weaknesses as a speaker. Identify the three primary aspects of speechmaking you most want to improve.

THE

3

Selecting a Topic and a Purpose

As you read through this book, you will find examples of hundreds of speeches that were delivered in classrooms, in the political arena, in community and business situations. Here is a very small sample of the topics they cover:

asthma	Native American art
Cesar Chavez	optical illusion
driverless cars	Paralympics
Everglades	Québec
fantasy football	Ramadan
Great Wall	Statue of Liberty
Habitat for Humanity	tropical fish
identity theft	water shortage
Jerusalem	X Games
knitting	Yellowstone
Martin Luther King	zoos

Undoubtedly you noticed that the list runs from A to Z. This array of topics wasn't planned. It happened naturally in the course of presenting many different kinds of speeches. The list is given here to show you that there are literally endless possibilities for speech topics—from A to Z.

Choosing a Topic

The first step in speechmaking is choosing a topic. For speeches outside the classroom this is seldom a problem. Usually the speech topic is determined by the occasion, the audience, and the speaker's qualifications. When Bill Clinton lectures at a college campus, he often speaks about global citizenship. Rachel Maddow will discuss current events. Spike Lee might share his views on new developments in film. The same is true of ordinary citizens. The doctor is asked to inform high-school athletes and their parents about sports injuries, the head of a neighborhood coalition speaks about zoning regulations, the florist discusses how to grow thriving houseplants.

topic

The subject of a speech.

In a public speaking class, the situation is different. Students generally have great leeway in selecting topics. This would appear to be an advantage, since it allows you to talk about matters of personal interest. Yet there may be no facet of speech preparation that causes more gnashing of teeth than selecting a topic.

It is a constant source of amazement to teachers that students who regularly chat with their friends about almost any subject under the sun become mentally paralyzed when faced with the task of deciding what to talk about in their speech class. Fortunately, once you get over this initial paralysis, you should have little trouble choosing a good topic.

There are two broad categories of potential topics for your classroom speeches: (1) subjects you know a lot about and (2) subjects you want to know more about. Let's start with the first.

TOPICS YOU KNOW A LOT ABOUT

Most people speak best about subjects with which they are most familiar. When thinking about a topic, draw on your own knowledge and experience. Everyone knows things or has done things that can be used in a speech.

Think for a moment about unusual experiences you may have had or special expertise you may have acquired. One student, who grew up in Turkey, presented a fascinating speech about daily life in that country. Another used her knowledge as a jewelry store salesperson to prepare a speech on how to judge the value of cut diamonds. A third student, who had lived through a tornado, gave a gripping speech about that terrifying experience.

Too dramatic? Nothing in your life is as interesting? Yet another student, who described herself as "just a housewife who is returning to school to finish the education she started 20 years ago," delivered a witty speech on the adjustments she had to make in coming back to college—sitting in class with students young enough to be her children, balancing her academic work against her family commitments, and the satisfaction of completing the education she had begun years earlier.

When you look for a speech topic, keep in mind special expertise you have or sports, hobbies, travel, and other personal experiences that would make for an interesting presentation.

Here are a few more examples of speech topics based largely on the students' personal knowledge and experience:

Interning at *The Daily Show*

The Basics of Snowboarding

Two Years in the Peace Corps

How to Have a Successful Job Interview

TOPICS YOU WANT TO KNOW MORE ABOUT

On the other hand, you may decide to make your speech a learning experience for yourself as well as for your audience. You may choose a subject about which you already have some knowledge or expertise but not enough to prepare a speech without doing additional research. You may even select a topic that you want to explore for the first time. Say, for example, you've always been interested in Stonehenge but never knew much about it. This would be a perfect opportunity to research a fascinating subject and turn it into a fascinating speech.

Or suppose you run across a subject in one of your other classes that catches your fancy. Why not investigate it further for your speech class? One student used this approach to develop a speech on the subject of neuromarketing, which uses recent advancements in neuroscience to study the way people respond to products and promotions. After hearing about the subject in her marketing class, the student researched the topic further. In the process, she learned that neuromarketing is currently being used by some of the biggest corporations in the world. Using what she learned in her research, she put together a captivating speech that kept everyone's attention from beginning to end.

connect

View an excerpt from "Neuromarketing: Whispers of the Brain" in the online Media Library for this chapter (Video 5.1).

Still another possibility—especially for persuasive speeches—is to think of subjects about which you hold strong opinions and beliefs. They may include national or international concerns such as school safety or environmental protection. Or perhaps you are closely involved in a local issue such as a school board election or a proposal to build a new student center. Not all such topics must be "political." They can deal with anything from graduation requirements to helping people with physical disabilities, from dormitory regulations to building a church recreation center.

BRAINSTORMING FOR TOPICS

brainstorming

A method of generating ideas for speech topics by free association of words and ideas.

After all this, you may still be thinking, "I *don't* care about neuromarketing. I've *never* been to Turkey. I'm *not* active in politics. WHAT am I going to talk about?" If you are having trouble selecting a topic, there are a number of brainstorming procedures you can follow to get started.

Personal Inventory

First, make a quick inventory of your experiences, interests, hobbies, skills, beliefs, and so forth. Jot down anything that comes to mind, no matter how silly or irrelevant it may seem. From this list may come a general subject area out of which you can fashion a specific topic. This method has worked for many students.

Clustering

If the first method doesn't work, try a technique called clustering. Take a sheet of paper and divide it into nine columns as follows: People, Places, Things, Events, Processes, Concepts, Natural Phenomena, Problems, and Plans and Policies. Then list in each column the first four or five items that come to mind. The result might look like this:

People	Places	Things
Mark Zuckerberg	Syria	drones
Sofía Vergara	Grand Canyon	smart guns
Barack Obama	Mars	4K TV
Erin Andrews	my hometown	movies

Events	Processes
graduation	fracking
Yom Kippur	cooking Indian food
Chinese New Year	creating an urban garden
Cinco de Mayo	writing a job resumé

Concepts	Natural Phenomena
time travel	sink holes
conservatism	earthquakes
sustainability	tornadoes
bioethics	lightning

Problems	Plans and Policies
campus crime	education reform
heroin	living wage
cyberbullying	legalizing marijuana
political gridlock	immigration policy

Very likely, several items on your lists will strike you as potential topics. If not, take the items you find most intriguing and compose sublists for each. Try to free-associate. Write down a word or idea. What does that trigger in your mind? Whatever it is, write that down next, and keep going until you have four or five ideas on your list. For example, working from the lists printed above, one student composed sublists for movies, campus crime, and lightning:

connect

For an additional resource on speech topics, check the Topic Helper under the Library tab in Connect.

Movies	Campus Crime	Lightning
Academy Awards	police	thunder
prizes	fingerprints	noise
lotteries	hands	traffic
gambling	gloves	air pollution

Can you follow her trail of association? In the first column, movies made her think of the Academy Awards. The Academy Awards are prizes. Prizes reminded her of lotteries. Lotteries are a form of gambling. Suddenly, this student remembered an article she had read on the problem of gambling addiction in America. The idea clicked in her mind. After considerable research, she developed an excellent speech titled "Gambling Addiction: Why You Can't Beat the Odds."

That's a far cry from movies! If you started out free-associating from movies, you would doubtless end up somewhere completely different. This is what clustering is all about.

Internet Search

By clustering, most people come up with a topic rather quickly. But if you are still stymied, try an Internet search. Browse through a subject-based Web site, an online encyclopedia, or some other reference portal until you come across what might be a good topic. As an experiment, one student scanned the *Merriam-Webster Online Dictionary,* limiting herself to the letter *s.* Within 10 minutes, she had come up with these potential topics:

salaries	sleepwalking	sushi	submarines
strip mining	stars	Sphinx	scuba diving
states' rights	Singapore	Sabbath	self-improvement
spiders	stock market	surfing	science fiction

Whatever the means you use for selecting a topic, *start early.* Pay attention to interesting subjects in conversation, on television and the Internet, in newspapers and magazines. Jot down ideas for topics as they occur to you.

Having an inventory of possible topics to choose from is much better than having to rack your brain for one at the last minute. If you get an early start on choosing a topic, you will have plenty of time to pick just the right one and prepare a first-rate speech.

Determining the General Purpose

general purpose

The broad goal of a speech.

Along with choosing a topic, you need to determine the general purpose of your speech. Usually it will fall into one of two overlapping categories—to inform or to persuade.

When your general purpose is to inform, you act as a teacher or lecturer. Your goal is to convey information clearly, accurately, and interestingly. If you describe how to lift weights, narrate the major events of the latest Middle East crisis, or report on your sorority's financial position, you are speaking to inform. Your aim is to enhance the knowledge and understanding of your listeners—to give them information they did not have before.

When your general purpose is to persuade, you act as an advocate or a partisan. You go beyond giving information to espousing a cause. You want to change or structure the attitudes or actions of your audience. If you try to convince your listeners that they should start a regular program of weight lifting, that the United States should modify its policy in the Middle East, or that your sorority should start a fund-raising drive to balance its budget, then you are speaking to persuade. In doing so, you cannot help but give information, but your primary goal is to win over your listeners to your point of view—to get them to believe something or do something as a result of your speech.

In speech classes, the general purpose is usually specified as part of the speech assignment. For speeches outside the classroom, however, you have to make sure of your general purpose yourself. Usually this is easy to do. Are you going to explain, report, or demonstrate something? Then your general purpose is to inform. Are you going to sell, advocate, or defend something? Then your general purpose is to persuade. But no matter what the situation, you must be certain of exactly what you hope to achieve by speaking.

Determining the Specific Purpose

specific purpose

A single infinitive phrase that states precisely what a speaker hopes to accomplish in his or her speech.

Once you have chosen a topic and a general purpose, you must narrow your choices to determine the specific purpose of your speech. The specific purpose should focus on one aspect of a topic. You should be able to state your specific purpose in a single infinitive phrase (to inform my audience about . . . ; to persuade my audience to . . .) that indicates *precisely* what you hope to accomplish with your speech.

For example, Duane Winfield, a student at a large state university, decided to give his first classroom speech on a topic from his personal experience. For the past two years, he had volunteered his time to perform music for patients in mental hospitals, nursing homes, and residences for disabled adults. He had seen how enthusiastically the patients responded to music, even when they remained unmoved by other kinds of stimuli. Duane's experience had given him a better understanding of the benefits of music therapy, and he wanted to share this understanding with his classmates. This gave him a topic and a general purpose, which he stated like this:

Topic: Music therapy

General Purpose: To inform

So far, so good. But what aspect of his topic would Duane discuss? The kinds of facilities in which he had worked? His specific role as a performer? The evidence that music therapy can improve patients' mental health? The needs of patients with different kinds of illnesses? He had to choose something interesting that he could cover in a six-minute speech. Finally, he settled on describing his most memorable experiences with patients to show how music therapy affected them. He stated his specific purpose this way:

Specific Purpose: To inform my audience about the benefits of music therapy for people with psychological or cognitive disabilities.

This turned out to be an excellent choice, and Duane's speech was among the best in the class.

Notice how clear the specific purpose statement is. Notice also how it relates the topic directly to the audience. That is, it states not only what the *speaker* wants to *say* but also what the speaker wants the *audience* to *know* as a result of the speech. This is very important, for it helps keep the audience at the center of your attention as you prepare your speech.

Using public speaking in your CAREER

Your communication degree has helped you land a job as spokesperson for the mayor of a medium-sized city on the West Coast. A year after starting the job, you are selected to organize an information campaign explaining the benefits of a new youth center proposed by the mayor.

To launch this campaign, you've decided to hold a news briefing at the end of the week. To open the briefing, you will present a short set of comments on the mayor's initiative. You decide to focus on four benefits of the youth center: (1) It will offer a range of activities—from sports to the arts—in a safe environment. (2) It will provide social networks for youths from all walks of life. (3) It will operate most hours of the day and night. (4) It will be free and open to everyone.

Following the format used in this chapter, state the general purpose, specific purpose, central idea, and main points of your comments.

Look what happens when the specific purpose statement does not include the audience.

Specific Purpose: To explain the benefits of music therapy for people with psychological or cognitive disabilities.

Explain to whom? To musicians? To medical students? To social workers? Those would be three different speeches. The musicians would want to know about the kinds of music Duane played. The medical students would want to hear about research on the benefits of music therapy. The social workers would want to learn how to implement a music program. Communicating effectively with each group would require preparing a different speech.

When the audience slips out of the specific purpose, it may slip out of the speaker's consciousness. You may begin to think that your task is the general one of preparing "an informative speech," when in fact your task is the specific one of informing a particular group of people. As we shall see in the next chapter, it is almost impossible to prepare a good speech without keeping constantly in mind the *people* for whom it is intended.

TIPS FOR FORMULATING THE SPECIFIC PURPOSE STATEMENT

Formulating a specific purpose is the most important early step in developing a successful speech. When writing your purpose statement, follow the general principles outlined on the following pages.

Write the Purpose Statement as a Full Infinitive Phrase, Not as a Fragment

Ineffective: avalanches.

More Effective: To inform my audience about the three major kinds of avalanches.

The ineffective statement is adequate as an announcement of the speech topic, but it is not thought out fully enough to indicate the specific purpose.

Express Your Purpose as a Statement, Not as a Question

Ineffective: What is Día de los Muertos?

More Effective: To inform my audience about the history of Mexico's Día de los Muertos celebration.

The question might arouse the curiosity of an audience, but it is not effective as a specific purpose statement. It gives no indication about what direction the speech will take or what the speaker hopes to accomplish.

Avoid Figurative Language in Your Purpose Statement

Ineffective: To persuade my audience that the campus policy on student parking really stinks.

Think of opinions you hold when looking for speech topics. One student spoke on the specific purpose "To persuade my audience that stronger measures should be taken to protect Siberian tigers."

More Effective: To persuade my audience that the campus policy on student parking should be revised to provide more spaces for students before 5 P.M.

Although the ineffective statement indicates something of the speaker's viewpoint, it does not state concisely what he or she hopes to achieve. Figurative language can reinforce ideas within a speech, but it is too ambiguous for a specific purpose statement.

Limit Your Purpose Statement to One Distinct Idea

Ineffective: To persuade my audience to become literacy tutors and to donate time to Meals on Wheels.

This purpose statement expresses two unrelated ideas, either of which could be the subject of a speech. The easiest remedy is to select one or the other as a focus for your presentation.

More Effective: To persuade my audience to become literacy tutors.

Or:

More Effective: To persuade my audience to donate time to Meals on Wheels.

Does this mean that you can never use the word "and" in your specific purpose statement? Not at all. Suppose your specific purpose is "To inform my audience about the causes and effects of epilepsy." In this case, "and" is appropriate because it connects two related parts of a unified topic. What you need to avoid is not simply the word "and," but a specific purpose statement that contains two unrelated ideas, either of which could be developed into a speech in its own right.

Make Sure Your Specific Purpose Is Not Too Vague or General

Ineffective: To persuade my audience that something should be done about unsafe school buses.

More Effective: To persuade my audience that the federal government should impose stronger safety standards for school buses in the United States.

The ineffective purpose statement falls into one of the most common traps—it is too broad and ill-defined. It gives no clues about what the speaker believes should be done about school buses. The more effective purpose statement is sharp and concise. It reveals clearly what the speaker plans to discuss.

The more precise your specific purpose, the easier it will be to prepare your speech. Consider this topic and specific purpose:

Topic: Hot-air balloons.

Specific Purpose: To inform my audience about hot-air balloons.

With such a hazy purpose, you have no systematic way of limiting your research or of deciding what to include in the speech and what to exclude. The origins of hot-air balloons, how they work, their current popularity—all could be equally relevant to a speech designed "to inform my audience about hot-air balloons."

In contrast, look at this topic and specific purpose:

Topic: Hot-air balloons.

Specific Purpose: To inform my audience about the scientific uses of hot-air balloons.

Now it is easy to decide what is germane and what is not. The origins of hot-air balloons, how they work, their popularity for recreation—all are interesting, but none is essential to the specific purpose of explaining "the scientific uses of hot-air balloons." Thus you need not worry about researching these matters or about explaining them in your speech. You can spend your preparation time efficiently.

QUESTIONS TO ASK ABOUT YOUR SPECIFIC PURPOSE

Sometimes you will arrive at your specific purpose almost immediately after choosing your topic. At other times you may do quite a bit of research before deciding on a specific purpose. Much will depend on how familiar you are with the topic, as well as on any special demands imposed by the assignment, the audience, or the occasion. But whenever you settle on your specific purpose, ask yourself the following questions about it.

Does My Purpose Meet the Assignment?

Students occasionally stumble over this question. Be sure you understand your assignment and shape your specific purpose to meet it. If you have questions, check with your instructor.

Can I Accomplish My Purpose in the Time Allotted?

Most classroom speeches are quite short, ranging from four to ten minutes. That may seem like a lot of time, but you will quickly find what generations of students have discovered—time flies when you are giving a speech!

Most people speak at an average rate of 120 to 150 words a minute. This means that a six-minute speech will consist of roughly 720 to 900 words. That is not long enough to develop a highly complex topic. Here are some specific purpose statements that would defy being handled well in the time normally allotted for classroom speeches:

> To inform my audience about the rise and fall of ancient Rome.
>
> To inform my audience about the role of technology in human history.
>
> To persuade my audience to convert to Buddhism.

You are much better off with a limited purpose that you have some reasonable hope of achieving in the short span of four to ten minutes.

IS THE PURPOSE RELEVANT TO MY AUDIENCE?

The price of retirement homes in Palm Springs might be an engrossing topic for older citizens who are in the market for such dwellings. And the quality

checklist

Specific Purpose

YES	NO	
☐	☐	1. Is the specific purpose written as a full infinitive phrase?
☐	☐	2. Does the specific purpose include a reference to the audience?
☐	☐	3. Is the specific purpose phrased as a statement rather than a question?
☐	☐	4. Is the specific purpose free of figurative language?
☐	☐	5. Is the specific purpose limited to one distinct subject?
☐	☐	6. Does the specific purpose indicate precisely what I plan to accomplish in the speech?
☐	☐	7. Does the specific purpose meet the requirements of the assignment?
☐	☐	8. Can the specific purpose be accomplished in the time allotted for the speech?
☐	☐	9. Is the specific purpose relevant to my audience?
☐	☐	10. Does the specific purpose deal with a nontrivial subject?
☐	☐	11. Is the specific purpose suitable for a nontechnical audience?

of hot lunches in the elementary schools is of great concern to the students who eat them and the parents who pay for them. But neither subject has much relevance for an audience of college students. No matter how well you construct your speeches, they are likely to fall flat unless you speak about matters of interest to your listeners.

This is not to say you must select only topics that pertain directly to the college student's daily experience. Most students have wide-ranging backgrounds, interests, ideas, and values. And most of them are intellectually curious. They can get involved in an astonishing variety of subjects. Follow your common sense and make sure *you* are truly interested in the topic. Also, when speaking on a subject that is not obviously relevant to your listeners, find a way to tie it in with their goals, values, interests, and well-being. We'll discuss how to do this in the next chapter.

Is the Purpose Too Trivial for My Audience?

Just as you need to avoid speech topics that are too broad or complicated, so you need to steer clear of topics that are too superficial. How to tie a perfect square knot might absorb a group of Cub Scouts, but your classmates would probably consider it frivolous. Unfortunately, there is no absolute rule for determining what is trivial to an audience and what is not. Here are some examples of specific purposes that most people would find too trivial for classroom speeches:

To inform my audience about the parts of a backpack.

To inform my audience how to do laundry.

To persuade my audience that espresso is better than cappuccino.

Is the Purpose Too Technical for My Audience?

Nothing puts an audience to sleep faster than a dry and technical speech. Beware of topics that are inherently technical and of treating ordinary subjects in a technical fashion. Although you may be familiar with the principles and vocabulary of international finance or clinical psychology, most of your classmates probably are not. There are aspects of these and similar subjects that can be treated clearly, with a minimum of jargon. But if you find that you can't fulfill your specific purpose without relying on technical words and concepts, you should reconsider your purpose.

Here are some examples of specific purposes that are overly technical for most classroom speeches:

To inform my audience about the solution to Fermat's Last Theorem.

To inform my audience about the principles of neutrino physics.

To inform my audience about the methods of encryption technology.

We will discuss the details of audience analysis and adaptation in Chapter 6. For the moment, remember to make sure that your specific purpose is appropriate for your listeners. If you have doubts, ask your instructor, or circulate a questionnaire among your classmates (see pages 110–113).

Phrasing the Central Idea

WHAT IS THE CENTRAL IDEA?

The specific purpose of a speech is what you hope to accomplish. The *central idea* is a concise statement of what you *expect to say.* Sometimes it is called the thesis statement, the subject sentence, or the major thought. Whatever the term, the central idea is usually expressed as a simple, declarative sentence that refines and sharpens the specific purpose statement.

central idea

A one-sentence statement that sums up or encapsulates the major ideas of a speech.

Imagine that you run into a friend on your way to speech class. She says, "I have to dash to my history lecture, but I hear you're giving a speech today. Can you tell me the gist of it in one sentence?" "Sure," you reply. "America's prison system suffers from three major problems—overcrowding of inmates, lack of effective rehabilitation programs, and high expense to taxpayers."

Your answer is the central idea of your speech. It is more precise than your topic (America's prison system) or your specific purpose statement ("To inform my audience of the three major problems facing America's prison system"). By stating exactly what the three major problems are, the central idea sums up your speech in a single sentence.

Another way to think of the central idea is as your *residual message*—what you want your audience to remember after they have forgotten everything else in the speech. Most of the time the central idea will encapsulate the main points to be developed in the body of the speech. To show how this works, let's take a few of the examples we saw earlier in this chapter and develop them from the topic, general purpose, and specific purpose to the central idea.

residual message

What a speaker wants the audience to remember after it has forgotten everything else in a speech.

We can start with the speech about music therapy.

Topic:	Music therapy.
General Purpose:	To inform.
Specific Purpose:	To inform my audience about the benefits of music therapy for people with psychological or cognitive disabilities.
Central Idea:	Music therapy developed as a formal mode of treatment during the 20th century, utilizes a number of methods, and is explained by several theories that account for its success.

Look carefully at this example. It shows how the speaker might start with a broad subject (music therapy) that becomes narrower and narrower as the speaker moves from the general purpose to the specific purpose to the central idea. Notice also how much more the central idea suggests about the content of the speech. From it we can expect the speaker to address three main points—the first summarizing the development of music therapy, the second looking at methods of music therapy, and the third exploring theories that account for the success of music therapy.

connect

View the introduction from "The Benefits of Music Therapy" in the online Media Library for this chapter (Video 5.2).

This sharpening of focus as one proceeds to the central idea is crucial. Here is another example:

Topic:	Día de los Muertos.
General Purpose:	To inform.

Specific Purpose: To inform my audience about the history of Mexico's Día de los Muertos celebration.

Central Idea: Día de los Muertos can be traced to the Aztecs, was moved from summer to fall by Spanish priests, and today is celebrated in a number of ways in different regions of Mexico.

This central idea is especially well worded. We can assume from it that the body of the speech will contain three main points: (1) on the Aztec origins of Día de los Muertos, (2) on how it was changed by the Spanish, and (3) on the ways it is celebrated today.

Notice in each of these examples how much more the central idea reveals about the content of the speech than does the specific purpose. This is not accidental. Often you can settle on a specific purpose statement early in preparing your speech. The central idea, however, usually emerges later—after you have done your research and have decided on the main points of the speech. The process may work like this:

> As an environmental science major, Marcia Esposito had learned that many experts fear the world may face a severe water shortage by the year 2025. She decided this would make a good topic for her informative speech. Tentatively, she adopted the following specific purpose statement: "To inform my audience about the seriousness of the growing international water crisis." Then Marcia started her research.
>
> An article in *Time* magazine, which she located through LexisNexis, explained how the population in countries such as China, India, and Pakistan is outstripping the available supply of fresh water. According to the article, 400 million Chinese do not have access to suitable drinking water and two-thirds of India's 1.1 billion people lack the water they need.
>
> Next Marcia found a report on the United Nations Web site about the impact of pollution on the water supply. The report stated that in developing countries "more than 90 percent of sewage and 70 percent of industrial wastewater is dumped untreated into surface water."
>
> Then Marcia hit upon the idea of interviewing one of her environmental science professors. In addition to confirming Marcia's research about the impact of population growth and pollution, the professor mentioned the problems caused by mismanagement of water supplies. Around the world, 65 to 70 percent of the water people use is lost to waste, evaporation, and other inefficiencies.
>
> Marcia digested all this information. Now she was ready to formulate her central idea: "Population growth, pollution, and mismanagement are creating a serious shortage of fresh water in many parts of the world."

GUIDELINES FOR THE CENTRAL IDEA

What makes a well-worded central idea? Essentially the same things that make a well-worded specific purpose statement. The central idea (1) should be expressed in a full sentence, (2) should not be in the form of a question, (3) should avoid figurative language, and (4) should not be vague or overly general.

Unlike the specific purpose, which you need to settle on early in the speech preparation process, the central idea usually takes shape later, as a result of your research and analysis of the topic.

Here, for example, are four poorly written central ideas. See if you can identify the problem with each and figure out how each might be phrased more effectively:

Ineffective: Paying college athletes a monthly stipend is a good idea.

Ineffective: Problems of fad diets.

Ineffective: What are nanorobots?

Ineffective: South Africa is an awesome place for a vacation.

The first is too general. To say that paying college athletes a monthly stipend is a "good idea" does not convey the speaker's viewpoint sharply and clearly. What does the speaker mean by a "good idea"? A revised central idea for this speech might be:

More Effective: Because college athletes in revenue-producing sports such as football and basketball generate millions of dollars in revenue for their schools, the NCAA should allow such athletes to receive a $300 monthly stipend as part of their scholarships.

The second ineffective central idea is also too general, but it suffers further from not being written as a complete sentence. "Problems of fad diets" does not reveal enough about the content of the speech to serve as the central idea. It should be rewritten as a full sentence that identifies the problems of fad diets to be discussed in the speech:

More Effective: Although fad diets produce quick weight loss, they can lead to serious health problems by creating deficiencies in vitamins and minerals and by breaking down muscle tissue as well as fat.

checklist

Central Idea

YES	NO	
☐	☐	1. Is the central idea written as a complete sentence?
☐	☐	2. Is the central idea phrased as a statement rather than a question?
☐	☐	3. Is the central idea free of figurative language?
☐	☐	4. Does the central idea clearly encapsulate the main points to be discussed in the body of the speech?
☐	☐	5. Can the central idea be adequately discussed in the time allotted for the speech?
☐	☐	6. Is the central idea relevant to the audience?
☐	☐	7. Is the central idea appropriate for a nontechnical audience?

The third poorly written central idea is phrased as a question rather than as a full declarative sentence. Asking "What are nanorobots?" might be a good way to catch the attention of listeners, but it does not encapsulate the main points to be developed in the speech. A more effective central idea would be:

More Effective: Microscopic in size, nanorobots are being developed for use in medicine, weaponry, and daily life.

The final ineffective central idea is flawed by its use of figurative language. To say that South Africa is an "awesome" place for a vacation does not indicate what characteristics of South Africa the speaker intends to discuss. A better central idea might be:

More Effective: South Africa has many attractions for vacationers, including beautiful scenery, exotic wildlife, and bustling cities.

Notice that in all these examples the more effective central idea sums up the main points of the speech in a single sentence. If you are having trouble phrasing your central idea, the reason may be that you do not yet have a firm grasp on the main points of your speech.

Don't worry too much about your central idea until after you have developed the body of your speech (see Chapter 9). If, at that point, you still can't come up with a clear, concise central idea, your speech itself may not be clear or concise. Keep working on the speech until you can compose a central idea that fits the criteria just discussed. The result will be a sharper central idea and a tighter, more coherent speech.

Summary

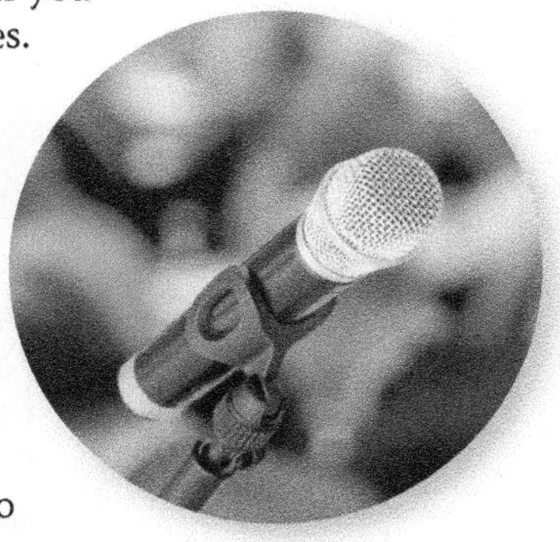

The first step in speechmaking is choosing a topic. For classroom speeches, you can choose a subject you know well or one you research especially for the speech. If you have trouble picking a topic, you can use one of three brainstorming procedures. First, make an inventory of your hobbies, interests, skills, beliefs, and so forth. Second, use clustering to list the first topics that come to mind in several categories. Third, use an Internet subject directory, encyclopedia, or similar reference site to help you scan possible topics.

The general purpose of your speech will usually be to inform or to persuade. When your general purpose is to inform, your goal is to communicate information clearly, accurately, and interestingly. When your general purpose is to persuade, your goal is to win listeners over to your point of view.

Once you know your topic and general purpose, you must focus on a specific purpose statement that indicates precisely what your speech seeks to achieve. The specific purpose statement should (1) be a full infinitive phrase; (2) be worded as a statement, not a question; (3) avoid figurative language; (4) concentrate on one distinct idea; (5) not be vague or general.

Keep several questions in mind as you formulate your specific purpose statement: Does my purpose meet the assignment? Can I accomplish my purpose in the time allotted? Is the purpose relevant to my audience? Is the purpose too trivial or too technical for my audience?

The central idea refines and sharpens your specific purpose. It is a concise statement of what you will say in your speech, and it usually crystallizes in your thinking after you have done your research and have decided on the main points of your speech. The central idea usually encapsulates the main points to be developed in the body of your speech.

Key Terms

topic (78)
brainstorming (80)
general purpose (82)
specific purpose (82)
central idea (89)
residual message (89)

Review Questions

After reading this chapter, you should be able to answer the following questions:

1. What three brainstorming methods can you follow if you are having trouble choosing a topic for your speech?
2. What are the two general purposes of most classroom speeches? How do they differ?
3. Why is determining the specific purpose such an important early step in speech preparation? Why is it important to include the audience in the specific purpose statement?

connect™

For further review, go to the LearnSmart study module for this chapter.

4. What are five tips for formulating your specific purpose?
5. What are five questions to ask about your specific purpose?
6. What is the difference between the specific purpose and the central idea of a speech? What are four guidelines for an effective central idea?

Exercises for Critical Thinking

1. Using one of the brainstorming methods described in this chapter, come up with three topics you might like to deal with in your next classroom speech. For each topic, devise a specific purpose statement suitable for the speech assignment. Make sure your specific purpose statements fit the guidelines discussed in the chapter.
2. Here are several specific purpose statements for classroom speeches. Identify the problem (or problems) with each.

   To inform my audience about Portugal.

   To persuade my audience that something has to be done about the problem of corporate tax loopholes.

   Donate blood.

   To inform my audience why square grooves are superior to U-shaped grooves on golf clubs.

   To persuade my audience that the U.S. government should increase funding for the national parks and send an astronaut to Mars by 2025.

   What is the Great Pacific Garbage Patch?

   To inform my audience how to register for classes.
3. Below are three sets of main points for speeches. For each set, supply the general purpose, specific purpose, and central idea.

   General Purpose:

   Specific Purpose:

   Central Idea:

   Main Points:
   I. You should support the school-bond referendum because it will improve classroom facilities.
   II. You should support the school-bond referendum because it will increase the number of teachers.
   III. You should support the school-bond referendum because it will upgrade instructional resources.

   General Purpose:

   Specific Purpose:

   Central Idea:

   Main Points:
   I. The first event in a triathlon is swimming.
   II. The second event in a triathlon is cycling.
   III. The third event in a triathlon is running.

General Purpose:

Specific Purpose:

Central Idea:

Main Points:

I. As a writer, Thomas Jefferson penned the Declaration of Independence and *Notes on the State of Virginia.*

II. As president, Thomas Jefferson negotiated the Louisiana Purchase and approved the Lewis and Clark expedition.

III. As an architect, Thomas Jefferson designed Monticello and the University of Virginia.

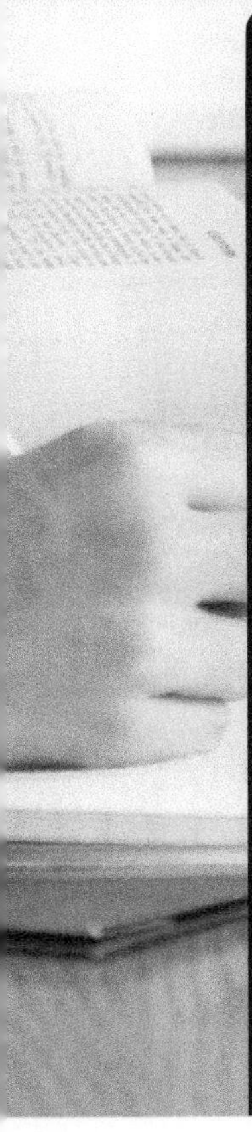

4

Outlining the Speech

Think what might happen if you tried to build a house without a floor plan or an architect's blueprint. You install a cathedral ceiling so you can have big windows and a huge ceiling fan, but the roof is so high it blocks your bedroom window upstairs. You put in sliding doors to the yard, but they can't be opened because they're too close to the fireplace to slide back without hitting it. You think it's a wonderful idea to have almost no interior walls. But when the first snowfall comes, your (unsupported) roof collapses.

Plans and blueprints are essential to architecture. So, too, are outlines essential to effective speeches. An outline is like a blueprint for your speech. It allows you to see the full scope and content of your speech at a glance. By outlining, you can judge whether each part of the speech is fully developed, whether you have adequate supporting materials for your main points, and whether the main points are properly balanced. An outline helps you make sure that related items are together, that ideas flow from one to another, that the structure of your speech will "stand up"—and not collapse.

Probably you will use two kinds of outlines for your speeches—one very detailed, for the planning stage, and one very brief, for the delivery of the speech.

The Preparation Outline

The preparation outline is just what its name implies—an outline that helps you prepare the speech. Writing a preparation outline means putting your speech together—deciding what you will say in the introduction, how you will organize the main points and supporting materials in the body, and what you will say in the conclusion.

GUIDELINES FOR THE PREPARATION OUTLINE

preparation outline

A detailed outline developed during the process of speech preparation that includes the title, specific purpose, central idea, introduction, main points, subpoints, connectives, conclusion, and bibliography of a speech.

Over the years, a relatively uniform system for preparation outlines has developed. It is explained below and is exemplified in the sample outline on pages 211–213. You should check with your teacher to see what format you are to follow.

State the Specific Purpose of Your Speech

The specific purpose statement should be a separate unit that comes before the outline itself. Including the specific purpose makes it easier to assess how well you have constructed the speech to accomplish your purpose.

Identify the Central Idea

Some instructors prefer that the central idea be given immediately after the purpose statement. Others prefer that it be given and identified in the text of the outline. Check to see which your instructor wants.

Label the Introduction, Body, and Conclusion

If you label the parts of your speech, you will be sure that you indeed *have* an introduction and conclusion and have accomplished the essential objectives of each. Usually the names of the speech parts are placed in the middle of the page or in the far left margin. They are technical labels only and are not included in the system of symbolization used to identify main points and supporting materials.

Use a Consistent Pattern of Symbolization and Indentation

In the most common system of outlining, main points are identified by Roman numerals and are indented equally so as to be aligned down the page. Subpoints (components of the main points) are identified by capital letters and are also indented equally so as to be aligned with each other.

Beyond this, there may be sub-subpoints and even sub-sub-subpoints. For example:

I. Main point
    A. Subpoint
    B. Subpoint
        1. Sub-subpoint
        2. Sub-subpoint
            a. Sub-sub-subpoint
            b. Sub-sub-subpoint

As blueprints are essential to architecture, so outlines are essential to speechmaking. Developing an outline helps ensure that the structure of your speech is clear and coherent.

II. Main point
  A. Subpoint
    1. Sub-subpoint
    2. Sub-subpoint
  B. Subpoint
    1. Sub-subpoint
    2. Sub-subpoint

The clear *visual framework* of this outline immediately shows the relationships among the ideas of the speech. The most important ideas (main points) are farthest to the left. Less important ideas (subpoints, sub-subpoints, and so on) are progressively farther to the right. This pattern reveals the structure of your entire speech.

visual framework

The pattern of symbolization and indentation in a speech outline that shows the relationships among the speaker's ideas.

Once you have organized the body of your speech (see Chapter 9), you should have identified the main points. You need only flesh out your outline with subpoints and sub-subpoints, as necessary, to support the main points. But suppose, as sometimes happens, you find yourself with a list of statements and are not sure which are main points, which are subpoints, and so forth. Such a list might look like this:

There were 13 people at the Last Supper—Jesus and his 12 disciples.

Many superstitions revolve around numbers.

In the United States, 13 is often omitted in the floor numbering of hotels and skyscrapers.

The number 13 has meant bad luck as long as anyone can remember.

Which statement is the main point? The second statement ("Many superstitions revolve around numbers"), which is broader in scope than any of the other statements. This would be one of the main ideas of your speech. The fourth statement is the subpoint; it immediately supports the main point. The other two statements are sub-subpoints; they illustrate the subpoint. Rearranged properly, they look like this:

I. Many superstitions revolve around numbers.
  A. The number 13 has meant bad luck as long as anyone can remember.
    1. There were 13 people at the Last Supper—Jesus and his 12 disciples.
    2. In the United States, 13 is often omitted in the floor numbering of hotels and skyscrapers.

Above all, remember that all points at the same level should immediately support the point that is just above and one notch to the left in your outline. If this sounds confusing, think of it as a business organization chart:

connect

For help formatting your outlines, use the automated Outline Tool in the online Speech Tools for this chapter.

I. President
  A. Vice president—Operations
    1. Manager—Domestic Operations
      a. Assistant manager—East
      b. Assistant manager—West
    2. Manager—International Operations
      a. Assistant manager—Europe
      b. Assistant manager—Asia
      c. Assistant manager—Americas
  B. Vice president—Administration
    1. Manager—Finance
    2. Manager—Personnel

As you can see, every person on this chart reports to the person who is above and one notch to the left—except, of course, the president, who is the "main point."

State Main Points and Subpoints in Full Sentences

Below are two sets of main points and subpoints for the same speech on the life of Martin Luther King.

Ineffective	**More Effective**
I. Montgomery	I. King began his civil rights career in the Montgomery bus boycott of 1955–1956.
II. 1960s	II. King's greatest triumphs came during the early 1960s.
A. Birmingham	A. In 1963, he campaigned against segregation in Birmingham, Alabama.
B. March	B. Later that year, he participated in the famous march on Washington, D.C.
1. 200,000	1. More than 200,000 people took part.
2. "Dream"	2. King gave his "I Have a Dream" speech.
C. Prize	C. In 1964, he received the Nobel Peace Prize.
III. Final years	III. King faced great turmoil during his final years.
A. Criticized	A. He was criticized by more militant blacks for being nonviolent.
B. Vietnam	B. He protested against the war in Vietnam.
C. Assassination	C. He was assassinated in Memphis, Tennessee, on April 4, 1968.

The sample at the left might serve as a speaking outline, but it is virtually useless as a preparation outline. It gives only vague labels rather than distinct ideas. It does not indicate clearly the content of the main points and subpoints. Nor does it reveal whether the speaker has thought out his or her ideas. But there is no concern about any of these matters with the outline on the right.

In sum, a skimpy preparation outline is of little value. Stating your main points and subpoints in full sentences will ensure that you develop your ideas fully.

Label Transitions, Internal Summaries, and Internal Previews

One way to make sure you have strong transitions, internal summaries, and internal previews is to include them in the preparation outline. Usually they are not incorporated into the system of symbolization and indentation but are labeled separately and inserted in the outline where they will appear in the speech.

Attach a Bibliography

You should include with the outline a bibliography that shows all the books, magazines, newspapers, and Internet sources you consulted, as well as any interviews or field research you conducted.

bibliography

A list of all the sources used in preparing a speech.

The two major bibliographic formats are those developed by the Modern Language Association (MLA) and the American Psychological Association (APA). Both are widely used by communication scholars; ask your instructor which he or she prefers. No matter which format you adopt, make sure your statement of sources is clear, accurate, and consistent. For help, turn to page 135 in Chapter 7, where you will find sample citations for the kinds of sources used most frequently in classroom speeches.

Give Your Speech a Title, If One Is Desired

In the classroom you probably do not need a title for your speech unless your teacher requires one. In some other situations, however, a speech title is necessary—as when the speech is publicized in advance or is going to be published. Whatever the reason, if you do decide to use a title, it should (1) be brief, (2) attract the attention of your audience, and (3) encapsulate the main thrust of your speech.

A good title need not have what Madison Avenue would call "sex appeal"—lots of glitter and pizzazz. By the same token, there is certainly nothing wrong with a catchy title—as long as it is germane to the speech. Here are two groups of titles. Those on the left are straightforward and descriptive. Those on the right are figurative alternatives to the ones on the left.

Group I	Group II
Gambling Addiction	Against All Odds
The Rage to Diet	The Art of Wishful Shrinking
Living with Deafness	The Sounds of Silence
Unsafe Drinking Water	Toxins on Tap

Which group do you prefer? There are advantages and disadvantages to both. Those in the first group clearly reveal the topic, but they are not as provocative as those in the second group. Those in the second group are sure to arouse interest, but they do not give as clear an idea of what the speeches are about.

checklist

Preparation Outline

YES	NO	
☐	☐	1. Does my speech have a title, if one is required?
☐	☐	2. Do I state the specific purpose before the text of the outline itself?
☐	☐	3. Do I state the central idea before the text of the outline itself?
☐	☐	4. Are the introduction, body, and conclusion clearly labeled?
☐	☐	5. Are main points and subpoints written in full sentences?
☐	☐	6. Are transitions, internal summaries, and internal previews clearly labeled?
☐	☐	7. Does the outline follow a consistent pattern of symbolization and indentation?
☐	☐	8. Does the outline provide a clear visual framework that shows the relationships among the ideas of my speech?
☐	☐	9. Does the bibliography identify all the sources I consulted in preparing the outline?
☐	☐	10. Does the bibliography follow the format required by my instructor?

There is one other kind of title you should consider—the question. Phrasing your title as a question can be both descriptive and provocative. Using this method, we can construct a third set of titles combining the virtues of groups I and II:

Group III

Do You Really Think You Can Beat the Odds?

Diets: How Effective Are They?

Can You See What I'm Saying?

Is Your Water Safe to Drink?

Sometimes you will choose a title for your speech very early. At other times you may not find one you like until the last minute. Either way, try to be resourceful about creating titles for your speeches. Experiment with several and choose the one that seems most appropriate.

SAMPLE PREPARATION OUTLINE WITH COMMENTARY

The following outline for a six-minute informative speech illustrates the principles just discussed. The commentary explains the procedures used in organizing the speech and writing the outline. (Check with your teacher to see if she or he wants you to include a title with your outline.)

Beneficial Bacteria

COMMENTARY

Stating your specific purpose and central idea as separate units before the text of the outline makes it easier to judge how well you have constructed the outline to achieve your purpose and to communicate your central idea.

Labeling the introduction marks it as a distinct section that plays a special role in the speech.

The opening gets attention and, as it progresses, reveals the topic of the speech.

Here the speaker establishes his credibility and previews the main points to be discussed in the body.

Including transitions ensures that the speaker has worked out how to connect one idea to the next. Notice that the transition is not included in the system of symbolization and indentation used for the rest of the speech.

Labeling the body marks it as a distinct part of the speech.

Main point I is phrased as a full sentence. The three subpoints of main point I are shown by the capital letters A, B, and C and are also written in full sentences to ensure that the speaker has thought them out fully.

OUTLINE

Specific Purpose: To inform my audience about the role of beneficial bacteria in our bodies and in the environment.

Central Idea: Beneficial bacteria are crucial to human health and to the health of our environment.

Introduction

I. Hold up your hand and look closely.
   A. You can't see them, but millions of creatures—bacteria—are living there.
   B. You've been taught to scrub off those bacteria in the sink.
   C. That's fine advice—but only up to a point.
II. The truth is that most bacteria are not something to be washed away.
III. Dr. Martin Blaser states in his book *Missing Microbes* that bacteria are vital to human life and to the world in general.
IV. I learned about the importance of bacteria in my biology class, and I did additional research for this speech.
V. Today, I'd like to inform you about some of the ways beneficial bacteria help our bodies and our environment.

(*Transition:* Let's start by looking at the beneficial bacteria inside us.)

Body

I. Beneficial bacteria play a crucial role in our bodies.
   A. All of us have had bacteria on—and in—our bodies since we were born.
      1. As stated in *Scientific American*, the human body is "a complex ecosystem . . . containing trillions of bacteria."
      2. Each square centimeter of your skin is home to as many as 100,000 bacteria.

The progressive indentation shows visually the relationships among main points, subpoints, and sub-subpoints.

3. There are more than 100 different kinds of bacteria in your mouth.
4. Overall, there are 10 times more bacteria in your body than there are human cells.

B. One positive function of bacteria is to help us digest food and maintain our body weight.
   1. Yogurt is famous for its positive bacteria.
   2. Other foods high in positive bacteria include sauerkraut, kefir, kimchi, and some soft cheeses.

Points below the level of subpoint are indicated by Arabic numerals and lowercase letters. Sometimes they are not written as full sentences. Check to see what your instructor prefers.

C. According to the *British Journal of Nutrition*, bacteria help our bodies in other ways as well.
   1. They strengthen our immune systems by helping cells divide and reproduce.
   2. They promote healthy organs by synthesizing the enzymes needed for vitamins.
   3. Perhaps most important, they help create the energy we need to live.

The transition shows how the speaker will get from main point I to main point II.

Like main point I, main point II is phrased as a full sentence.

(*Transition:* Just as important as the bacteria in our bodies are the bacteria in the world around us.)

II. Beneficial bacteria play a crucial role in our environment.
   A. The Web site for the master gardener program at Colorado State University notes that healthy soil is "a dynamic living ecosystem."
      1. In every cup of soil, you'll find some 200 million bacteria.
      2. These bacteria help produce nutrients in the soil that allow plants to grow.
      3. In other words, a good garden requires good bacteria.

Notice the pattern of subordination in this section. Subpoint B states that beneficial bacteria can combat pollution. Sub-subpoint 2 notes that bacteria can help clean up oil spills. Because items a and b expand upon the point about oil spills, they are subordinated to it.

   B. In addition to enriching the soil, bacteria play an important role in combatting pollution.
      1. As a natural part of the environment, bacteria reduce contaminants in lakes, rivers, and oceans.
      2. Scientists are now using bacteria to help clean up oil spills.
         a. Remember the Deepwater Horizon oil spill in the Gulf of Mexico a few years ago?
         b. A recent article in *U.S. News and World Report* states that bacteria released by scientists ate through a significant portion of the oil.
      3. Some bacteria can even eat through discarded plastic and radioactive waste.

Labeling the conclusion marks it as a distinct part of the speech.

Summarizing the main points is standard procedure in an informative speech.

The speaker's closing quotation reinforces his central idea.

Conclusion

I. While bacteria can be dangerous, many are so beneficial that life as we know it could not survive without them.

II. The health of our bodies and the health of our environment both depend on beneficial bacteria.

III. In the words of award-winning science writer Richard Conniff, we should see bacteria "not as enemies, but as intimate partners" in our journey through life.

This is the final bibliography. It lists the sources actually used in writing the speech and is shorter than the preliminary bibliography compiled in the early stages of research. (See Chapter 7 for a discussion of the preliminary bibliography.)

This bibliography follows the Modern Language Association (MLA) format. Check with your instructor to see what format you should use for your bibliography.

Bibliography

Ackerman, Jennifer. "The Ultimate Social Network." *Scientific American* June 2012: 36–43. Print.

Alonso, Virginia Robles, and Francisco Guarner. "Linking the Gut Microbiota to Human Health." *British Journal of Nutrition* Jan. 2013: S21–S26. Print.

Blaser, Martin J. *Missing Microbes: How the Overuse of Antibiotics Is Fueling Our Modern Plagues*. New York: Henry Holt, 2014. Print.

Colorado Master Gardener Program. "The Living Soil." *Colorado State University Extension*. Colorado State University, Dec. 2011. Web. 5 Apr. 2014.

Conniff, Richard. "The Body Eclectic: You're Not Just Human." *Smithsonian Magazine* May 2013: 40. Print.

Koebler, Jason. "Study: Oil-Eating Bacteria Mitigated Deepwater Horizon Oil Spill." *U.S. News & World Report* 8 Apr. 2013. Web. 7 Apr. 2014.

Still have questions about outlining? If you log on to Connect, you will find additional resources to help you create effective preparation outlines. The Outline Tool will help you construct your own outlines from scratch following the guidelines in this chapter. There is also a program called EasyBib that can automatically format your speech bibliography in either APA or MLA format. Like many students before you, you can take advantage of these resources to improve your command of outlining principles and practices.

connect

The Outline Tool and EasyBib can be accessed through the Library tab on the Connect home page.

The Speaking Outline

"I was never so excited by public speaking before in my life," wrote one listener in 1820 after listening to Daniel Webster. "Three or four times I thought my temples would burst with the gush of blood. . . . I was beside myself, and am so still."[1]

Such reactions were not unusual among Webster's audiences. He thrilled two generations of Americans with his masterful orations. Incredible as it seems today, he did so while speaking for several hours at a time, often without using any notes! A reporter once asked how he managed this. "It is my memory," Webster said. "I can prepare a speech, revise and correct it in my memory, then deliver the corrected speech exactly as finished."[2]

Few people have Webster's remarkable powers of memory. Fortunately, it is no longer customary to speak from memory. Today most people speak extemporaneously—which means the speech is carefully prepared and practiced in advance, but much of the exact wording is selected while the speech is being delivered (see Chapter 13). Your speeches will probably be of this type. You should know, then, about the *speaking outline*—the most widely recommended form of notes for extemporaneous speeches.

speaking outline

A brief outline used to jog a speaker's memory during the presentation of a speech.

The aim of a speaking outline is to help you remember what you want to say. In some ways, it is a condensed version of your preparation outline. It should contain key words or phrases to jog your memory, as well as essential statistics and quotations that you don't want to risk forgetting. But it should also include material *not* in your preparation outline—especially cues to direct and sharpen your delivery.

Most speakers develop their own variations on the speaking outline. As you acquire more experience, you, too, should feel free to experiment. But for now, your best bet is to follow the basic guidelines below and to use the sample speaking outline on pages 216–217 as your model.

GUIDELINES FOR THE SPEAKING OUTLINE

Follow the Visual Framework Used in the Preparation Outline

Your speaking outline should use the same visual framework—the same symbols and the same pattern of indentation—as your preparation outline. This will make it much easier to prepare the speaking outline. More important, it will allow you to see instantly where you are in the speech at any given moment while you are speaking. You will find this a great advantage. As you speak, you will look down at your outline periodically to make sure you are covering the right ideas in the right order.

Compare the following two versions of a partial speaking outline. They are from an informative speech about the history of the U.S. women's rights movement.

Ineffective

I. 1840–1860
A. World Anti-Slavery Convention
B. Seneca Falls convention
1. Lucretia Mott
2. Elizabeth Cady Stanton
3. Declaration of Sentiments
II. 1900–1920
A. National American Woman Suffrage Association
1. Founding
2. Objectives
B. Nineteenth Amendment
1. Campaign
2. Ratification

More Effective

- I. 1840–1860
    - A. World Anti-Slavery Convention
    - B. Seneca Falls convention
        - 1. Lucretia Mott
        - 2. Elizabeth Cady Stanton
        - 3. Declaration of Sentiments
- II. 1900–1920
    - A. National American Woman Suffrage Association
        - 1. Founding
        - 2. Objectives
    - B. Nineteenth Amendment
        - 1. Campaign
        - 2. Ratification

The wording of both outlines is exactly the same. But the visual framework of the one on the right makes it easier to take in at a glance and reduces the odds of the speaker losing her or his place.

Make Sure the Outline Is Legible

Your speaking outline is all but worthless unless it is instantly readable at a distance. When you make your outline, use large lettering, leave extra space between lines, provide ample margins, and write or type on only one side of the paper.

Some speakers put their notes on index cards. Most find the 3 × 5 size too cramped and prefer the 4 × 6 or 5 × 8 size instead. Other people write their speaking outlines on regular paper. Either practice is fine, as long as your notes are immediately legible to you while you are speaking.

Many experienced speakers are more comfortable with a brief set of notes, or no notes at all, which allows them to communicate directly with the audience.

Keep the Outline as Brief as Possible

If your notes are too detailed, you will have difficulty maintaining eye contact with your audience. A detailed outline will tempt you to look at it far too often, as one student discovered:

Angela Rossi was speaking about the benefits of Pilates. She had prepared the speech thoroughly and practiced it until it was nearly perfect. But when she delivered the speech in class, she referred constantly to her detailed notes. As a result, her delivery was choppy and strained. After the speech, Angela's classmates remarked on how often she had looked at her notes, and she was amazed. "I didn't even know I was doing it," she said. "Most of the time I wasn't even paying attention to the outline. I knew the speech cold."

Using public speaking in your CAREER

As the defense attorney in a car theft case, you need to prepare your closing argument to the jury before it begins its deliberations. After reviewing evidence from the trial, you decide to stress the following points to demonstrate the innocence of your client:

a. The stolen car was found abandoned three hours after the theft with the engine still warm; at the time the car was found, your client was at the airport to meet the flight of a friend who was flying into town.
b. Lab analysis of muddy shoe prints on the floor mat of the car indicates that the prints came from a size 13 shoe; your client wears a size 10.
c. Lab analysis shows the presence of cigarette smoke in the car, but your client does not smoke.
d. The only eyewitness to the crime, who was 50 feet from the car, said the thief "looked like" your client; yet the eyewitness admitted that at the time of the theft she was not wearing her glasses, which had been prescribed for improving distance vision.
e. The car was stolen at about 1 P.M.; your client testified that he was in a small town 250 miles away at 11 A.M.
f. In a statement to police, the eyewitness described the thief as blond; your client has red hair.

As you work on the outline of your speech, you see that these points can be organized into three main points, each with two supporting points. Compose an outline that organizes the points in this manner.

Many students have had the same experience. "As long as I have plenty of notes," they feel, "disaster will not strike." In fact, most beginning speakers use too many notes. Like Angela, they don't need all of them to remember the speech, and they find that too many notes can actually interfere with good communication.

To guard against this, keep your speaking outline as brief as possible. It should contain key words or phrases to help you remember major points, subpoints, and connectives. If you are citing statistics, you will probably want to include them in your notes. Unless you are good at memorizing quotations, write them out fully as well. Finally, there may be two, three, or four key ideas whose wording is so important that you want to state them in simple complete sentences. The best rule is that your notes should be the *minimum* you need to jog your memory and keep you on track.

Give Yourself Cues for Delivering the Speech

A good speaking outline reminds you not only of *what* you want to say but also of *how* you want to say it. As you practice the speech, you will decide that certain ideas and phrases need special emphasis—that they should be spoken more loudly, softly, slowly, or rapidly than other parts of the speech. You will also determine how you want to pace the speech—how you will control its timing, rhythm, and momentum. But no matter how you work these things out ahead of time, no matter how often you practice, it is easy to forget them once you get in front of an audience.

delivery cues

Directions in a speaking outline to help a speaker remember how she or he wants to deliver key parts of the speech.

The solution is to include in your speaking outline *delivery cues*—directions for delivering the speech. One way to do this is by underlining or otherwise highlighting key ideas that you want to be sure to emphasize. Then, when you reach them in the outline, you will be reminded to stress them. Another way is to jot down on the outline explicit cues such as "pause," "repeat," "slow down," "louder," and so forth. Both techniques are good aids for beginning speakers, but they are also used by experienced speakers.

SAMPLE SPEAKING OUTLINE WITH COMMENTARY

Below is a sample speaking outline for a six-minute informative talk about beneficial bacteria. By comparing it with the preparation outline for the same speech on pages 211–213, you can see how a detailed preparation outline is transformed into a concise speaking outline.

COMMENTARY

These comments remind the speaker to establish eye contact and not to race through the speech.

Including the main points of the introduction helps keep the speaker on track at the start of the speech.

OUTLINE

Eye Contact!!

Slow Down

I. Hold up hand—look closely.
   A. Can't see millions of creatures there—bacteria.
   B. Taught to scrub off in sink.
   C. Fine—up to a point.
II. Most bacteria should <u>not</u> be washed away.
III. Dr. Martin Blaser, *Missing Microbes*: co-exist with bacteria vital to human life and the world.

IV. Learned in biology; did additional research.
V. Today: bacteria help bodies, environment.

(Start with bacteria in us.)

It's usually a good idea to pause briefly before launching into the first main point. This is another way of signaling that you are moving from the introduction to the body.

—*Pause*—

Most speakers label the body of the speech in the speaking outline as well as in the preparation outline.

Notice how the body of the speech follows the same visual format as the preparation outline. This makes the outline easy to read at a glance.

Body

I. Beneficial bacteria in bodies.
  A. We have all lived with bacteria since birth.
    1. *Scientific American*: Human body is "a complex ecosystem . . . containing trillions of bacteria."
    2. Each square centimeter—100,000.
    3. 100 kinds in mouth.
    4. 10 times more in body than human cells.
  B. One positive function: digest food, maintain weight.
    1. Yogurt.
    2. Others: sauerkraut, kefir, kimchi, soft cheeses.
  C. *British Journal of Nutrition*: help other ways.
    1. Strengthen immune systems.
    2. Promote healthy organs.
    3. Create energy needed to live.

Throughout the outline, key words are used to jog the speaker's memory. Because the final wording of an extemporaneous speech is chosen at the moment of delivery, it will not be exactly the same as that in the preparation outline.

(Just as important as bacteria in the body are bacteria in the world.)

Inserting transitions makes sure the speaker doesn't forget them.

Quotations are usually written out in full in the speaking outline.

Underlining reminds the speaker to stress key words or ideas.

II. Beneficial bacteria in environment.
  A. Web site for master gardener program at Colorado State: healthy soil "a dynamic living ecosystem."
    1. Cup of soil—200 million.
    2. Provide nutrients that allow plants to grow.
    3. Good garden—good bacteria.
  B. In addition to enriching soil, bacteria can combat pollution.
    1. Reduce contaminants in lakes, rivers, oceans.
    2. Scientists use to clean up oil spills.
      a. Remember Deepwater Horizon?
      b. *U.S. News and World Report*: bacteria ate oil.
    3. Can also eat plastic and radioactive waste.

Sources of statistics or testimony should be included in the speaking outline to make sure the speaker identifies them in the speech.

It's usually a good idea to pause before entering the conclusion.

—*Pause*—

Conclusion

Including key ideas and phrases from the conclusion jogs the speaker's memory and ensures that the speech will end as planned.

I. Some bacteria dangerous, many beneficial.
II. Health of bodies, health of environment depend on them.
III. Science writer Richard Conniff: see bacteria "not as enemies, but as intimate partners" in journey through life.

Summary

Outlines are essential to effective speeches. By outlining, you make sure that related ideas are together, that your thoughts flow from one to another, and that the structure of your speech is coherent. You will probably use two kinds of outlines for your speeches—the detailed preparation outline and the brief speaking outline.

In the preparation outline, you state your specific purpose and central idea; label the introduction, body, and conclusion; and designate transitions, internal summaries, and internal previews. You should identify main points, subpoints, and sub-subpoints by a consistent pattern of symbolization and indentation. Your instructor may require a bibliography with your preparation outline.

The speaking outline should contain key words or phrases to jog your memory, as well as essential statistics and quotations. Make sure your speaking outline is legible, follows the same visual framework as your preparation outline, and includes cues for delivering the speech.

Key Terms

preparation outline (206)
visual framework (207)
bibliography (209)
speaking outline (213)
delivery cues (216)

Review Questions

connect
For further review, go to the LearnSmart study module for this chapter.

After reading this chapter, you should be able to answer the following questions:

1. Why is it important to outline your speeches?
2. What is a preparation outline? What are the eight guidelines discussed in this chapter for writing a preparation outline?
3. What is a speaking outline? What are four guidelines for your speaking outline?

Exercises for Critical Thinking

1. In the left-hand column on page 219 is a partially blank outline from a speech about the Golden Gate Bridge. In the right-hand column, arranged in random order, are the subpoints to fill in the outline. Choose the appropriate subpoint for each blank in the outline.

Outline

I. More than 20 years passed from the time the Golden Gate Bridge was proposed to the time it opened.

A.

B.

C.

D.

II. Now nearly 80 years old, the Golden Gate Bridge remains a marvel of engineering.

A.

1.

2.

B.

1.

2.

Subpoints

Today, those towers make it the world's fourth tallest suspension bridge.

Construction finally began in 1933 and ended in 1937.

The span between its towers is 4,200 feet.

At the time it was built, the Golden Gate was also the longest suspension bridge in the world.

In 1923, the State of California passed legislation authorizing construction of the bridge.

Its two towers rise almost 750 feet above the waters of the Pacific Ocean.

Once construction of the bridge was authorized, it took ten years to approve the design and financing.

That span makes it the twelfth longest suspension bridge in the world today.

At the time it was built, the Golden Gate was the tallest suspension bridge in the world.

The bridge was originally proposed in 1916 but faced years of legal hurdles.

connect

For additional practice with scrambled outlines, go to the LearnSmart module for this chapter.

2. From the preparation outline on the Golden Gate Bridge you constructed in Exercise 1, create a speaking outline that you might use in delivering the speech. Follow the guidelines for a speaking outline discussed in this chapter.

Ins

5

Speaking to Inform

- Types of Informative Speeches: Analysis and Organization
- Guidelines for Informative Speaking
- Sample Speech with Commentary

Hayley Walden is the chief designer at a fast-growing company that creates and sells innovative sportswear. On a bright Tuesday in October, Hayley begins her workday by talking to a colleague from tech support about her computer problems. She shows what goes wrong when she boots up, and she explains the mistakes in her internal backup system.

Later that morning, Hayley has a long meeting with her design team. They discuss their new line of spring products, going over everything from the manufacturing process to the marketing campaign. As the other team members talk, Hayley takes careful notes and asks questions to make sure she doesn't miss anything.

In the afternoon, Hayley rushes to a meeting with the company president, so she can report on what the design team discussed earlier in the day. She reviews the manufacturing process for the new outfits, discusses the distribution chain, and explains different marketing options. Afterward, the president compliments Hayley for giving such a clear presentation. "Anyone who can communicate that well," the president says, "is going to go a long way in this company."

Hayley doesn't consider herself a "public speaker," but much of her job involves absorbing and communicating information clearly and effectively. Although Hayley is just a single person, her experience is not unusual. In one survey, graduates from five U.S. colleges were asked to rank the speech skills most important to their jobs. They rated informative speaking number one. In another survey, 62 percent of the respondents said they used informative speaking "almost constantly."[1]

Public speaking to inform occurs in a wide range of everyday situations. The business manager explains next year's budget. The architect reviews plans for a new building. The union leader informs members about a new contract. The church worker outlines plans for a fund drive. There are endless situations in which people need to inform others. Competence in this form of communication will prove valuable to you throughout your life.

informative speech

A speech designed to convey knowledge and understanding.

One of your first classroom assignments probably will be to deliver an informative speech in which you will act as a lecturer or teacher. You may describe an object, show how something works, report on an event, explain a concept. Your aim will be to convey knowledge and understanding—not to advocate a cause. Your speech will be judged in light of three general criteria:

Is the information communicated accurately?

Is the information communicated clearly?

Is the information made meaningful and interesting to the audience?

In this chapter, we will look at four types of informative speeches and the basic principles of informative speaking. Along the way, we will apply various general principles discussed in previous chapters.

Types of Informative Speeches: Analysis and Organization

There are many ways to classify informative speeches. Here we focus on the kinds you are most likely to give in your speech class: (1) speeches about objects, (2) speeches about processes, (3) speeches about events, and (4) speeches about concepts.

SPEECHES ABOUT OBJECTS

object

Anything that is visible, tangible, and stable in form.

As the word is used here, "objects" include anything that is visible, tangible, and stable in form. Objects may have moving parts or be alive; they may include places, structures, animals, even people. Here are examples of subjects for speeches about objects:

Legos	service dogs
graphene	Susan B. Anthony
Matterhorn	dreamcatchers

You will not have time to tell your classmates everything about any of these subjects. Instead, you will choose a specific purpose that focuses on one aspect of your subject. Working from the topics presented above, the following are examples of good specific purpose statements for informative speeches about objects:

> To inform my audience about three major kinds of service dogs.
>
> To inform my audience about the role of Susan B. Anthony in the U.S. women's rights movement.
>
> To inform my audience about the worldwide fascination with Legos.

Notice how precise these statements are. As we saw in Chapter 5, you should select a specific purpose that is not too broad to achieve in the allotted time. "To inform my audience about Pablo Picasso" is far too general for a classroom speech. "To inform my audience about the major contributions of Pablo Picasso to modern art" is more precise and is a purpose you could reasonably hope to achieve in a brief talk.

If your specific purpose is to explain the history or evolution of your subject, you will put your speech in *chronological* order. For example:

Specific Purpose: To inform my audience about the major achievements of Frederick Douglass.

Central Idea: Although born in slavery, Frederick Douglass became one of the greatest figures in American history.

Main Points:

I. Douglass spent the first 20 years of his life as a slave in Maryland.

II. After escaping to the North, Douglass became a leader in the abolitionist movement to end slavery.

III. During the Civil War, Douglass helped establish black regiments in the Union Army.

IV. After the war, Douglass was a tireless champion of equal rights for his race.

If your specific purpose is to describe the main features of your subject, you may organize your speech in *spatial* order:

Specific Purpose: To inform my audience about the geographical regions of the Mississippi River.

Central Idea: The Mississippi River is divided into three sections, each with its own unique features.

Main Points:

I. The upper Mississippi is known for its scenic parks and system of dams and locks.

II. The middle Mississippi is known for its wildlife refuges and fishing opportunities.

III. The lower Mississippi is known for its heavy river traffic and connection to the Gulf of Mexico.

As often as not, you will find that speeches about objects fall into *topical* order. For example:

Specific Purpose: To inform my audience about the three major features of the Taj Mahal.

Central Idea: The three major features of the Taj Mahal are the mausoleum, the garden, and the reflecting pool.

Main Points:

I. The Taj Mahal's mausoleum is famous for its brilliant white marble and massive dome.

II. The Taj Mahal's garden is famous for its symmetry and carefully sculpted greenery.

III. The Taj Mahal's reflecting pool is famous for its mirror-like surface and expansive layout.

No matter which of these organizational methods you use—chronological, spatial, or topical—be sure to follow the guidelines discussed in Chapter 9: (1) limit your speech to between two and five main points; (2) keep main points separate; (3) try to use the same pattern of wording for all main points; (4) balance the amount of time devoted to each main point.

SPEECHES ABOUT PROCESSES

process

A systematic series of actions that leads to a specific result or product.

A process is a systematic series of actions that leads to a specific result or product. Speeches about processes explain how something is made, how something is done, or how something works. Here are examples of good specific purpose statements for speeches about processes:

To inform my audience how flash floods develop.

To inform my audience how to write an effective job resumé.

To inform my audience how U.S. currency is made.

As these examples suggest, there are two kinds of informative speeches about processes. One kind explains a process so that listeners will *understand* it better. Your goal is to have your audience know the steps of the process and how they relate to one another. If your specific purpose is "To inform my audience how a nuclear power plant works," you will explain the basic procedures of a nuclear power plant. You will not instruct your listeners on how they can *operate* a nuclear power plant.

A second kind of speech explains a process so listeners will be better able to *perform* the process themselves. Your goal in this kind of speech is to have the audience learn a skill. Suppose your specific purpose is "To inform my audience how to take pictures like a professional photographer." You will present photographic techniques and show your listeners how they can utilize them. You want the audience to be able to *use* the techniques as a result of your speech.

Both kinds of speeches about processes may require visual aids. At the very least, you should prepare a chart outlining the steps or techniques of your process. In some cases you will need to demonstrate the steps or techniques by performing them in front of your audience. One student did sleight-of-hand magic tricks to show the techniques behind them. Another executed elementary tai chi maneuvers. In each case, the demonstration not only

Informative speeches can be organized in many ways. A speech on the history of the Taj Mahal would likely be in chronological order, while a speech on its major features would fall into topical order.

clarified the speaker's process, but captivated the audience as well. (If you are using visual aids of any kind, be sure to review Chapter 14.)

When informing about a process, you will usually arrange your speech in *chronological* order, explaining the process step by step from beginning to end. For example:

Specific Purpose: To inform my audience about the three major stages of dementia.

Central Idea: Dementia is a loss of cognitive ability that proceeds through early, middle, and late stages.

Main Points:

I. The early stage of dementia includes forgetfulness, losing track of time, and being uncomfortable in familiar places.

II. The middle stage of dementia includes serious memory lapses, anxiety, and social withdrawal.

III. The late stage of dementia includes inability to recognize family members and full dependence on others.

Sometimes, rather than moving through a process step by step, you will focus on the major principles or techniques involved in performing the process. Then you will organize your speech in *topical* order. Each main point will deal with a separate principle or technique. For example:

Specific Purpose: To inform my audience of the common methods used by stage magicians to perform their tricks.

Central Idea: Stage magicians use two common methods to perform their tricks—mechanical devices and sleight of hand.

Main Points:

I. Many magic tricks rely on mechanical devices that may require little skill by the magician.

II. Other magic tricks depend on the magician's skill in fooling people by sleight-of-hand manipulation.

Concise organization is especially important in speeches about processes. You must make sure each step is clear and easy to follow. If your process has more than four or five steps, group the steps into units to limit the number of main points. For example, in a speech explaining how to set up a home aquarium, a student presented the following main points:

I. First you must choose the size of your tank.
II. Then you must determine the shape of your tank.
III. You must also decide how much you can afford to pay for a tank.
IV. Once you have the tank, you need a filter system.
V. A heater is also absolutely necessary.
VI. You must also get an air pump.
VII. Once this is done, you need to choose gravel for the tank.
VIII. You will also need plants.
IX. Other decorations will round out the effects of your aquarium.
X. Now you are ready to add the fish.
XI. Freshwater fish are the most common.
XII. Saltwater fish are more expensive and require special care.

Not surprisingly, this was too much for the audience to follow. The speaker should have organized the points something like this:

I. The first step in establishing a home aquarium is choosing a tank.
  A. The size of the tank is important.
  B. The shape of the tank is important.
  C. The cost of the tank is important.
II. The second step in establishing a home aquarium is equipping the tank.
  A. You will need a filter system.
  B. You will need a heater.
  C. You will need an air pump.
  D. You will need gravel.
  E. You will need plants.
  F. You may also want other decorations.
III. The third step in establishing a home aquarium is adding the fish.
  A. Freshwater fish are the most common for home aquariums.
  B. Saltwater fish are more expensive and require special care.

The subpoints cover the same territory as the original twelve points, but three main points are much easier to understand and remember.

SPEECHES ABOUT EVENTS

event

Anything that happens or is regarded as happening.

The *Random House Dictionary* defines an event as "anything that happens or is regarded as happening." By this definition, the following are examples of suitable topics for informative speeches about events:

Boston Marathon	cyberterrorism
sleep deprivation	Battle of Little Big Horn
Festival of the Sun	therapeutic massage

As usual, you will need to narrow your focus and pick a specific purpose you can accomplish in a short speech. Here are examples of good specific purpose statements for informative speeches about events:

> To inform my audience about the events at Peru's Festival of the Sun ceremony.
>
> To inform my audience about the major types of therapeutic massage.
>
> To inform my audience about what occurred at the Battle of Little Big Horn.

There are many ways to discuss events. If your specific purpose is to recount the history of an event, you will organize your speech in *chronological* order, relating the incidents one after another in the order they occurred. For example:

Specific Purpose: To inform my audience about the history of the Paralympics.

Central Idea: Olympic-style games for athletes with physical disabilities have made great strides since the first competition more than 60 years ago.

Main Points:

I. What would eventually become the Paralympics began in 1948 with a sports competition in Great Britain involving World War II veterans with spinal cord injuries.

II. In 1952, the event expanded when athletes from the Netherlands took part.

III. In 1960, the first Paralympic Games for international athletes took place in Rome.

IV. In 2001, an agreement was signed officially holding the Paralympic Games alongside the summer and winter Olympic Games.

You can approach an event from almost any angle or combination of angles—features, origins, implications, benefits, future developments, and so forth. In such cases, you will put your speech together in *topical* order. And you should make sure your main points subdivide the subject logically and consistently. For instance:

Specific Purpose: To inform my audience about three aspects of the Mardi Gras celebration in New Orleans.

Central Idea: The Mardi Gras celebration in New Orleans is renowned for its parades, costumes, and food.

Main Points:

I. The parades are lavish events that take place over the course of several weeks.

II. The costumes include disguises, medallions, and the official Mardi Gras colors of purple, green, and gold.

III. The food features Cajun and Creole dishes common to southern Louisiana.

SPEECHES ABOUT CONCEPTS

concept

A belief, theory, idea, notion, principle, or the like.

Concepts include beliefs, theories, ideas, principles, and the like. They are more abstract than objects, processes, or events. The following are examples of subjects for speeches about concepts:

numerology	sustainability
philosophies of education	original-intent doctrine
Net neutrality	Confucianism

Taking a few of these general subjects, here are some specific purpose statements for speeches about concepts:

> To inform my audience about the philosophy of Net neutrality.
>
> To inform my audience about the doctrine of original intent in constitutional interpretation.
>
> To inform my audience about the basic principles of Confucianism.

Speeches about concepts are usually organized in *topical* order and focus on the main features or aspects of your concept. For example:

Specific Purpose: To inform my audience about the basic principles of nonviolent resistance.

Central Idea: The basic principles of nonviolent resistance stress using moral means to achieve social change, refusing to inflict violence on one's enemies, and using suffering as a social force.

Main Points:

I. The first major principle of nonviolent resistance is that social change must be achieved by moral means.

II. The second major principle of nonviolent resistance is that one should not inflict violence on one's enemies.

III. The third major principle of nonviolent resistance is that suffering can be a powerful social force.

Another approach is to define the concept you are dealing with, identify its major elements, and illustrate it with specific examples. An excellent instance of this came in a student speech about homeschooling:

Specific Purpose: To inform my audience about different philosophies of homeschooling.

Central Idea: Approaches to homeschooling include the classical model, the Charlotte Mason model, the Montessori model, and the unschooling model.

Main Points:

I. The classical model focuses on language, critical thinking, and communication skills.

II. The Charlotte Mason model focuses on hands-on learning and the study of nature.

The need to communicate information is essential for most occupations. Here Austin, Texas, police chief Art Acevedo briefs the press on a crime investigation.

III. The Montessori model focuses on an interactive environment that children navigate on their own.

IV. The unschooling model focuses on escaping formal instruction and letting children learn through experience.

Speeches about concepts are often more complex than other kinds of informative speeches. When dealing with concepts, pay special attention to avoiding technical language, to defining terms clearly, and to using examples and comparisons to illustrate the concepts.

Look, for example, at Video 15.1 in the online Media Library for this chapter, which presents an excerpt from a student speech about the Chinese philosophy of Confucianism. Notice how the student defines Confucianism and then explains its unifying principle of *jen*. If you give an informative speech about a concept, give special thought to how you can make that concept clear and comprehensible to your listeners.

connect

View an excerpt from "Confucianism" in the online Media Library for this chapter (Video 15.1).

The lines dividing speeches about objects, processes, events, and concepts are not absolute. Some subjects could fit into more than one category, depending on how you develop the speech. For example, a speech about the destruction of ancient Pompeii by the eruption of Mount Vesuvius would probably deal with its subject as an event, but a speech on what causes volcanoes to erupt would most likely treat its subject as a process. The important step is to decide whether you will handle your subject as an object, a process, an event, or a concept. Once you do that, you can develop the speech accordingly.

Regardless of how you approach your topic, be sure to give listeners plenty of help in sorting out facts and ideas. One way is by using enough transitions, internal previews, internal summaries, and signposts (see Chapter 9). Another way is to follow the old maxim "Tell 'em what you're going to say; say it; then tell 'em what you've said." In other words, preview the main points of your speech in the introduction and summarize them in the conclusion. This will make your speech easier to understand and easier to remember.

Guidelines for Informative Speaking

All the previous chapters of this book relate to the principles of informative speaking. Selecting a topic and specific purpose, analyzing the audience, gathering materials, choosing supporting details, organizing the speech, using words to communicate meaning, delivering the speech—all must be done effectively if an informative speech is to be a success. Here we emphasize six additional points that will help make yours a success.

DON'T OVERESTIMATE WHAT THE AUDIENCE KNOWS

In a speech about meteorology, a student said, "If modern methods of weather forecasting had existed in 1900, the Galveston hurricane disaster would never have taken place." Then he was off to other matters, leaving his listeners to puzzle over what the Galveston hurricane was, when it happened, and what kind of destruction it wreaked.

The speaker assumed his audience already knew these things. But they were not experts on meteorology or on American history. Even those who had heard of the hurricane had only a fuzzy notion of it. Only the speaker knew that the hurricane, which killed more than 6,000 people when it unexpectedly struck on September 8, 1900, is still the deadliest natural disaster in American history.

As many speakers have discovered, it is easy to overestimate the audience's stock of information. In most informative speeches, your listeners will be only vaguely knowledgeable (at best) about the details of your topic. You cannot *assume* they will know what you mean. Rather, you must be *sure* to explain everything so thoroughly that they cannot help but understand. As you work on your speech, always consider whether it will be clear to someone who is hearing about the topic for the first time.

Suppose you are talking about bulletproof vests. Surely all of your classmates have heard of bulletproof vests, but most probably don't know how the vests work. How will you tell them? Here's one way:

> Ballistic vests, more commonly known as bulletproof vests, are pieces of personal body armor that protect human beings from damage incurred by explosively propelled projectiles. How? Intricately woven synthetic fibers such as Kevlar form a powerful mesh that laterally disperses a projectile's kinetic energy while at the same time deforming the projectile and stopping its momentum.

To someone who knows a lot about physics or textiles, this is probably perfectly clear. But someone who does not may get lost along the way. The tone of the statement is that of a speaker reviewing information already familiar to the audience—not of a speaker introducing new information.

Here, in contrast, is another explanation of bulletproof vests:

> So how do bulletproof vests actually stop bullets? Let me explain with an example.
>
> Imagine a police officer investigating a strange noise down a dark alley. He startles a drug dealer trying to make a sale, and before he knows it, bang! Luckily, the officer was wearing his bulletproof vest.
>
> Instead of entering the officer's body, the bullet enters layer upon layer of strong, tightly woven fibers. Because of their strength and intricate pattern, the fibers begin to twist and deform the bullet. The fibers are so strong that they flatten the bullet out and absorb its energy. While the bullet may go through a couple of layers of fabric, it stops well before going through the entire vest.
>
> Thanks to these strong, tightly woven fibers, our police officer lives to put the drug dealer in cuffs.

This explanation is clear and simple. Its tone is that of a teacher unraveling a new subject.

Is it too simple? Not at all. The test of a good speaker is to communicate even the most complex ideas clearly and simply. Anyone can go to a book and find a learned-sounding definition of a bulletproof vest. But to say in plain English how a bulletproof vest works—that takes hard work and creative thinking.

Also, remember that readers can study a printed passage again and again until they extract its meaning, but listeners don't have that luxury. They must understand what you say in the time it takes you to say it. The more you assume they know about the topic, the greater your chances of being misunderstood.

RELATE THE SUBJECT DIRECTLY TO THE AUDIENCE

> The British dramatist Oscar Wilde arrived at his club after the disastrous opening-night performance of his new play.
>
> "Oscar, how did your play go?" asked a friend.
>
> "Oh," Wilde quipped, "the play was a great success, but the audience was a failure."

Speakers have been known to give much the same answer in saving face after a dismal informative speech. "Oh," they say, "the speech was fine, but

Informative speeches take place in a wide range of situations. Here journalist Rachel Maddow presents a lecture at the John F. Kennedy School of Government.

the audience just wasn't interested." And they are at least partly right—the audience *wasn't* interested. But there is no such thing as a fine speech that puts people to sleep. It is the speaker's job to get listeners interested—and to keep them interested.

Informative speakers have one big hurdle to overcome. They must recognize that what is fascinating to them may not be fascinating to everybody. Once you have chosen a topic that could possibly be interesting to your listeners, you should take special steps to relate it to them. You should tie it in with their interests and concerns.

Start in the introduction. Instead of saying,

> I want to talk with you about the Ironman competition.

you could say:

> Your body can't go any further. Your toenails fell off long ago. Your lungs are on fire. Your heart is one beat away from exploding. Are you dying? Are you dreaming? Neither. You're about to cross the finish line of your first Ironman competition—and nothing could feel better.

connect

View this excerpt from "Not Your Everyday Competition" in the online Media Library for this chapter (Video 15.2).

But don't stop with the introduction. Whenever you can, put your listeners into the body of the speech. After all, nothing interests people more than themselves. Find ways to talk about your topic in terms of your listeners. Bring your material home to them. Get it as close to them as possible.

Here's an example. Let's say you are explaining how bed bugs spread from person to person and location to location. You have plenty of facts and could recite them like this:

> High-traffic areas provide ideal environmental conditions for bed bugs to spread. High-density locations such as dormitories, apartment buildings, and transportation terminals are among the most likely places to find bed bugs. Because bed bugs are attracted to items that allow them to hide, they often attach themselves to clothing, backpacks, purses, and the like. Bed bugs also thrive in cluttered locations that have a lot of items lying about.

This is valuable information, but it is not related to the audience. Let's try again:

> Bed bugs spread most rapidly in places that have lots of people coming and going. If *you* live in the dorms or an apartment, if *you* travel through airports, train stations, and bus stations, or if *you* stay in hotels and motels, *you're* passing through prime breeding grounds for bed bugs.
>
> Bed bugs are like tiny hitchhikers. They'll insert themselves in *your* clothes, *your* luggage, *your* purse, *your* backpack, *your* coat—anything that has fabric and folds.
>
> Bed bugs are also drawn to locations where they can hide easily. So the more clutter *you* have in *your* environment, the more bed bugs will like to be *your* tiny companions.

connect

View this excerpt from "Don't Let the Bed Bugs Bite" in the online Media Library for this chapter (Video 15.3).

Look at the frequent use of "you" and "your." The facts are the same, but now they are pointed directly at the audience. Research shows that using personal terms such as "you" and "your" in an informative speech significantly increases audience understanding of the speaker's ideas.[2]

DON'T BE TOO TECHNICAL

What does it mean to say that an informative speech is too technical? It may mean the subject matter is too specialized for the audience. Any subject can be popularized—but only up to a point. The important thing for a speaker to know is what can be explained to an ordinary audience and what cannot.

Say your subject is power amplifiers. It's no trick to demonstrate how to operate an amplifier (how to turn it on and off, adjust the volume, set the tone and balance controls). It's also relatively easy to explain what an amplifier does (it boosts the sound received from a DVD, mobile device, or live performance). But to give a full scientific account of how an amplifier works cannot be done in any reasonable time unless the audience knows the principles of audio technology. The material is just too technical for a general audience.

Even when the subject matter is not technical, the language used to explain it may be. Every activity has its jargon, whether it be golf (bogey, wedge, match play); chemistry (colloid, glycogen, heavy water); or financial analysis (covered call, reverse bid, toehold acquisition). If you are talking to a group of specialists, you can use technical words and be understood. But you must do all you can to avoid technical words when informing a general audience such as your speech class.

Here, for instance, are two statements explaining graphene, a revolutionary material that is thin and bendable, yet incredibly strong. The first is heavily laden with specialized language that would have little impact on ordinary listeners:

> Graphene is a two-dimensional material composed of a single layer of carbon atoms. The structure of graphene is a hexagonal lattice of 0.33-nanometer thickness. A semi-metal or zero-gap semiconductor, graphene allows electrons to flow through it at one one-hundredth the speed of light, as if they carried no mass.

Using public speaking in your CAREER

As a financial planner at a local investment firm, you have been asked to speak to a group of recent college graduates about long-term financial planning. After considering what recent college graduates need to know about saving for their future, you decide to organize your presentation around four general stages of investing:

1. The early years of investing, which include putting aside small amounts of money that will grow over time.
2. The years of acquisition, which include balancing investments with large expenses such as raising children and paying a mortgage.
3. The years of accumulation, which include putting away as much money as possible in anticipation of retirement.
4. The retirement years, which include living off of savings and adjusting investments as needed.

As you look over these stages of investing, you think back to the public speaking course you took in college. You remember that informative speakers should relate their speech directly to the audience, should not be too technical, should not overestimate what the audience knows about the subject, and should be creative. How might each of these guidelines influence your presentation to recent college graduates? Be specific.

The second statement is perfectly understandable and shows how technical information can be made clear to the average person:

> It's the strongest, thinnest, most conductive material in the world. The *New York Times* calls it the "material of tomorrow." But you can call it by its official name—graphene.
>
> Nick Bilton, technology writer for the *Times,* explains graphene's miraculous properties. A million times thinner than a single hair on your head, it is 200 times stronger than steel and can conduct electricity faster than anything known to exist. It is also bendable and can be stretched by up to 20 percent of its original length.
>
> Cell phones made of graphene will be the width of a piece of paper. Airplanes made of it will be lighter, stronger, and faster. In these ways—and countless others—graphene will transform our lives in the years to come.

Much clearer, isn't it? The only specialized word in the whole passage is "graphene." The rest of the language is straightforward, the ideas easy to grasp. This is what you should strive for in your informative speeches.

AVOID ABSTRACTIONS

"My task," said the novelist Joseph Conrad, "is, before all, to make you see." And make the reader see is just what Conrad did. Witness this passage, in which Conrad describes the aftermath of an explosion aboard a ship:

> The first person I saw was Mahon, with eyes like saucers, his mouth open, and the long white hair standing straight on end round his head like a silver halo. . . . I stared at him in unbelief, and he stared at me with a queer kind of shocked curiosity. I did not know that I had no hair, no eyebrows, no eyelashes, that my young mustache was burnt off, that my face was black, one cheek laid open, my nose cut, and my chin bleeding.[3]

A speech is not a novel. Still, many informative speeches would be vastly improved by the novelist's bent for color, specificity, and detail.

description

A statement that depicts a person, event, idea, or the like with clarity and vividness.

One way to avoid abstractions is through *description.* When we think of description, we usually think of external events such as the explosion described by Conrad. But description is also used to communicate internal feelings. Here is how one student tried to convey to his audience the sensations he experienced when he first began sky diving:

> As we wait for the plane to climb to the jump altitude of 12,000 feet, my mind races with a frenzied jumble of thoughts: "OK, this is the moment you've been waiting for. It's going to be great. Am I really going to jump out of an airplane from 12,000 feet? What if something goes wrong? Can I still back out? Come on now, don't worry. It'll be fine."

Even if we have not been sky diving, we have all had the same kinds of emotions on similar occasions. So what happened next?

> Now it is time to jump. My palms are sweating and my heart is pounding so hard I think it may burst. "Get ready," yells the instructor. As I jump into the blue, I wonder, "What am I doing here?"

Yes—and then what?

> The blast of air resistance blows me backward like a leaf at the mercy of an autumn wind. In about 10 seconds my body levels out and accelerates to a speed of 120 miles an hour. The air supports my body like an invisible flying carpet. There is no sound except for the wind rushing around my face. Any fears or doubts I had are gone in the exhilaration of free flight. Every nerve in my body is alive with sensation; yet I am overcome by a peaceful feeling and the sense that I am at one with the sky.

As we listen to the speaker we share his thoughts, feel his heart pound, and join his exhilaration as he floats effortlessly through the sky. The vivid description lends reality to the speech and draws us further in.

Another way to escape abstractions is with *comparisons* that put your subject in concrete, familiar terms. Do you want to convey what would happen if a comet or large asteroid struck the earth? You could say this:

comparison

A statement of the similarities among two or more people, events, ideas, etc.

> If a comet or large asteroid struck the earth, the impact would be devastating.

True, but the statement is vague and abstract. It does not communicate your meaning clearly and concretely. Now suppose you add this:

> To give you an idea how devastating the impact would be, it would be like all the nuclear bombs in the world going off at one spot.

Now you have made the abstract specific and given us a sharp new slant on things.

Like comparison, *contrast* can put an idea into concrete terms. Suppose you want to illustrate the size of the fantasy football market in the United States. You could say, "Americans spend a whopping $15 billion playing fantasy football every year." The word "whopping" suggests that you consider $15 billion a significant amount, but significant in comparison to what? One speaker offered this contrast:

contrast

A statement of the differences among two or more people, events, ideas, etc.

> Last year, Americans spent $15 billion playing fantasy football. In contrast, the total revenue for the National Football League was only $10 billion. Think about it: Americans spend $5 billion more on NFL fantasy football than they do on the real thing.

This puts an abstract fact into meaningful perspective.

PERSONALIZE YOUR IDEAS

Listeners want to be entertained as they are being enlightened.[4] Nothing takes the edge off an informative speech more than an unbroken string of facts and figures. And nothing enlivens a speech more than personal illustrations. Whenever possible, you should try to *personalize* your ideas and dramatize them in human terms.

personalize

To present one's ideas in human terms that relate in some fashion to the experience of the audience.

Let's say you are talking about family homelessness, which most often involves mothers and their children living on the streets, in cars, or in shelters. You would surely note that 41 percent of the homeless population

Whether in the classroom or out, effective informative speakers work to communicate their ideas in clear, nontechnical language that relates the topic to their listeners' knowledge and interests.

consists of families, leaving 1.6 million children without a home. You would also note that these children are much more likely than their peers to experience violence, physical and mental health problems, and developmental difficulties.

But these are dry facts and figures. If you really want to get your audience involved, you will weave in some examples of families who have experienced homelessness. One speaker began by telling this story:

> Lydia. She was the new girl in school. We were in a couple of the same classes, sometimes we sat together at lunch, and we would see each other during recess. Lydia was kind, funny, and supportive. But for six months, I didn't know the secret she was hiding.
>
> Lydia didn't like to talk about her family. She never wanted me to meet her mom, and she never invited me over to her house. She always insisted that we meet somewhere like the mall. But then one day I found out why: Lydia never invited me to her house because she did not have a house. For more than a year she, her mother, and her little brother had been homeless. They had been living in shelters, staying with relatives, and resting their heads wherever they could.

During the body of the speech, the speaker mentioned Lydia twice more to illustrate different aspects of family homelessness. Then, at the end of the speech, she brought Lydia's story to a hopeful conclusion:

> We have seen how family homelessness affects millions of Americans and can lead to poor physical and mental health, episodes of violence, and a range of developmental difficulties. Homelessness is not just the

disheveled man sitting by himself on the street—the image we've seen countless times in the media. Homelessness affects families; it affects people like Lydia.

Or, I should say, it *used* to affect Lydia. After two difficult years, her mother found a job that paid her enough to rent an apartment. Lydia herself now works part time and takes classes at a community college. She made it through the stressful time that affects far too many families. And she remains my friend.

connect

View this excerpt from "Family Homelessness" in the online Media Library for this chapter (Video 15.4).

It was a powerful ending. By putting a human face on the topic, the speaker took family homelessness out of the realm of statistics and social services and communicated it in personal terms.

BE CREATIVE

Whether you are seeking alternatives to technical language, avoiding abstractions, personalizing ideas, or adapting to the audience's knowledge about the topic, you need to be creative in thinking about ways to achieve your objectives. A good informative speech is not an oral encyclopedia article. Like any other kind of speech, it requires a healthy dose of creativity.

If you look back at the examples on the previous few pages, you will see that all of them involve creative thinking by the speaker. As in these examples, creativity is often a matter of using language imaginatively and resourcefully. But creativity can involve *any* aspect of an informative speech, including visual aids—as can be seen in the speech on the Statue of Liberty that is reprinted on pages 300–302.

Part of the speech deals with the architecture of the statue. The exterior of the Statue of Liberty is made of thin copper, which is supported by a massive iron skeleton. Because the skeleton can't be seen in photographs, the speaker needed to find a way to make it visible for his audience. He did so by using a PowerPoint slide in which a photograph of the statue faded away and black lines representing the iron skeleton appeared in coordination with the speaker's words. The black lines seemed to "build" the skeleton right before the audience's eyes. As you can see from Video 15.5, it was an effective—and creative—solution.

connect

View this excerpt from "Lady Liberty" in the online Media Library for this chapter (Video 15.5).

If, like this speaker, you think creatively when constructing your informative speech, you are much more likely to be successful.

Sample Speech with Commentary

The following classroom speech provides an excellent example of how to apply the guidelines for informative speaking discussed in this chapter. Notice how the speaker takes what could be a dry and technical topic and makes it interesting. Well-chosen supporting materials and superb visual aids help the speech come alive—as does the speaker's dynamic delivery. You can view the speech in the online Media Library for this chapter.

connect

View "Lady Liberty" in the online Media Library for this chapter (Video 15.6).

Lady Liberty

COMMENTARY	SPEECH
The speaker gains attention and interest by arousing the audience's curiosity. After identifying the topic, he displays a photo of the Statue of Liberty.	If you've ever been to New York, you've probably seen it. I used to see it almost every day growing up on Staten Island, in New York Harbor. And even though its skin has turned green with age, it remains vibrant. I'm talking, of course, about the Statue of Liberty. This 220 tons of copper and iron is a powerful symbol of our country.
The speaker relates his subject directly to the audience and explains why it is important. His repeated use of "we" creates common ground with the audience.	Now, America isn't perfect, and we sometimes fall short of our ideals, but the Statue of Liberty remains a part of our lives. We see it all the time in movies, on television, and in advertisements. The statue has become so familiar that we sometimes don't think about it. But we should. As Neil Kotler, an historian at the Smithsonian Institute, says, the statue is "a monument of breathtaking proportions."
The speaker establishes his credibility, previews the main points to be discussed in the rest of the speech, and provides a transition to the body.	I've been fascinated with the Statue of Liberty ever since I was a kid, but I never knew just how amazing it is until I started researching it for this speech. This morning, I'd like to tell you a bit about its symbolism, its history, and its architecture. By the end, I hope you'll understand why this familiar structure is a modern marvel. Let's start with its symbolism, moving from the top of the statue to the bottom.
Main point one deals with the Statue of Liberty's symbolism, starting with the torch at the top of the statue. As you can see from the video, the speaker uses well-chosen photographs throughout the body to help illustrate his points.	At the top is the statue's most famous symbol—the torch. Ever since the statue was built, the torch has been a beacon to immigrants. It's the torch that prompted the poet Emma Lazarus to pen the famous lines that are inscribed on the pedestal of the statue: "Give me your tired, your poor, your huddled masses yearning to breathe free. . . . I lift my lamp beside the golden door!"
Here the speaker explains the symbolism of the statue's crown.	Down from the torch is the Statue of Liberty's crown. Coming out from the crown are seven rays—one for each continent. As the National Park Service explains on its Statue of Liberty Web site, these rays symbolize the importance of liberty around the world.
The speaker completes his look at the statue's symbolism by discussing the broken chains at the foot of the statue.	Less famous than the crown and the torch are the chains at the foot of the Statue of Liberty. As you can see here, the chains are broken. *National Geographic* explains that the broken chains represent the abolition of slavery and the Union's victory in the U.S. Civil War, which ended not long before the statue was built.

A signpost signals that the speaker is moving to his second main point, on the history of the Statue of Liberty. As in other parts of the speech, he relies on expert testimony to support his ideas. Notice how clearly he identifies the source he is citing.

As we shall see next, the symbolism of the statue takes on added significance when we take a look at its history. Historian Edward Berenson, author of *The Statue of Liberty: A Transatlantic Story*, explains how the statue was created. At a dinner party in France in 1865, two men, Edouard de Laboulaye and Frederic Bartholdi, came up with the idea of building a statue for the United States. Laboulaye was an expert on American politics and wanted to commemorate the end of slavery. Bartholdi was a brilliant young sculptor who envisioned a colossal monument he called "Liberty Enlightening the World."

This paragraph focuses on construction of the Statue of Liberty. The speaker's dramatic photographs complement his words and keep the audience involved.

Construction of the statue began in 1876 and was completed 10 years later. All the building was done in France. You can see in this photo what the statue looked like with the buildings of Paris in the background. After the statue was finished, it was taken down as you can see here, put in boxes, and shipped to New York, where it was reconstructed.

Throughout the speech, vivid descriptions help bring the speaker's ideas to life.

When the statue was unveiled in New York, more than 1 million people flocked to the harbor to see it. Shown in this painting, the celebration was one of the biggest in American history. "Liberty Enlightening the World" had finally found its permanent home.

Now the speaker begins his third main point, which deals with the statue's architecture.

Today we take the Statue of Liberty for granted, but it was considered an architectural marvel when it was built. If you look at the statue from the outside, it looks solid—like it's made completely of stone. But looks can be deceiving.

By comparing the thickness of the statue's exterior to that of a penny, the speaker turns an abstraction into a concrete image.

The statue's exterior is not made of stone, but of copper. And it's only 2.4 millimeters thick—not much thicker than this penny. Yet despite its thin copper skin, the statue stands 151 feet tall and towers 305 feet above the water, if you include the pedestal. Think about the wind and the weather that have beaten against it for 130 years. The thin copper skin wouldn't be able to survive without something really strong underneath.

This paragraph is a fine example of how to communicate technical information clearly and concisely. In addition to his words, the speaker employs a creative visual aid to help listeners visualize the statue's internal structure.

So what is underneath? As represented in this slide, there's an iron skeleton underneath the copper skin. Darcy Grigsby, author of the 2012 book *Colossal*, explains that the skeleton is made of a 92-foot-tall pylon that is stuck deep in the stone pedestal. The skeleton has flat metal bars that connect the copper skin to the pylon. These bars work like springs; they provide the strength and flexibility that allow the Statue of Liberty to survive the harsh weather of New York Harbor.

A comparison with the Eiffel Tower further clarifies the engineering principles employed in the Statue of Liberty.

If the interior design of the Statue of Liberty reminds you at all of this structure, that's because it was created by the same man who would later build the Eiffel Tower. You can definitely see similarities between the open structure of the Eiffel Tower and the engineering principles employed in the interior design of the Statue of Liberty.

As in other places, the speaker's use of high-quality expert testimony lends credibility to his statements.

Architectural historian Yasmin Sabina Khan says in her 2010 book *Enlightening the World* that the statue's design was such a stunning technical achievement that people referred to it at the time as the eighth wonder of the world.

"In conclusion" signals that the speech is coming to an end. After summarizing the main points of the body, the speaker closes by echoing language from the introduction.

In conclusion, I hope I've shown you some of the reasons why the Statue of Liberty remains a wonder of the world. Its symbolism, history, and architecture make this 220 tons of copper and iron a modern marvel. So the next time you're in New York City, the next time you see the statue on television, in movies, in magazines, just remember—there's a lot more to it than meets the eye.

Summary

Speaking to inform occurs in a wide range of everyday situations. Improving your ability to convey knowledge effectively will be valuable to you throughout your life.

Informative speeches may be grouped into four categories—speeches about objects, speeches about processes, speeches about events, and speeches about concepts.

Objects include places, structures, animals, even people. Speeches about objects usually are organized in chronological, spatial, or topical order. A process is a series of actions that work together to produce a final result. Speeches about processes explain how something is made, how something is done, or how something works. The most common types of organization for speeches about processes are chronological and topical.

An event is anything that happens or is regarded as happening. Speeches about events are usually arranged in chronological or topical order. Concepts include beliefs, theories, ideas, and principles. Speeches about concepts are often more complex than other kinds of informative speeches, and they typically follow a topical pattern of organization.

No matter what the subject of your informative speech, be careful not to overestimate what your audience knows about it. Explain everything so thoroughly that they can't help but understand. Avoid being too technical. Make sure your ideas and your language are fully comprehensible to someone who has no specialized knowledge about the topic.

Equally important, recognize that what is fascinating to you may not be fascinating to everybody. It is your job to make your informative speech interesting and meaningful to your audience. Find ways to talk about the topic in terms of your listeners. Avoid too many abstractions. Use description, comparison, and contrast to make your audience *see* what you are talking about. Try to personalize your ideas and dramatize them in human terms. Finally, be creative in thinking of ways to communicate your ideas.

Key Terms

informative speech (284)
object (284)
process (286)
event (288)
concept (290)
description (296)
comparison (297)
contrast (297)
personalize (297)

Review Questions

After reading this chapter, you should be able to answer the following questions:

1. What are the four types of informative speeches discussed in the chapter? Give an example of a good specific purpose statement for each type.
2. Why must informative speakers be careful not to overestimate what the audience knows about the topic? What can you do to make sure your ideas don't pass over the heads of your listeners?
3. What should you do as an informative speaker to relate your topic directly to the audience?
4. What two things should you watch out for in making sure your speech is not overly technical?
5. What are three methods you can use to avoid abstractions in your informative speech?
6. What does it mean to say that informative speakers should personalize their ideas?
7. Why is it important for informative speakers to be creative in thinking about ways to communicate their ideas?

connect™

For further review, go to the LearnSmart study module for this chapter.

Exercises for Critical Thinking

1. Below is a list of subjects for informative speeches. Your task is twofold: (a) Select four of the topics and prepare a specific purpose statement for an informative speech about each of the four. Make sure your four specific purpose statements include at least one that deals with its topic as an object, one that deals with its topic as a process, one that deals with its topic as an event, and one that deals with its topic as a concept. (b) Explain what method of organization you would most likely use in structuring a speech about each of your specific purpose statements.

hobbies	sports	education
animals	music	media
science	cultural customs	technology

2. Analyze "Medical Robots: From Science Fiction to Science Fact" in the appendix of sample speeches that follows Chapter 19. Identify the specific purpose, central idea, main points, and method of organization. Evaluate the speech in light of the guidelines for informative speaking discussed in this chapter.

Understanding the Basics of Argument

CUL DE SAC **BY RICHARD THOMPSON**

READ: What is the situation? What is the reaction of the younger children? What does the older boy try to do?

REASON: Why is the older boy frustrated?

REFLECT/WRITE: What can happen to those who lack scientific knowledge?

In this section we will explore the processes of thinking logically and analyzing issues to reach informed judgments. Remember: Mature people do not need to agree on all issues to respect one another's good sense, but they do have little patience with uninformed or illogical statements masquerading as argument.

CHARACTERISTICS OF ARGUMENT

Argument Is Conversation with a Goal

When you enter into an argument (as speaker, writer, or reader), you become a participant in an ongoing debate about an issue. Since you are probably not the first to address the issue, you need to be aware of the ways that the issue has been debated by others and then seek to advance the conversation, just as you would if you were having a more casual conversation with friends. If the time of the movie is set, the discussion now turns to whose car to take or where to meet. If you were to just repeat the time of the movie, you would add nothing useful to the conversation. Also, if you were to change the subject to a movie you saw last week, you would annoy your friends by not offering useful information or showing that you valued the current conversation. Just as with your conversation about the movie, you want your argument to stay focused on the issue, to respect what others have already contributed, and to make a useful addition to our understanding of the topic.

Argument Takes a Stand on an Arguable Issue

A meaningful argument focuses on a debatable issue. We usually do not argue about facts. "Professor Jones's American literature class meets at 10:00 on Mondays" is not arguable. It is either true or false. We can check the schedule of classes to find out. (Sometimes the facts change; new facts replace old ones.) We also do not debate personal preferences for the simple reason that they are just that—personal. If the debate is about the appropriateness of boxing as a sport, for you to declare that you would rather play tennis is to fail to advance the conversation. You have expressed a personal preference, interesting perhaps, but not relevant to the debate.

Argument Uses Reasons and Evidence

Some arguments merely "look right." That is, conclusions are drawn from facts, but the facts are not those that actually support the assertion, or the conclusion is not the only or the best explanation of those facts. To shape convincing arguments, we need more than an array of facts. We need to think critically, to analyze the issue, to see relationships, to weigh evidence. We need to avoid the temptation to "argue" from emotion only, or to believe that just stating our opinion is the same thing as building a sound argument.

Argument Incorporates Values

Arguments are based not just on reason and evidence but also on the beliefs and values we hold and think that our audience may hold as well. In a reasoned debate, you want to make clear the values that you consider relevant to the argument. In an editorial defending the sport of boxing, one editor wrote that boxing "is a sport because the world has not yet become a place in which the qualities that go into excellence in boxing [endurance, agility, courage] have no value" (*Washington Post,* February 5, 1983). But James J. Kilpatrick also appeals to values when he argues, in an editorial critical of boxing, that we should not want to live in a society "in which deliberate brutality is legally authorized and publicly applauded" (*Washington Post,* December 7, 1982). Observe, however, the high level of seriousness in the appeal to values. Neither writer settles for a simplistic personal preference: "Boxing is exciting," or "Boxing is too violent."

Argument Recognizes the Topic's Complexity

Much false reasoning (the logical fallacies discussed in Chapter 6) results from a writer's oversimplifying an issue. A sound argument begins with an understanding that most issues are terribly complicated. The wise person approaches such ethical concerns as abortion or euthanasia or such public policy issues as tax cuts or trade agreements with the understanding that there are many philosophical, moral, and political issues that complicate discussions of these topics. Recognizing an argument's complexity may also lead us to an understanding that there can be more than one "right" position. The thoughtful arguer respects the views of others, seeks common ground when possible, and often chooses a conciliatory approach.

THE SHAPE OF ARGUMENT: WHAT WE CAN LEARN FROM ARISTOTLE

Still one of the best ways to understand the basics of argument is to reflect on what the Greek philosopher Aristotle describes as the three "players" in any argument: the *writer* (or *speaker*), the *argument itself,* and the *reader* (or *audience*). Aristotle also reminds us that the occasion or "situation" (*kairos*) is important in understanding and evaluating an argument. Let's examine each part of this model of argument.

Ethos (about the Writer/Speaker)

It seems logical to begin with *ethos* because without this player we have no argument. We could, though, end with the writer because Aristotle asserts that this player in any argument is the most important. No argument, no matter how logical, no matter how appealing to one's audience, can succeed if the audience rejects the arguer's credibility, his or her *ethical* qualities.

Think how often in political contests those running attack their opponent's character rather than the candidate's programs. Remember the smear campaign against Obama—he is (or was) a Muslim and therefore unfit to be president, the first point an error of fact, the second point an emotional appeal to voters' fears. Candidates try these smear tactics, even without evidence, because they understand that every voter they can convince of an opponent's failure of *ethos* is a citizen who will vote for them.

Many American voters want to be assured that a candidate is patriotic, religious (but of course not fanatic!), a loyal spouse, and a loving parent. At times, we even lose sight of important differences in positions as we focus on the person instead. But, this tells us how much an audience values their sense of the arguer's credibility. During his campaign for reelection, after the Watergate break-in, Nixon was attacked with the line "Would you buy a used car from this guy?" (In defense of used-car salespeople, not all are untrustworthy!)

Logos (about the Logic of the Argument)

Logos refers to the argument itself—to the assertion and the support for it. Aristotle maintains that part of an arguer's appeal to his or her audience lies in the logic of the argument and the quality of the support provided. Even the most credible of writers will not move thoughtful audiences with inadequate evidence or sloppy reasoning. Yes, "arguments" that appeal to emotions, to our needs and fantasies, will work for some audiences—look at the success of advertising, for example. But, if you want to present a serious claim to critical readers, then you must pay attention to your argument. Paying attention means not only having good reasons but also organizing them clearly. Your audience needs to see *how* your evidence supports your point. Consider the following argument in opposition to the war on Iraq.

> War can be justified only as a form of self-defense. To initiate a war, we need to be able to show that our first strike was necessary as a form of self-defense. The Bush administration argued that Iraq had weapons of mass destruction and intended to use them against us. Responding to someone's "intent" to do harm is always a difficult judgment call. But, in this case, there were no weapons of mass destruction so there could not have been any intent to harm the United States, or at least none that was obvious and immediate. Thus we must conclude that this war was not the right course of action for the United States.

You may disagree (many will) with this argument's assertion, but you can respect the writer's logic, the clear connecting of one reason to the next. One good way to strengthen your credibility is to get respect for clear reasoning.

Pathos (about Appeals to the Audience)

Argument implies an audience, those whose views we want to influence in some way. Aristotle labels this player *pathos,* the Greek word for both passion and suffering (hence *pathology,* the study of disease). Arguers need to be aware of their audience's feelings on the issue, the attitudes and values that will affect their response to the argument. There are really two questions arguers must answer: "How can I engage my audience's interest?" and "How can I engage their sympathy for my position?"

Some educators and health experts believe that childhood obesity is a major problem in the United States. Other Americans are much more focused on the economy—or their own careers. Al Gore is passionately concerned about the harmful effects of global warming; others, though increasingly fewer, think he lacks sufficient evidence of environmental degradation. How does a physician raise reader interest in childhood obesity? How does Gore convince doubters that we need to reduce carbon emissions? To prepare an effective argument, we need always to plan our approach with a clear vision of how best to connect to a specific audience—one which may or may not agree with our interests or our position.

Kairos (about the Occasion or Situation)

While *ethos, logos,* and *pathos* create the traditional three-part communication model, Aristotle adds another term to enhance our understanding of any argument "moment." The term *kairos* refers to the occasion for the argument, the situation that we are in. What does this moment call for from us? Is the lunch table the appropriate time and place for an argument with your coworker over her failure to meet a deadline that is part of a joint project? You have just received a 65 on your history test; is this the best time to e-mail your professor to protest

Personal confrontation at a business meeting: Not cool.

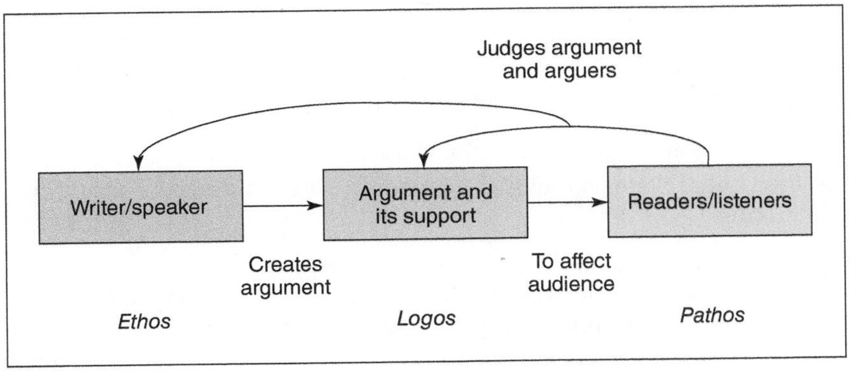

FIGURE 3.1 Aristotelian Structure of Argument

the grade? Would the professor's office be the better place for your discussion than an e-mail sent from your BlackBerry minutes after you have left class?

The concept of *kairos* asks us to consider what is most appropriate for the occasion, to think through the best time, place, and genre (type of argument) to make a successful argument. This concept has special meaning for students in a writing class who sometimes have difficulty thinking about audience at all. When practicing writing for the academic community, you may need to modify the language or tone that you use in other situations.

We argue in a specific context of three interrelated parts, as illustrated in Figure 3.1.

We present support for an assertion to a specific audience whose expectations and character we have given thought to when shaping our argument. And we present ourselves as informed, competent, and reliable so that our audience will give us their attention.

THE LANGUAGE OF ARGUMENT

We could title this section the *languages* of argument because arguments come in visual language as well as in words. But visual arguments—cartoons, photos, ads—are almost always accompanied by some words: figures speaking in bubbles, a caption, a slogan (Nike's "Just Do It!"). So we need to think about the kinds of statements that make up arguments, whether those arguments are legal briefs or cartoons, casual conversations or scholarly essays. To build an argument we need some statements that support other statements that present the main idea or claim of the argument.

- Claims: usually either inferences or judgments, for these are debatable assertions.
- Support: facts, opinions based on facts (inferences), or opinions based on values, beliefs, or ideas (judgments) or some combination of the three.

Let's consider what kinds of statements each of these terms describes.

Facts

Facts are statements that are verifiable. Factual statements refer to what can be counted or measured or confirmed by reasonable observers or trusted experts.

> There are twenty-six desks in Room 110.
>
> In the United States about 400,000 people die each year as a result of smoking.

These are factual statements. We can verify the first by observation—by counting. The second fact comes from medical records. We rely on trusted record-keeping sources and medical experts for verification. By definition, we do not argue about the facts. Usually. Sometimes "facts" change, as we learn more about our world. For example, only in the last thirty years has convincing evidence been gathered to demonstrate the relationship between smoking and various illnesses of the heart and lungs. And sometimes "facts" are false facts. These are statements that sound like facts but are incorrect. For example: Nadel has won more Wimbledon titles than Federer. Not so.

Inferences

Inferences are opinions based on facts. Inferences are the conclusions we draw from an analysis of facts.

> There will not be enough desks in Room 110 for upcoming fall-semester classes.
>
> Smoking is a serious health hazard.

Predictions of an increase in student enrollment for the coming fall semester lead to the inference that most English classes scheduled in Room 110 will run with several more students per class than last year. The dean should order new desks. Similarly, we infer from the number of deaths that smoking is a health problem; statistics show more people dying from tobacco than from AIDS, or murder, or car accidents, causes of death that get media coverage but do not produce nearly as many deaths.

Inferences vary in their closeness to the facts supporting them. That the sun will "rise" tomorrow is an inference, but we count on its happening, acting as if it is a fact. However, the first inference stated above is based not just on the fact of twenty-six desks but on another inference—a projected increase in student enrollment—and two assumptions. The argument looks like this:

FACT:	There are twenty-six desks in Room 110.
INFERENCE:	There will be more first-year students next year.
ASSUMPTIONS:	1. English will remain a required course.
	2. No additional classrooms are available for English classes.
CLAIM:	There will not be enough desks in Room 110 for upcoming fall-semester classes.

This inference could be challenged by a different analysis of the facts supporting enrollment projections. Or, if additional rooms can be found, the dean will not need to order new desks. Inferences can be part of the support of an argument, or they can be the claim of an argument.

Judgments

Judgments are opinions based on values, beliefs, or philosophical concepts. (Judgments also include opinions based on personal preferences, but we have already excluded these from argument.) Judgments concern right and wrong, good and bad, better or worse, should and should not:

> No more than twenty-six students should be enrolled in any English class.
>
> Cigarette advertising should be eliminated, and the federal government should develop an antismoking campaign.

NOTE: Placing such qualifiers as "I believe," "I think," or "I feel" in an assertion does not free you from the need to support that claim. The statement "I believe that President Bush was a great president" calls for an argument based on evidence and reasons.

To support the first judgment, we need to explain what constitutes overcrowding, or what constitutes the best class size for effective teaching. If we can support our views on effective teaching, we may be able to convince the college president that ordering more desks for Room 110 is not the best solution to an increasing enrollment in English classes. The second judgment also offers a solution to a problem, in this case a national health problem. To reduce the number of deaths, we need to reduce the number of smokers, either by encouraging smokers to quit or nonsmokers not to start. The underlying assumption: Advertising does affect behavior.

EXERCISE: Facts, Inferences, and Judgments

Compile a list of three statements of fact, three inferences, and three judgments. Try to organize them into three related sets, as illustrated here:

- Smoking is prohibited in some restaurants.
- Secondhand smoke is a health hazard.
- Smoking should be prohibited in all restaurants.

We can classify judgments to see better what kind of assertion we are making and, therefore, what kind of support we need to argue effectively.

FUNCTIONAL JUDGMENTS (guidelines for judging how something or someone works or could work)

Tiger Woods is the best golfer to play the game.

Antismoking advertising will reduce the number of smokers.

AESTHETIC JUDGMENTS (guidelines for judging art, literature, music, or natural scenes)

The sunrise was beautiful.

The Great Gatsby's structure, characters, and symbols are perfectly wedded to create the novel's vision of the American dream.

ETHICAL JUDGMENTS (guidelines for group or social behavior)

Lawyers should not advertise.

It is discourteous to talk during a film or lecture.

MORAL JUDGMENTS (guidelines of right and wrong for judging individuals and for establishing legal principles)

Taking another person's life is wrong.

Equal rights under the law should not be denied on the basis of race or gender.

Functional and aesthetic judgments generally require defining key terms and establishing criteria for the judging or ranking made by the assertion. How, for example, do we compare golfers? On the amount of money won? The number of tournaments won? Or the consistency of winning throughout one's career? What about the golfer's quality and range of shots? Ethical and moral judgments may be more difficult to support because they depend not just on how terms are defined and criteria established but on values and beliefs as well. If taking another person's life is wrong, why isn't it wrong in war? Or is it? These are difficult questions that require thoughtful debate.

EXERCISES: Understanding Assumptions, Facts, False Facts, Inferences, and Judgments

1. Categorize the judgments you wrote for the previous exercise (p. 77) as either aesthetic, moral, ethical, or functional. Alternatively, compile a list of three judgments that you then categorize.
2. For each judgment listed for exercise 1, generate one statement of support, either a fact or an inference or another judgment. Then state any underlying assumptions that are part of each argument.
3. Read the following article and then complete the exercise that follows. This exercise tests both careful reading and your understanding of the differences among facts, inferences, and judgments.

YOUR BRAIN LIES TO YOU

SAM WANG and SANDRA AAMODT

Dr. Samuel S. H. Wang is a professor of molecular biology and neuroscience at Princeton, where he manages a research lab. Dr. Sandra Aamodt, former editor of *Nature Neuroscience*, is a freelance science writer. Drs. Wang and Aamodt are the authors of *Welcome to Your Brain: Why You Lose Your Car Keys but Never Forget How to Drive and Other Puzzles of Everyday Life* (2008). The following article appeared on June 27, 2008, in the *New York Times*.

False beliefs are everywhere. Eighteen percent of Americans think the sun revolves around the earth, one poll has found. Thus it seems slightly less egregious that, according to another poll, 10 percent of us think that Senator Barack Obama, a Christian, is instead a Muslim. The Obama campaign has created a Web site to dispel misinformation. But this effort may be more difficult than it seems, thanks to the quirky way in which our brains store memories—and mislead us along the way. 1

The brain does not simply gather and stockpile information as a computer's hard drive does. Current research suggests that facts may be stored first in the hippocampus, a structure deep in the brain about the size and shape of a fat man's curled pinkie finger. But the information does not rest there. Every time we recall it, our brain writes it down again, and during this re-storage, it is also reprocessed. In time, the fact is gradually transferred to the cerebral cortex and is separated from the context in which it was originally learned. For example, you know that the capital of California is Sacramento, but you probably don't remember how you learned it. 2

This phenomenon, known as source amnesia, can also lead people to forget whether a statement is true. Even when a lie is presented with a disclaimer, people often later remember it as true. 3

With time, this misremembering only gets worse. A false statement from a non-credible source that is at first not believed can gain credibility during the months it takes to reprocess memories from short-term hippocampal storage to longer-term cortical storage. As the source is forgotten, the message and its implications gain strength. This could explain why, during the 2004 presidential campaign, it took some weeks for the Swift Boat Veterans for Truth campaign against Senator John Kerry to have an effect on his standing in the polls. 4

Even if they do not understand the neuroscience behind source amnesia, campaign strategists can exploit it to spread misinformation. They know that if their message is initially memorable, its impression will persist long after it is debunked. In repeating a falsehood, someone may back it up with an opening line like "I think I read somewhere" or even with a reference to a specific source. 5

In one study, a group of Stanford students was exposed repeatedly to an unsubstantiated claim taken from a Web site that Coca-Cola is an effective paint thinner. Students who read the statement five times were nearly one-third more likely than those who read it only twice to attribute it to *Consumer Reports* (rather than *The National Enquirer*, their other choice), giving it a gloss of credibility. 6

7 Adding to this innate tendency to mold information we recall is the way our brains fit facts into established mental frameworks. We tend to remember news that accords with our worldview, and discount statements that contradict it.

8 In another Stanford study, 48 students, half of whom said they favored capital punishment and half of whom said they opposed it, were presented with two pieces of evidence, one supporting and one contradicting the claim that capital punishment deters crime. Both groups were more convinced by the evidence that supported their initial position.

9 Psychologists have suggested that legends propagate by striking an emotional chord. In the same way, ideas can spread by emotional selection, rather than by their factual merits, encouraging the persistence of falsehoods about Coke—or about a presidential candidate.

10 Journalists and campaign workers may think they are acting to counter misinformation by pointing out that it is not true. But by repeating a false rumor, they may inadvertently make it stronger. In its concerted effort to "stop the smears," the Obama campaign may want to keep this in mind. Rather than emphasize that Mr. Obama is not a Muslim, for instance, it may be more effective to stress that he embraced Christianity as a young man.

11 Consumers of news, for their part, are prone to selectively accept and remember statements that reinforce beliefs they already hold. In a replication of the study of students' impressions of evidence about the death penalty, researchers found that even when subjects were given a specific instruction to be objective, they were still inclined to reject evidence that disagreed with their beliefs.

12 In the same study, however, when subjects were asked to imagine their reaction if the evidence had pointed to the opposite conclusion, they were more open-minded to information that contradicted their beliefs. Apparently, it pays for consumers of controversial news to take a moment and consider that the opposite interpretation may be true.

13 In 1919, Justice Oliver Wendell Holmes of the Supreme Court wrote that "the best test of truth is the power of the thought to get itself accepted in the competition of the market." Holmes erroneously assumed that ideas are more likely to spread if they are honest. Our brains do not naturally obey this admirable dictum, but by better understanding the mechanisms of memory perhaps we can move closer to Holmes's ideal.

Source: Originally appeared in the *New York Times*, June 27, 2008. Reprinted by permission of the authors.

Label each of the following sentences as F (fact), FF (false fact), I (inference), or J (judgment).

_____ 1. Campaigns have trouble getting rid of misinformation about their candidate.

_____ 2. When we reprocess information we may get the information wrong, but we always remember the source.

_____ 3. The Obama campaign should stress that he became a Christian as a young man.

_____ 4. Most of us remember information that matches our view of the world.

_____ 5. When students were told to be objective in evaluating evidence, they continued to reject evidence they disagreed with.

_____ 6. Coke is an effective paint thinner.

_____ 7. True statements should be accepted and false statements rejected.

_____ 8. Justice Holmes was wrong about the power of truth to spread more widely than falsehood.

_____ 9. The more we understand about the way the world works, the better our chances of separating truth from falsehood.

_____ 10. Americans do not seem to understand basic science.

THE SHAPE OF ARGUMENT: WHAT WE CAN LEARN FROM TOULMIN

British philosopher Stephen Toulmin adds to what we have learned from Aristotle by focusing our attention on the basics of the argument itself. First, consider this definition of argument: *An argument consists of evidence and/or reasons presented in support of an assertion or claim that is either stated or implied.* For example:

CLAIM:	We should not go skiing today
GROUNDS:	because it is too cold.
GROUNDS:	Because some laws are unjust,
CLAIM:	civil disobedience is sometimes justified.
GROUNDS:	It's only fair and right for academic institutions to
CLAIM:	accept students only on academic merit.

The parts of an argument, Toulmin asserts, are actually a bit more complex than these examples suggest. Each argument has a third part that is not stated in the preceding examples. This third part is the "glue" that connects the support—the evidence and reasons—to the argument's claim and thus fulfills the logic of the argument. Toulmin calls this glue an argument's *warrants.* These are the principles or assumptions that allow us to assert that our evidence or reasons—what Toulmin calls the *grounds*—do indeed support our claim. (Figure 3.2 illustrates these basics of the Toulmin model of argument.)

CLAIM:	Academic institutions should accept students only on academic merit.
GROUNDS:	It is only fair and right.
WARRANT:	(1) Fair and right are important values. (2) Academic institutions are only about academics.

FIGURE 3.2 **The Toulmin Structure of Argument**

Look again at the sample arguments to see what warrants must be accepted to make each argument work:

CLAIM:	We should not go skiing today.
GROUNDS:	It is too cold.
WARRANTS:	When it is too cold, skiing is not fun; the activity is not sufficient to keep one from becoming uncomfortable. AND: Too cold is what is too cold for me.
CLAIM:	Civil disobedience is sometimes justified.
EVIDENCE:	Some laws are unjust.
WARRANTS:	To get unjust laws changed, people need to be made aware of the injustice. Acts of civil disobedience will get people's attention and make them aware that the laws need changing.
CLAIM:	Academic institutions should accept students only on academic merit.
EVIDENCE:	It is fair and right.
WARRANTS:	Fair and right are important values. AND: Academic institutions are only about academics.

Warrants play an important role in any argument, so we need to be sure to understand what they are. Note, for instance, the second warrant operating in the first argument: The temperature considered uncomfortable for the speaker will also be uncomfortable for her companions—an uncertain assumption. In the second argument, the warrant is less debatable, for acts of civil disobedience usually get media coverage and thus dramatize the issue. The underlying assumptions in the third example stress the need to know one's warrants. Both warrants will need to be defended in the debate over selection by academic merit only.

COLLABORATIVE EXERCISE: Building Arguments

With your class partner or in small groups, examine each of the following claims. Select two, think of one statement that could serve as evidence for each claim, and then think of the underlying assumption(s) that complete each of the arguments.

1. Professor X is not a good instructor.
2. Americans need to reduce the fat in their diets.
3. Tiger Woods is a great golfer.
4. Military women should be allowed to serve in combat zones.
5. College newspapers should be free of supervision by faculty or administrators.

Toulmin was particularly interested in the great range or strength or probability of various arguments. Some kinds of arguments are stronger than others because of the language or logic they use. Other arguments must, necessarily, be heavily qualified for the claim to be supportable. Toulmin developed his language to provide a strategy for analyzing the degree of probability in a given argument and to remind us of the need to qualify some kinds of claims. You have already seen how the idea of warrants, or assumptions, helps us think about the "glue" that presumably makes a given argument work. Taken together, Toulmin terms and concepts help us analyze the arguments of others and prepare more convincing arguments of our own.

Claims

A claim is what the argument asserts or seeks to prove. It answers the question "What is your point?" In an argumentative speech or essay, the claim is the speaker's or writer's main idea or thesis. Although an argument's claim "follows" from reasons and evidence, we often present an argument—whether written or spoken—with the claim stated near the beginning of the presentation. We can better understand an argument's claim by recognizing that we can have claims of fact, claims of value, and claims of policy.

Claims of Fact

Although facts usually support claims, we do argue over some facts. Historians and biographers may argue over what happened in the past, although they are more likely to argue over the significance of what happened. Scientists also argue over the facts, over how to classify an unearthed fossil, or whether the fossil indicates that the animal had feathers. For example:

CLAIM: The small, predatory dinosaur *Deinonychus* hunted its prey in packs.

This claim is supported by the discovery of several fossils of *Deinonychus* close together and with the fossil bones of a much larger dinosaur. Their teeth have also been found in or near the bones of dinosaurs that have died in a struggle.

Assertions about what will happen are sometimes classified as claims of fact, but they can also be labeled as inferences supported by facts. Predictions about a future event may be classified as claims of fact:

CLAIM: The United States will win the most gold medals at the 2012 Olympics.

CLAIM: I will get an A on tomorrow's psychology test.

What evidence would you use to support each of these claims? (And, did the first one turn out to be correct?)

Claims of Value

These include moral, ethical, and aesthetic judgments. Assertions that use such words as *good* or *bad, better* or *worse,* and *right* or *wrong* will be claims of value. The following are all claims of value:

CLAIM: Roger Federer is a better tennis player than Andy Roddick.

CLAIM: *Adventures of Huckleberry Finn* is one of the most significant American novels.

CLAIM: Cheating hurts others and the cheater too.

CLAIM: Abortion is wrong.

Arguments in support of judgments demand relevant evidence, careful reasoning, and an awareness of the assumptions one is making. Support for claims of value often include other value statements. For example, to support the claim that censorship is bad, arguers often assert that the free exchange of ideas is good and necessary in a democracy. The support is itself a value statement.

Claims of Policy

Finally, claims of policy are assertions about what should or should not happen, what the government ought or ought not to do, how to best solve social problems. Claims of policy debate, for example, college rules, state gun laws, or federal aid to Africans suffering from AIDS. The following are claims of policy:

CLAIM: College newspapers should not be controlled in any way by college authorities.

CLAIM: States should not have laws allowing people to carry concealed weapons.

CLAIM: The United States must provide more aid to African countries where 25 percent or more of the citizens have tested positive for HIV.

Claims of policy are often closely tied to judgments of morality or political philosophy, but they also need to be grounded in feasibility. That is, your claim needs to be doable, to be based on a thoughtful consideration of the real world and the complexities of public policy issues.

Grounds (or Data or Evidence)

The term *grounds* refers to the reasons and evidence provided in support of a claim. Although the words *data* and *evidence* can also be used, note that *grounds* is the most general term because it includes reasons or logic as well as examples or statistics. We determine the grounds of an argument by asking the question "Why do you think that?" or "How do you know that?" When writing your own arguments, you can ask yourself these questions and answer by using a *because* clause:

CLAIM: Smoking should be banned in restaurants because

GROUNDS: secondhand smoke is a serious health hazard.

CLAIM: Federer is a better tennis player than Roddick because

GROUNDS:	1. he was ranked number one longer, 2. he won more tournaments than Roddick, and 3. he won more major tournaments than Roddick.

Warrants

Why should we believe that your grounds do indeed support your claim? Your argument's warrants answer this question. They explain why your evidence really is evidence. Sometimes warrants reside in language itself, in the meanings of the words we are using. If I am *younger* than my brother, then my brother must be *older* than I am. In a court case attempting to prove that Jones murdered Smith, the relation of evidence to claim is less assured. If the police investigation has been properly managed and the physical evidence is substantial, then Smith may be Jones's murderer. The prosecution has—presumably beyond a reasonable doubt—established motive, means, and opportunity for Smith to commit the murder. In many arguments based on statistical data, the argument's warrant rests on complex analyses of the statistics—and on the conviction that the statistics have been developed without error.

Still, without taking courses in statistics and logic, you can develop an alertness to the "good sense" of some arguments and the "dubious sense" of others. You know, for example, that good SAT scores are a predictor of success in college. Can you argue that you will do well in college because you have good SATs? No. We can determine only a statistical probability. We cannot turn probabilities about a group of people into a warrant about one person in the group. (In addition, SAT scores are only one predictor. Another key variable is motivation.)

What is the warrant for the Federer claim?

CLAIM:	Federer is a better tennis player than Roddick.
GROUNDS:	The three facts listed above.
WARRANT:	It is appropriate to judge and rank tennis players on these kinds of statistics. That is, the better player is one who has held the number-one ranking for the longest time, has won the most tournaments, and also has won the most major tournaments.

Backing

Standing behind an argument's warrant may be additional *backing*. Backing answers the question "How do we know that your evidence is good evidence?" You may answer this question by providing authoritative sources for the data used (for example, the Census Bureau or the U.S. Tennis Association). Or, you may explain in detail the methodology of the experiments performed or the surveys taken. When scientists and social scientists present the results of their research, they anticipate the question of backing and automatically provide a detailed explanation of the process by which they acquired their evidence. In criminal trials, defense attorneys challenge the backing of the prosecution's argument. They question the handling of blood samples sent to labs for DNA testing, for instance. The defense attorneys want jury members to doubt the *quality* of the evidence.

This discussion of backing returns us to the point that one part of any argument is the audience. To create an effective argument, ask yourself: Will my warrants and backing be accepted? Is my audience likely to share my values, religious beliefs, or scientific approach? If you are speaking to a group at your church, then backing based on the religious beliefs of that church may be effective. If you are preparing an argument for a general audience, then using specific religious assertions as warrants or backing probably will not result in an effective argument.

Qualifiers

Some arguments are absolute; they can be stated without qualification. *If I am younger than my brother, then he must be older than I am.* Most arguments need some qualification; many need precise limitations. If, when playing bridge, I am dealt eight spades, then my opponents and partner together must have five spade cards—because there are thirteen cards of each suit in a deck. My partner *probably* has one spade but *could* be void of spades. My partner *possibly* has two or more spades, but I would be foolish to count on it. When bidding my hand, I must be controlled by the laws of probability. Look again at the smoking-ban claim. Observe the absolute nature of both the claim and its support. If secondhand smoke is indeed a health hazard, it will be that in *all* restaurants, not just in some. With each argument ask what qualification is needed for a successful argument.

Sweeping generalizations often come to us in the heat of a debate or when we first start to think about an issue. For example: *Gun control is wrong because it restricts individual rights.* But on reflection surely you would not want to argue against all forms of gun control. (Remember: An unqualified assertion is understood by your audience to be absolute.) Would you sell guns to felons in jail or to children on the way to school? Obviously not. So, let's try the claim again, this time with two important qualifiers:

QUALIFIED	**Adults without a criminal record should not be restricted in the**
CLAIM:	**purchase of guns.**

Others may want this claim further qualified to eliminate particular types of guns or to control the number purchased or the process for purchasing. The gun-control debate is not about absolutes; it is all about which qualified claim is best.

Rebuttals

Arguments can be challenged. Smart debaters assume that there are people who will disagree with them. They anticipate the ways that opponents can challenge their arguments. When you are planning an argument, you need to think about how you can counter or rebut the challenges you anticipate. Think of yourself as an attorney in a court case preparing your argument *and* a defense of the other attorney's challenges to your argument. If you ignore the important role of rebuttals, you may not win the jury to your side.

USING TOULMIN'S TERMS TO ANALYZE ARGUMENTS

Terms are never an end in themselves; we learn them when we recognize that they help us to organize our thinking about a subject. Toulmin's terms can aid your reading of the arguments of others. You can "see what's going on" in an argument if you analyze it, applying Toulmin's language to its parts. Not all terms will be useful for every analysis because, for example, some arguments will not have qualifiers or rebuttals. But to recognize that an argument is *without qualifiers* is to learn something important about that argument.

First, here is a simple argument broken down into its parts using Toulmin's terms:

GROUNDS:	Because Dr. Bradshaw has an attendance policy,
CLAIM:	students who miss more than seven classes will
QUALIFIER:	most likely (last year, Dr. Bradshaw did allow one student, in unusual circumstances, to continue in the class) be dropped from the course.
WARRANT:	Dr. Bradshaw's syllabus explains her attendance policy, a
BACKING:	policy consistent with the concept of a discussion class that depends on student participation and consistent with the attendance policies of most of her colleagues.
REBUTTAL:	Although some students complain about an attendance policy of any kind, Dr. Bradshaw does explain her policy and her reasons for it the first day of class. She then reminds students that the syllabus is a contract between them; if they choose to stay, they agree to abide by the guidelines explained on the syllabus.

This argument is brief and fairly simple. Let's see how Toulmin's terms can help us analyze a longer, more complex argument. Read actively and annotate the following essay while noting the existing annotations using Toulmin's terms. Then answer the questions that follow the article.

THE THREAT TO FREE SPEECH AT UNIVERSITIES

GREG LUKIANOFF

An attorney, Greg Lukianoff holds degrees from American University and Stanford Law School. He is the president of the Foundation for Individual Rights in Education (FIRE), a regular columnist at *Huffington Post,* and the author of *Unlearning Liberty: Campus Censorship and the End of the American Debate* (2012). The following argument was published January 6, 2012.

PREREADING QUESTIONS Are there good reasons to have campus speech codes? Are there problems with speech codes?

Toulmin's Terms

1 Activists embarked on a campaign in the 1980s to eradicate hurtful, bigoted and politically incorrect speech by enacting speech codes at universities across the country. Although the movement presented itself as a forward-thinking way to make campuses welcoming, the initiative stood in stark contrast to the celebrated "free speech movement" of the 1960s, whose proponents understood that vague exceptions to free speech were inevitably used by those in power to punish opinions they dislike or disagree with. And unfortunately the effort gained momentum as prestigious institutions passed speech codes.

Rebutted—universities wrongly motivated

Claim implied in word choice

2 The legal fig leaf upon which the speech-codes movement relied was the concept of "hostile work environment" harassment. Because civil rights laws, chief among them Title IX, banned sexual discrimination on campuses, harassment jurisprudence—sometimes combined with other tenuous rationales—became the primary legal tool universities used to formulate speech codes.

Grounds

3 Courts, however, understood that merely naming a restriction a "harassment" code did not inoculate it from First Amendment scrutiny. In nearly a dozen courtroom losses between 1989 and 2010, harassment-based speech codes have been defeated at campuses from the University of Michigan to Stanford. Amazingly, these defeats have not slowed the spread of these codes. The Foundation for Individual Rights in Education (FIRE), of which I am president, conducts an extensive annual study of campus speech codes; our 2012 report found that 65 percent of nearly 400 top colleges maintain codes that prohibit substantial amounts of clearly protected speech.

4 Overly broad harassment codes remain the weapon of choice on campus to punish speech that administrators dislike. In a decade fighting campus censorship, I have seen harassment defined as expressions as mild as "inappropriately directed laughter" and used to police students for references to a student government candidate as a "jerk and a fool" (at the University of Central Florida in 2006) and a factually verifiable if unflattering piece on Islamic extremism in a conservative student magazine (at Tufts University in 2007). Other examples abound. Worryingly, such broad codes and heavy-handed enforcement are teaching a generation of students that it may be safer to keep their mouths shut when important or controversial issues arise. Such illiberal lessons on how to live in a free society are poison to freewheeling debate and thought experimentation and, therefore, to the innovative thinking that both higher education and our democracy need.

Warrant

Grounds

5 The Education Department's Office for Civil Rights (OCR), which enforces Title IX on college campuses, tried in 2003 to put a stop to the "government made me do it" excuse for speech codes. It issued a letter to every college receiving federal funds—so, virtually all—making clear that harassment requires a serious pattern of discriminatory behavior, not just mere offense. Since then, the number of campus speech codes has slowly begun to decline.

Rebuttal

6 But last year the OCR backpedaled. The agency issued a 19-page letter in April dictating to colleges the procedures they must follow in sexual harassment and assault cases. Among its many troubling points, including a requirement that sexual harassment cases be adjudicated using the lowest possible standard of evidence allowable in court, is the fact that the letter makes no mention of the First Amendment or free speech. This ignores the role that vague and broad definitions of harassment have played in justifying campus speech codes and censorship over the past few decades. By mandating so many procedural steps colleges must take to respond to allegations of sexual harassment while simultaneously failing to mandate a consistent, limited and constitutional definition of harassment, the OCR encourages those on campus who are already inclined to use such codes to punish speech they simply dislike.

Backing, with claim in paragraph 8

7 Rather than proffer shifting rules, the OCR should end the threat of harassment-based campus speech codes once and for all. The Supreme Court offered its only guidance on the thorny issue of student-on-student harassment in the 1999 case *Davis v. Monroe County Board of Education*. The justices recognized the necessity of carefully defining what constitutes "harassment" in the educational context, lest everyday interactions be rendered a federal offense. The court defined harassment as discriminatory conduct, directed at an individual, that is "so severe, pervasive, and objectively offensive" that "victim-students are effectively denied equal access to an institution's resources and opportunities."

8 This definition, if applied fairly, poses little threat to free speech and effectively prohibits real harassment

Backing-support for claim

9 This week, FIRE and a broad coalition of organizations (the Tully Center for Free Speech at Syracuse University, National Coalition Against Censorship, the Heartland Institute, National Association of Scholars, Alliance Defense Fund Center for Academic Freedom, Feminists for Free Expression, Woodhull Sexual Freedom Alliance, American Booksellers Foundation for Free Expression, Accuracy in Academia, and the American Council of Trustees and Alumni) are writing to the OCR to request that it publicly affirm the *Davis* standard as the controlling definition for harassment on campus.

Claim restated

10 By simply following the Supreme Courts guidance, the OCR would assure that serious harassment is punished on campus while free speech is robustly protected. In one move, OCR could rid campuses of a substantial portion of all speech codes while protecting institutions from losing still more First Amendment lawsuits. Most important, by recognizing the *Davis* standard, the OCR would send a message that free speech and free minds are essential to—not incompatible with—the development of creative, critical and innovative thinkers on our nations campuses.

Warrant

QUESTIONS FOR READING

1. What is Lukianoff's subject? (Free speech is not sufficiently precise as an answer.)
2. What is the legal basis for colleges' speech codes? How has this law been challenged in the past?
3. Explain the shifting positions of the Office of Civil Rights; what does the author want this office to do now?

QUESTIONS FOR REASONING AND ANALYSIS

4. What is Lukianoff's claim?
5. What is his primary support? (Add a "because" clause to his claim to find his grounds.)
6. Review the author's comments about college authorities—those he holds responsible for speech codes. What, in Lukianoff's view, is their reason for wanting speech codes? Does the author provide evidence for this warrant? Is support needed?

QUESTIONS FOR REFLECTION AND WRITING

7. Reflect on the author's position that codes let colleges punish views they don't like. Is this the only reason for speech codes? Do you agree that it is the primary motivation of college officials?
8. Lukianoff asserts that it is possible to punish "serious harassment" on campus without restricting free speech. How should colleges do this? (One student's free speech is often another's perceived insult.) What suggestions do you have for writing clear guidelines for students that will define the author's desired balance?
9. How can colleges create a sense of community with mutual respect while still embracing the free exchange of ideas?

Toulmin's terms can help you to see what writers are actually "doing" in their arguments. Just remember that writers do not usually follow the terms in precise order. Indeed, you can find both grounds and backing in the same sentence, or claim and qualifiers in the same paragraph, and so on. Still, the terms can help you to sort out your thinking about a claim you want to support. Now use your knowledge of argument as you read and analyze the following arguments.

FOR ANALYSIS AND DEBATE

CHEERING FREE SPEECH | JEFFREY MATEER AND ERIN LEU

Jeff Mateer is General Counsel of Liberty Institute, overseeing the legal team in the organization's commitment to the support of religious liberty. His law degree is from Southern Methodist University, and he is admitted to the bar in Texas. Erin Leu, a graduate of Harvard Law School, was an attorney at Liberty and represented the Kountze cheerleaders. She is now an associate with a law firm in the Dallas area. Their article was published November 5, 2012.

PREREADING QUESTIONS Once you read the opening sentence, can you appreciate the title's clever play with words? What do you expect the essay to be about?

Cheerleaders in Kountze, Tex., recently learned an invaluable lesson about the Constitution and the importance of individual expression without government censorship. Ironically, it's a lesson they had to watch a court teach their school district. 1

Controversy arose this fall when the cheerleaders at Kountze High School decided to model good sportsmanship by replacing the often-violent messages on their banners, such as "Scalp the Indians," with encouraging religious messages. The only complaints came from an antireligion advocacy group more than 1,000 miles away. In response, the Kountze superintendent issued an unlawful directive banning all such religious speech. 2

The cheerleaders sued their school district to preserve their rights to free speech and religious expression. Their cause gained international support, from tens of thousands of individuals across six continents. Texas Gov. Rick Perry and state Attorney General Greg Abbott spoke out, applauding the students for standing up for their rights and denouncing government hostility toward religion. 3

Two weeks ago a Texas court issued a temporary injunction allowing the cheerleaders to display their banners for at least the remainder of the season. Free speech prevailed, reminding us of the well-established principle that students do not shed their constitutional rights to freedom of speech or expression at the schoolhouse gate. 4

People from all political persuasions should be celebrating this decision. Many are mistakenly arguing, however, that the outcome is incorrect because the Supreme Court struck down school-sponsored prayer at football games in the 2000 case *Santa Fe v. Doe*. But *Santa Fe* recognized that "there is a crucial difference between *government* speech endorsing religion, which the Establishment Clause forbids, and *private* speech endorsing religion, which the Free Speech and Free Exercise Clauses protect." 5

In *Santa Fe,* the court held that a school policy that created a majoritarian election on religion and explicitly encouraged prayer created government speech. Conversely, in this case, both Texas law and the school's policies affirm that when students speak at school events, including football games, they are engaging in private speech and their views do not reflect the position of the school. Indeed, the policies at issue in *Kountze* create a forum for student speech and require the school district to remain neutral toward all viewpoints. *Santa Fe* involved government speech; Kountze involves private student speech. 6

The Kountze cheerleaders alone decide what message to place on their banners. The team is student-run, with school officials present only to monitor safety. Each week two cheerleaders take turns leading the team, including choosing whether to create banners and, if so, what messages they should bear. The supplies to create the banners are paid for with private funds, as are the cheerleaders' uniforms, further demonstrating the private nature of their speech. 7

In *Santa Fe,* the court stated that: "By no means do [the Religion Clauses] impose a prohibition on all religious activity in our public schools. . . . Indeed, the common purpose of the Religion Clauses is to secure religious liberty." When football players or cheerleaders are on the field in uniform, they do not become 8 agents of the state. No one would argue that high school football players are prohibited from praying together. In the same manner, just because cheerleaders wear uniforms and are on school property does not mean that they become instruments of the school or that they must surrender their right to free speech.

9 High school students' rights to free speech should be robustly protected. These students are nearly adults; they are about to enter college, military service or the workforce. Schools should be teaching students about the First Amendment and the free marketplace of ideas, including that other individuals may advocate for messages with which they disagree, instead of censoring speech that some might find offensive. As the Supreme Court has stated: "The vigilant protection of constitutional freedoms is nowhere more vital than in the community of American schools."

10 This is because "[t]he Nation's future depends upon leaders trained through wide exposure to that robust exchange of ideas which discovers truth out of a multitude of tongues, [rather] than through any kind of authoritative selection."

11 We better serve our students by educating them about our country's commitment to free expression rather than shutting out certain views. Otherwise, our schools do a great disservice to students and fail to prepare them to be citizens of our free society.

12 Nonetheless, the character of the Kountze cheerleaders should give us hope for the future. With young adults like these ready to respectfully stand for our Constitution, our freedoms are more secure.

Source: *Washington Post*, November 5, 2012. Reprinted by permission of the authors.

QUESTIONS FOR READING

1. What is the situation that led to this essay? What did the cheerleaders do?
2. What was the court's ruling? The authors write that Texas law has supported the cheerleaders, but is this case closed?

QUESTIONS FOR REASONING AND ANALYSIS

3. What is the authors' claim? What grounds (reasons/evidence) do they provide?
4. Mateer and Leu agree with the court's ruling that football players can pray on the field. They argue that the cheerleaders' religious signs are not the same. How do they defend the similarity?
5. Study the final four paragraphs; what makes them an effective conclusion? How are the authors "defining" the issue in these paragraphs?

QUESTIONS FOR REFLECTION AND WRITING

6. The core of this argument is that the cheerleaders' signs are private speech because they do not represent the school. Do you agree with their position? If you agree, how would you add to their discussion? If you disagree, how would you challenge it?
7. If you were the judge making the final ruling on this case, how would you rule? Why?

HOW CAN WE BAN INSULTS AGAINST JEWS BUT NOT MUSLIMS?

WILLIAM SALETAN

A graduate of Swarthmore College, William Saletan writes about science, technology, and politics for the online magazine *Slate*. He has published several books, including *Bearing Right: How Conservatives Won the Abortion War* (2004). The following article was posted September 28, 2012.

PREREADING QUESTIONS Does your college have rules against hate speech? Are such rules consistent with First Amendment rights?

How can we ban hate speech against Jews while defending mockery of Muslims? Jews have too much influence over U.S. foreign policy. Gay men are too promiscuous. Muslims commit too much terrorism. Blacks commit too much crime. 1

Each of those claims is poorly stated. Each, in its clumsy way, addresses a real problem or concern. And each violates laws against hate speech. In much of what we call the free world, for writing that paragraph, I could be jailed. 2

Libertarians, cultural conservatives, and racists have complained about these laws for years. But now the problem has turned global. Islamic governments, angered by an anti-Muslim video that provoked protests and riots in their countries, are demanding to know why insulting the Prophet Mohammed is free speech but vilifying Jews and denying the Holocaust isn't. And we don't have a good answer. 3

If we're going to preach freedom of expression around the world, we have to practice it. We have to scrap our hate-speech laws. 4

Muslim leaders want us to extend these laws. At this week's meeting of the U.N. General Assembly, they lobbied for tighter censorship. Egypt's president said freedom of expression shouldn't include speech that is "used to incite hatred" or "directed towards one specific religion." Pakistan's president urged the "international community" to "criminalize" acts that "endanger world security by misusing freedom of expression." Yemen's president called for "international legislation" to suppress speech that "blasphemes the beliefs of nations and defames their figures." The Arab League's secretary-general proposed a binding "international legal framework" to "criminalize psychological and spiritual harm" caused by expressions that "insult the beliefs, culture and civilization of others." 5

President Obama, while condemning the video, met these proposals with a stout defense of free speech. Switzerland's president agreed: "Freedom of opinion and of expression are core values guaranteed universally which must be protected." And when a French magazine published cartoons poking fun at Mohammed, the country's prime minister insisted that French laws protecting free speech extend to caricatures. 6

This debate between East and West, between respect and pluralism, isn't a crisis. It's a stage of global progress. The Arab spring has freed hundreds of millions of Muslims from the political retardation of dictatorship. They're taking responsibility for governing themselves and their relations with other countries. They're debating one another and challenging us. And they should, because we're hypocrites. 7

Pakistani activists of the hard line Sunni party Jamaat-e-Islami (JI) burn a U.S. flag during a protest against an anti-Islam movie in Peshawar on September 18, 2012. Police used tear gas to disperse a crowd of more than 2,000 protesters trying to reach the US consulate in northwest Pakistan as fresh demonstrations erupted against an anti-Islam film.

8 From Pakistan to Iran to Saudi Arabia to Egypt to Nigeria to the United Kingdom, Muslims scoff at our rhetoric about free speech. They point to European laws against questioning the Holocaust. Monday on CNN, Iranian President Mahmoud Ahmedinejad needled British interviewer Piers Morgan: "Why in Europe has it been forbidden for anyone to conduct any research about this event? Why are researchers in prison? . . . Do you believe in the freedom of thought and ideas, or no?" On Tuesday, Pakistan's U.N. ambassador, speaking for the Organization of Islamic Cooperation, told the U.N. Human Rights Council:

> 9 We are all aware of the fact that laws exist in Europe and other countries which impose curbs, for instance, on anti-Semitic speech, Holocaust denial, or racial slurs. We need to acknowledge, once and for all, that Islamophobia in particular and discrimination on the basis of religion and belief are contemporary forms of racism and must be dealt with as such. Not to do so would be a clear example of double standards. Islamophobia has to be treated in law and practice equal to the treatment given to anti-Semitism.

10 He's right. Laws throughout Europe forbid any expression that "minimizes," "trivializes," "belittles," "plays down," "contests," or "puts in doubt" Nazi crimes. Hungary, Poland, and the Czech Republic extend this prohibition to communist atrocities. These laws carry jail sentences of up to five years. Germany adds two years for anyone who "disparages the memory of a deceased person."

Hate speech laws go further. Germany punishes anyone found guilty of "insulting" or "defaming segments of the population." The Netherlands bans anything that "verbally or in writing or image, deliberately offends a group of people because of their race, their religion or beliefs, their hetero- or homosexual orientation or their physical, psychological or mental handicap." It's illegal to "insult" such a group in France, to "defame" them in Portugal, to "degrade" them in Denmark, or to "expresses contempt" for them in Sweden. In Switzerland, it's illegal to "demean" them even with a "gesture." Canada punishes anyone who "willfully promotes hatred." The United Kingdom outlaws "insulting words or behavior" that arouse "racial hatred." Romania forbids the possession of xenophobic "symbols." 11

What have these laws produced? Look at the convictions upheld or accepted by the European Court of Human Rights. Four Swedes who distributed leaflets that called homosexuality "deviant" and "morally destructive" and blamed it for AIDS. An Englishman who displayed in his window a 9/11 poster proclaiming, "Islam out of Britain." A Turk who published two letters from readers angry at the government's treatment of Kurds. A Frenchman who wrote an article disputing the plausibility of poison gas technology at a Nazi concentration camp. 12

Look at the defendants rescued by the court. A Dane "convicted of aiding and abetting the dissemination of racist remarks" for making a documentary in which three people "made abusive and derogatory remarks about immigrants and ethnic groups." A man "convicted of openly inciting the population to hatred" in Turkey by "criticizing secular and democratic principles and openly calling for the introduction of Sharia law." Another Turkish resident "convicted of disseminating propaganda" after he "criticized the United States' intervention in Iraq and the solitary confinement of the leader of a terrorist organization." Two Frenchmen who wrote a newspaper article that "portrayed Marshal Pétain in a favorable light, drawing a veil over his policy of collaboration with the Nazi regime." 13

Beyond the court's docket, you'll find more prosecutions of dissent. A Swedish pastor convicted of violating hate-speech laws by preaching against homosexuality. A Serb convicted of discrimination for saying, "We are against every gathering where homosexuals are demonstrating in the streets of Belgrade and want to show something, which is a disease, like it is normal." An Australian columnist convicted of violating the Racial Discrimination Act by suggesting that "there are fair-skinned people in Australia with essentially European ancestry . . . who, motivated by career opportunities available to Aboriginal people or by political activism, have chosen to falsely identify as Aboriginal." 14

My favorite case involves a Frenchman who sought free-speech protection under Article 10 of the European Convention on Human Rights: 15

Denis Leroy is a cartoonist. One of his drawings representing the attack on the World Trade Centre was published in a Basque weekly newspaper . . . with a caption which read: "We have all dreamt of it . . . Hamas did it." Having been sentenced to payment of a fine for "condoning terrorism," Mr Leroy argued that his freedom of expression had been infringed. 16

The Court considered that, through his work, the applicant had glorified the violent destruction of American imperialism, expressed moral support for the 17 perpetrators of the attacks of 11 September, commented approvingly on the violence perpetrated against thousands of civilians and diminished the dignity of the victims. Despite the newspaper's limited circulation, the Court observed that the drawing's publication had provoked a certain public reaction, capable of stirring up violence and of having a demonstrable impact on public order in the Basque Country. The Court held that there had been no violation of Article 10.

18 How can you justify prosecuting cases like these while defending cartoonists and video makers who ridicule Mohammed? You can't. Either you censor both, or you censor neither. Given the choice, I'll stand with Obama. "Efforts to restrict speech," he warned the U. N., "can quickly become a tool to silence critics and oppress minorities."

19 That principle, borne out by the wretched record of hate-speech prosecutions, is worth defending. But first, we have to live up to it.

QUESTIONS FOR READING

1. What event has led to Saletan's article?
2. Which groups/countries want to extend hate speech laws? Which countries have defended free speech?
3. What is the Muslim world's view of the West's "commitment" to free speech?

QUESTIONS FOR REASONING AND ANALYSIS

4. What is Saletan's claim? (Be precise; he isn't just taking a position on hate speech laws.)
5. What evidence does the author provide? What is especially significant about the ruling on the cartoonist Leroy?
6. Examine Saletan's opening paragraphs; what makes his opening effective?

QUESTIONS FOR REFLECTION AND WRITING

7. Were you aware of the extent of hate speech laws in the West? Are you surprised? Should you be more surprised by the inconsistency in rulings? Reflect on these questions.
8. Has Saletan convinced you that we do not practice what we preach? Why or why not? If you disagree, how would you refute Saletan?
9. Is it possible to understand hate speech restrictions in Western Europe relative to the Holocaust? Is it possible to understand and still oppose prosecution of someone who wants to argue that there was no Holocaust? Is it possible to legislate against ignorance or stupidity? Reflect on these questions.

SUGGESTIONS FOR DISCUSSION AND WRITING

1. Compare the style and tone of Mateer/Leu's and Saletan's essays. Has each one written in a way that works for the author's approach to this issue? Be prepared to explain your views or develop them into a comparative analysis of style.
2. Reread and study the essay "Your Brain Lies to You" (pp. 79–80) and then analyze the argument's parts, using Toulmin's terms.

GOING ONLINE

Another issue on college campuses is student drinking. Should colleges find ways to crack down on underage student alcohol use and binge drinking? You may be able to offer some answers to this question based on your knowledge and experience. You may also want to go online for some statistics about college drinking and health and safety risks. Drawing on both experience and data, what claim can you support?

7

Speaking to Persuade

- The Importance of Persuasion
- Ethics and Persuasion
- The Psychology of Persuasion
- Persuasive Speeches on Questions of Fact
- Persuasive Speeches on Questions of Value
- Persuasive Speeches on Questions of Policy
- Sample Speech with Commentary

Nicolás Navarro started his day on campus by stopping at his history professor's office hours. "I don't normally do this," he said, "but I'm wondering if I can have a 24-hour extension on my paper. I have two exams on the same day and I've really been overwhelmed lately." The professor hemmed and hawed. Then she said, "Okay. You've turned in all your other work just fine, so you can have an extension this one time."

With a sigh of relief, Nicolás headed off for classes. Walking across the quad, he ran into some friends. "Are we still on for basketball today?" one of them asked. "I wish I could," Nicolás said, "but I'm handing out flyers for the dance marathon for the children's hospital. Next week, though, for sure."

In the afternoon, Nicolás went to his part-time job at the marketing department of a local independent music label. "I've been thinking about how we can keep people interested in our music," he said at a meeting with other members of the marketing team. "People have a great time at our concerts, and we want them to remember that. What if we gave away audio from the concerts—kind of like the Grateful Dead used to? This would increase interest among our fans, and we already record the concerts."

The head of marketing looked skeptical, but then replied: "Okay. Let's try it for a few months and see what happens. But first I want you to figure out the details."

If you asked Nicolás how he spent his day, he might say, "I talked to my history professor. I handed out flyers for the dance marathon. I had a staff meeting at work." In fact, he spent a large part of his day *persuading*—persuading people to do things they were reluctant to do or that had not occurred to them.

The Importance of Persuasion

persuasion

The process of creating, reinforcing, or changing people's beliefs or actions.

Persuasion is the process of creating, reinforcing, or changing people's beliefs or actions.[1] The ability to speak (and write) persuasively will benefit you in every part of your life, from personal relations to community activities to career aspirations. When economists added up the number of people—lawyers, sales representatives, public relations specialists, counselors, administrators, and others—whose jobs depend largely on persuading people to adopt their point of view, they concluded that persuasion accounts for 26 percent of the U.S. gross domestic product![2]

Understanding the principles of persuasion is also vital to being an informed citizen and consumer. Politicians and advertisers, salespeople and interest groups, fund-raisers and community activists—all vie for your attention, votes, money, time, and support. The more you know about persuasion, the more effective you can be in using your powers of critical thinking to assess the barrage of persuasive messages you are exposed to every day.

Although persuasion has been studied for more than 2,000 years, it is still the subject of lively debate among scholars. There are a number of scientific models of the persuasive process and a wide range of respected theories about how persuasion works. In this chapter and the next, we will explore the principles of persuasion as they apply to public speaking.

When you speak to persuade, you act as an advocate. Your job is to get listeners to agree with you and, perhaps, to act on that belief. Your goal may be to defend an idea, to refute an opponent, to sell a program, or to inspire people to action. Because persuasive speakers must communicate information clearly and concisely, you will need all the skills you used in speaking to inform. But you will also need new skills that take you from giving information to affecting your listeners' attitudes, beliefs, or actions.

Ethics and Persuasion

No matter what the speaking situation, you need to make sure your goals are ethically sound and that you use ethical methods to communicate your ideas. Meeting these obligations can be especially challenging when you speak to persuade. Would you be willing to shade the truth "just a bit" if it would guarantee a successful speech? How about juggling statistics, doctoring quotations, passing off opinions as facts, or pandering to prejudice and stereotypes?

Unfortunately, there is no shortage of speakers—and other persuaders—who are willing to take ethical shortcuts to achieve their objectives. Yet, as Martin Luther King stated years ago, it is not possible to bring about a truly beneficial result by using unethical methods. Maintaining the bond of trust with listeners is also vital to a speaker's credibility. As in other kinds of public speaking, the ideal of effective persuasion is the good person speaking well.

When you work on your persuasive speech, keep in mind the guidelines for ethical speaking discussed in Chapter 2. Make sure your goals are ethically sound and that you can defend them if they are questioned or challenged. Study the topic thoroughly so you won't mislead your audience through shoddy research or muddled thinking. Learn about all sides of an issue, seek out competing viewpoints, and get your facts right.

But knowing the facts is not enough. You also need to be honest in what you say. There is no place in ethical speechmaking for deliberately false or deceptive statements. Also be on guard against more subtle forms of dishonesty such as quoting out of context, portraying a few details as the whole story, and misrepresenting the sources of facts and figures. Take care to present statistics, testimony, and other kinds of evidence fairly and accurately.

Keep in mind as well the power of language and use it responsibly. Show respect for the rights of free speech and expression, and stay away from name-calling and other forms of abusive language. Finally, check the section of Chapter 17 that discusses the role of emotional appeal (pages 348–352). Make sure that any emotional appeal you use is appropriate to the topic and that you build your speech on a firm base of facts and logic before appealing to your audience's emotions. Aim at the highest standards and construct your speech so it will be both convincing *and* ethically sound.[3]

The Psychology of Persuasion

Persuasion is a psychological process. It occurs in a situation where two or more points of view exist. The speaker supports right-to-work laws, but many listeners do not. The speaker considers genetic screening unethical, but some in the audience think it is justified in certain circumstances. The different points of view may be completely opposed, or they may simply be different in degree. Whichever the case, there must be a disagreement, or else there would be no need for persuasion.

THE CHALLENGE OF PERSUASIVE SPEAKING

Of all the kinds of public speaking, persuasion is the most complex and the most challenging. Your objective is more ambitious than in speaking to inform, and audience analysis and adaptation become much more demanding. In some persuasive speeches, you will deal with controversial topics that touch on your listeners' basic attitudes, values, and beliefs. This may increase their resistance to persuasion and make your task more difficult.

It is much easier, for example, to explain the history of the war on drugs than to persuade an audience either that marijuana should be legalized in every state or once again be outlawed across the country. In the persuasive speech, you must contend not only with your audience's knowledge about marijuana but also with their attitudes toward recreational drugs and their beliefs about the impact of marijuana use on human health and social mores.

Lines of argument that work with one part of the audience may fail with—or even upset—another part. What seems perfectly logical to some listeners may seem wildly irrational to others. No matter how expert you are on the topic, no matter how skillfully you prepare the speech, no matter how captivating your delivery—some listeners will not agree with you.

This does not mean that persuasion is impossible. It does mean you should have a realistic sense of what you can accomplish. You can't expect a group of die-hard Democrats to become Republicans or a steak lover to turn vegetarian as a result of one speech.

In every persuasive speech, you will face some listeners who are strongly in favor of your position, some who are neutral, and some who are adamantly opposed. If listeners are neutral or only moderately committed one way or another, you can realistically hope your speech will move at least some of them toward your side. If listeners are strongly opposed to your position, you can consider your speech a success if it leads even a few to reexamine their views.

When thinking about the range of persuasive responses, you may find it helpful to visualize listeners on a scale such as that shown in Figure 16.1 (below). Persuasion involves any movement by a listener from left to right on the scale, no matter where the listener begins and no matter how great or small the movement.[4]

How successful you are in any particular persuasive speech will depend above all on how well you tailor your message to the values, attitudes, and beliefs of your audience. In Chapter 6, we considered the general principles of audience analysis and adaptation. Here we emphasize two additional principles that are crucial to the psychology of persuasion. The first deals with how listeners process and respond to persuasive messages. The second pertains to the target audience for persuasive speeches.

HOW LISTENERS PROCESS PERSUASIVE MESSAGES

We often think of persuasion as something a speaker does *to* an audience. In fact, persuasion is something a speaker does *with* an audience. Listeners do not

FIGURE 16.1

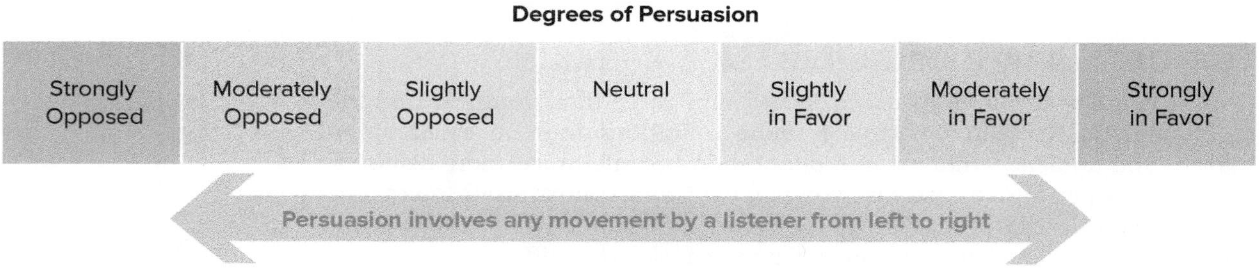

No matter what the situation, a persuasive speaker needs to adapt to the target audience. Here Washington University student Daniel Giuffra speaks in support of the Youth Tobacco Prevention Campaign.

just sit passively and soak in everything the speaker has to say. Instead, they engage in a mental give-and-take with the speaker. While they listen, they assess the speaker's credibility, delivery, supporting materials, language, reasoning, and emotional appeals. They may respond positively at one point, negatively at another. At times they may argue, inside their own minds, with the speaker. This mental give-and-take is especially vigorous when listeners are highly involved with the topic and believe it has a direct bearing on their lives.[5]

In a sense, the psychological interaction between a speaker and audience during a persuasive speech is similar to what happens vocally during a conversation—as in this example:

Karyn: It's better to donate your time to charity than to donate your money. Plenty of charities are well supported financially, but they lack the volunteers they need.

Naomi: It's true that volunteering is important, but most of us just don't have the time. It's easier to send a donation online. I'm sure the charities would rather have me give money than nothing at all.

Karyn: You're right about that. But you'd be surprised how easy it is to find an hour or two a week. Between classes, on the weekends, in the evenings—most people have more flexibility than they realize.

Naomi: Perhaps, but showing up at some strange place to volunteer makes me nervous. Even if I could find the time, I get uncomfortable in new situations like that.

Karyn: I used to feel the same way, but charities are set up to help volunteers feel welcome. I got over my nervousness quickly, and now I'm excited to volunteer.

Much the same kind of interaction might occur during a persuasive speech, except that the listener would respond internally rather than out loud.

mental dialogue with the audience

The mental give-and-take between speaker and listener during a persuasive speech.

What does this mean to you as a speaker? It means you must think of your persuasive speech as a kind of *mental dialogue* with your audience. You must anticipate possible objections the audience will raise to your point of view and answer them in your speech. You cannot convert skeptical listeners unless you deal directly with the reasons for their skepticism.

As you prepare your persuasive speech, put yourself in the place of your audience and imagine how they will respond. Be as tough on your speech as your audience will be. Every place they will raise a question, answer it. Every place they will have a criticism, deal with it. Every place they will see a hole in your argument, fill it. Leave nothing to chance.[6]

THE TARGET AUDIENCE

Unfortunately, no matter how carefully you plot your speech, you will seldom be able to persuade all your listeners. Like most audiences, yours will probably contain some listeners who are hostile to your position, some who favor it, some who are undecided, and some who just don't care. You would like to make your speech equally appealing to everyone, but this is rarely possible. Most often you will have a particular *part* of the whole audience that you want to reach with your speech. That part is called the *target audience.*

target audience

The portion of the whole audience that the speaker most wants to persuade.

Advertising gives us an effective model. Successful commercials are aimed at particular segments of the market. Investment funds now direct many of their advertisements at women. Why? Because more and more women are investing in the stock market. Beer commercials, on the other hand, are directed at men because they drink the most beer.

For your classroom speeches, you don't have the sophisticated research capability of a large advertising agency. But as we saw in Chapter 6, you can use questionnaires to find out where your classmates stand on your speech topic. This is your equivalent of market research. Once you know where your target audience stands, you can tailor your speech to fit their values and concerns—aim at the target, so to speak.

Here, for example, is how one student, Vivian Xu, determined her target audience for a persuasive speech advocating lifetime GPS tracking of high-risk serial sex offenders:

> There are 22 students in my audience. My audience-analysis questionnaires show that 4 are absolutely opposed to my plan. I can't persuade them no matter what I say. My questionnaires also show that 6 already support my position. I don't need to persuade them. The other 12 students could be persuaded if they knew more about how the GPS tracking program would work and about its privacy implications.

Not only did Vivian pinpoint her target audience, she also knew from her audience-analysis questionnaire the issues she would have to discuss to be convincing:

> The members of my target audience break down this way: 5 give "concerns over cost" as their primary concern; 5 are worried about "privacy and government surveillance"; and 2 think sex offenders will just remove the monitoring devices.

With all this information, Vivian was able to put together a speech that focused directly on her classmates' attitudes and beliefs. As a result, she was able to convince several to support her position.

In the next chapter, we'll discuss the methods you can use to hit the target in your persuasive speeches. In the rest of this chapter, we focus on the three major kinds of persuasive speeches and how to organize them most effectively.

Persuasive Speeches on Questions of Fact

WHAT ARE QUESTIONS OF FACT?

What college basketball team has won the most games since 2000? Who was the first African American to sit on the U.S. Supreme Court? How far is it from Los Angeles to Cairo? These questions of fact can be answered absolutely. The answers are either right or wrong.

question of fact

A question about the truth or falsity of an assertion.

But many questions of fact cannot be answered absolutely. There is a true answer, but we don't have enough information to know what it is. Some questions like this involve prediction: Will the economy be better or worse next year? Who will win the Super Bowl this season?

Other questions deal with issues on which the facts are murky or inconclusive. Is there intelligent life in other parts of the solar system? What will happen next in the Middle East? No one knows the final answers to these questions, but that doesn't stop people from speculating about them or from trying to convince other people that they have the best possible answers.

ANALYZING QUESTIONS OF FACT

In some ways, a persuasive speech on a question of fact is similar to an informative speech. But the two kinds of speeches take place in different kinds of situations and for different purposes.

The situation for an informative speech is *nonpartisan*. The speaker acts as a lecturer or a teacher. The aim is to give information as impartially as possible, not to argue for a particular point of view.

On the other hand, the situation for a persuasive speech on a question of fact is *partisan*. The speaker acts as an advocate. The aim is not to be impartial, but to present one view of the facts as persuasively as possible. The speaker may mention competing views of the facts, but only to refute them.

For example, consider the assassination of John F. Kennedy. After 50 years, there is still much debate about what really happened in Dallas on November 22, 1963. Did Lee Harvey Oswald act alone, or was he part of a conspiracy? How many shots were fired at President Kennedy and from what locations? If there was a conspiracy, who was involved in it? The informative speaker would recite the known facts on both sides of these questions without drawing a conclusion about which side is correct. The persuasive speaker, however, would draw a conclusion from the known facts and try to convert listeners to his or her point of view.

If there were no possibility of dispute on questions of fact, there would be no need for courtroom trials. In a criminal trial there is usually at least one known fact—a crime has been committed. But did the defendant commit the crime? The prosecuting attorney tries to persuade the jury that the defendant is guilty. The defense attorney tries to persuade the jury that the defendant is innocent. The jury must decide which view of the facts is more persuasive.[7]

ORGANIZING SPEECHES ON QUESTIONS OF FACT

Persuasive speeches on questions of fact are usually organized *topically.* Suppose, for example, that you want to convince your classmates that an earthquake of 9.0 or above on the Richter scale will hit California within the next ten years. Each main point in your speech will present a *reason* why someone should agree with you:

Specific Purpose: To persuade my audience that an earthquake of 9.0 or above on the Richter scale will hit California in the next ten years.

Central Idea: There are three good reasons to believe that an earthquake of 9.0 or above on the Richter scale will hit California in the next ten years.

Main Points:

I. California is long overdue for a major earthquake.

II. Many geological signs indicate that a major earthquake may happen soon.

III. Experts agree that an earthquake of 9.0 or above could strike California any day.

To take another example, suppose you are trying to persuade your classmates that the plays attributed to William Shakespeare were not actually written by him. Your specific purpose, central idea, and main points might be:

Specific Purpose: To persuade my audience that William Shakespeare did not write the plays attributed to him.

Central Idea: There is considerable evidence that the plays attributed to William Shakespeare were actually written by Francis Bacon or Edward de Vere.

Main Points:

I. Biographical and textual evidence suggest that William Shakespeare did not write the plays attributed to him.

II. Historical evidence indicates that Shakespeare's plays were probably written by either Sir Francis Bacon or Edward de Vere, 17th Earl of Oxford.

Notice in these examples that the speaker's purpose is limited to persuading the audience to accept a particular view of the facts. Sometimes, however, the dispute that gives rise to a persuasive speech will go beyond a question of fact and will turn on a question of value.

Many persuasive speeches revolve around questions of fact. There is much debate, for example, about the impact of climate change on violent weather events around the world.

Persuasive Speeches on Questions of Value

WHAT ARE QUESTIONS OF VALUE?

What is the best movie of all time? Is solitary confinement morally justifiable? What are the ethical responsibilities of journalists? Such questions not only involve matters of fact, but they also demand *value judgments*—judgments based on a person's beliefs about what is right or wrong, good or bad, moral or immoral, proper or improper, fair or unfair.

question of value

A question about the worth, rightness, morality, and so forth of an idea or action.

Take the issue of solitary confinement. It can be discussed at a purely factual level by asking such questions as "What are the laws about solitary confinement?" or "How widespread is solitary confinement as a punishment in American prisons?" These are factual questions. The answers you reach are independent of your belief about the morality of solitary confinement.

But suppose you ask, "Is it morally justifiable to keep prisoners in solitary confinement for extended periods of time?" Now you are dealing with a question of value. How you answer will depend not only on your factual knowledge about solitary confinement, but also on your moral values.

ANALYZING QUESTIONS OF VALUE

Contrary to what many people think, questions of value are not simply matters of personal opinion or whim. If you say, "I enjoy bicycle riding," you do not have to give a reason why you enjoy it. You are making a statement about your personal taste. Even if bicycle riding were the most unpleasant activity ever invented, it could still be one of your favorites.

On the other hand, if you say, "Bicycle riding is the ideal form of land transportation," you are making a statement about a question of value. Whether bicycling is the ideal form of land transportation does not depend on your own likes and dislikes. To defend the statement, you cannot say, "Bicycle riding is the ideal form of land transportation because I like it."

Instead, you must *justify* your claim. The first step is to define what you mean by an "ideal form of land transportation." Do you mean a mode of transportation that gets people where they want to go as fast as possible? That is relatively inexpensive? That is fun? Nonpolluting? Beneficial for the user? In other words, you must establish your *standards* for an "ideal form of land transportation." Then you can show how bicycle riding measures up against those standards.

Whenever you give a speech on a question of value, be sure to give special thought to the standards for your value judgment.

ORGANIZING SPEECHES ON QUESTIONS OF VALUE

Persuasive speeches on questions of value are almost always organized *topically*. The most common approach is to devote your first main point to establishing the standards for your value judgment and your second main point to applying those standards to the subject of your speech.

Think back for a moment to the speech about bicycle riding as the ideal form of land transportation. If you organized this speech in topical order, your first main point would identify the standards for an ideal form of land transportation. Your second main point would show how biking measures up against those standards. Here is how your specific purpose, central idea, and main points might look:

Specific Purpose: To persuade my audience that bicycle riding is the ideal form of land transportation.

Central Idea: Bicycle riding is the ideal form of land transportation because it is faster than walking or running, is nonpolluting, and promotes the health of the rider.

Main Points:

I. An ideal form of land transportation should meet three major standards.
   A. It should be faster than running or walking.
   B. It should be nonpolluting.
   C. It should be beneficial for the person who uses it.

II. Bicycle riding meets all these standards for an ideal form of land transportation.
   A. Bicycle riding is faster than walking or running.
   B. Bicycle riding is not a source of air, land, water, or noise pollution.
   C. Bicycle riding is extremely beneficial for the health of the rider.

When you speak on a question of value, you must make sure to justify your judgment against some identifiable standards. In the following example, notice how the speaker devotes her first main point to judging capital punishment against moral standards and her second main point to judging it against legal standards:

Specific Purpose:	To persuade my audience that capital punishment is morally and legally wrong.
Central Idea:	Capital punishment violates both the Bible and the U.S. Constitution.
Main Points:	I. Capital punishment violates the biblical commandment "Thou shalt not kill."
	II. Capital punishment violates the constitutional ban on "cruel and unusual punishment."

As you can see, speeches on questions of value may have strong implications for our actions. A person who is persuaded that capital punishment is morally and legally wrong is more likely to support legislation abolishing the death penalty. But speeches on questions of value do not argue directly for or against particular courses of action. Once you go beyond arguing right or wrong to arguing that something should or should not be done, you move from a question of value to a question of policy.

Persuasive Speeches on Questions of Policy

WHAT ARE QUESTIONS OF POLICY?

Questions of policy arise daily in almost everything we do. At home we debate what to do during spring vacation, whether to buy a new laptop, which movie to see on the weekend. At work we discuss whether to ask for a raise, what strategy to use in selling a product, how to improve communication between management and employees. As citizens we ponder whether to vote for or against a political candidate, what to do about national defense, how to promote economic growth.

All these are questions of policy because they deal with specific courses of action. Questions of policy inevitably involve questions of fact. (How can we decide whether to vote for a candidate unless we know the facts of her or his stand on the issues?) They may also involve questions of value. (The policy you favor on abortion will be affected by whether you think abortion is moral or immoral.) But questions of policy *always* go beyond questions of fact or value to decide whether something should or should not be done.

question of policy

A question about whether a specific course of action should or should not be taken.

When put formally, questions of policy usually include the word "should," as in these examples:

What measures should be taken to protect people's privacy online?

Should the electoral college be abolished?

What steps should be taken to reduce the erosion of America's coastlines?

TYPES OF SPEECHES ON QUESTIONS OF POLICY

When you speak on a question of policy, your goal may be either to gain passive agreement or to motivate immediate action from your listeners. Deciding which goal you want to achieve will affect almost every aspect of your speech.

Speeches to Gain Passive Agreement

speech to gain passive agreement

A persuasive speech in which the speaker's goal is to convince the audience that a given policy is desirable without encouraging the audience to take action in support of the policy.

If your goal is passive agreement, you will try to get your audience to agree with you that a certain policy is desirable, but you will not necessarily encourage the audience to do anything to enact the policy. For example, suppose you want to persuade people that the United States should abolish the electoral college and elect the President by direct popular vote. If you seek passive agreement, you will try to get your audience to concur, but you will not urge them to take any action right now to help change presidential election procedures.

Here are some specific purpose statements for policy speeches that seek passive agreement:

> To persuade my audience that there should be stricter safety standards on amusement-park rides.
>
> To persuade my audience that the U.S. patent system should be overhauled so as to promote innovation.
>
> To persuade my audience that a balanced-budget amendment should be added to the U.S. Constitution.

In each case, the speaker's aim is to convince listeners that the speaker's policy is necessary and practical. The speaker is not trying to get listeners to take action in support of the policy.

Speeches to Gain Immediate Action

speech to gain immediate action

A persuasive speech in which the speaker's goal is to convince the audience to take action in support of a given policy.

When your goal is immediate action, you want to do more than get your listeners to nod their heads in agreement. You want to motivate them to action—to sign a petition for abolishing the electoral college, to campaign for lower tuition, to contribute to a fund drive, and so forth.

Here are some examples of specific purpose statements for policy speeches that seek immediate action:

> To persuade my audience to participate in alternate spring break.
>
> To persuade my audience to give time to Big Brothers or Big Sisters.
>
> To persuade my audience to establish retirement accounts early in their careers.

Some experts say you should seek action from your audience whenever possible. Although it is much easier to evoke passive agreement than to elicit action, the listener is not making much of a commitment by thinking, "Sure, I agree with you." Within a day or two that same listener may forget entirely about your speech—and about her or his agreement with it.

Action, however, reinforces belief. A great deal of research shows that if you can persuade a listener to take some kind of action—even if it is no more than signing a petition, putting a bumper sticker on a car, or attending a meeting—you have gained a more serious commitment. Once a listener acts on behalf of a speaker's position, she or he is more likely to remain committed to it.[8]

When you call for action in a persuasive speech, you should make your recommendations as specific as possible. Don't just urge listeners to "do something." Tell them exactly what to do and how to do it.

For an excellent example, look at Video 16.1 in the online Media Library for this chapter. The speaker's aim was to convince her classmates to donate time to the Special Olympics. After talking about the mission of Special

connect

View this excerpt from "Making a Difference Through the Special Olympics" in the online Media Library for this chapter (Video 16.1).

Persuasive speeches on questions of policy are given whenever people debate specific courses of action. Here U.S. Senator Elizabeth Warren presents a plan to improve wages for American workers.

Olympics, the need for volunteers, and the rewarding feelings experienced by volunteers, she explained how students can get involved for whatever amount of time they are able to commit at the moment. She also brought along brochures with additional information to pass out after her speech. When you construct your persuasive speech, remember that the more specific your instructions, the more likely it is that your call to action will succeed.[9]

ANALYZING QUESTIONS OF POLICY

Regardless of whether your aim is to elicit passive agreement or to gain immediate action, you will face three basic issues whenever you discuss a question of policy—need, plan, and practicality.

Need

There is no point in arguing for a policy unless you can show a need for it:

> Is there a need for more student parking on campus?
>
> Is there a need for the school district to replace traditional textbooks with e-textbooks?
>
> Is there a need for a national ID card in the United States?

Your first step is to convince listeners that there is a serious problem with things as they are. People are not inclined to adopt a new policy unless they are convinced that the old one is not working. This is why the *burden of proof* always rests with the speaker who advocates change. (Of course, you may be defending present policy, in which case you will argue that there is *no* need to change—that things are already working as well as can be expected.)

need

The first basic issue in analyzing a question of policy: Is there a serious problem or need that requires a change from current policy?

burden of proof

The obligation facing a persuasive speaker to prove that a change from current policy is necessary.

Plan

The second basic issue of policy speeches is plan. Once you have shown that a problem exists, you must explain your plan for solving it:

> What can we do to get more student parking on campus?
>
> How much will e-textbooks cost? Who will pay for them? What devices will students use to read them?
>
> What information should be included on a national ID card? Who will be responsible for collecting the information and creating the cards?

plan

The second basic issue in analyzing a question of policy: If there is a problem with current policy, does the speaker have a plan to solve the problem?

Answering such questions is especially important if you call for a new policy. It's easy to complain about problems; the real challenge is developing solutions.

In most classroom speeches, you will not have time to describe your plan in detail, but you should at least identify its major features. Look, for example, at the plan section in the speech on puppy mills in the online Media Library for this chapter. First, the speaker proposes legal measures to punish dog breeders that do not take proper care of their animals. Second, he presents four steps that individual listeners can take when buying a dog to make sure they are not supporting puppy mills. The speech would have been much less persuasive if the speaker had not spelled out the major features of his plan.

connect

View this excerpt from "The Horrors of Puppy Mills" in the online Media Library for this chapter (Video 16.2).

Practicality

The third basic issue of policy speeches is practicality. Once you have presented a plan, you must show that it will work. Will it solve the problem? Or will it create new and more serious problems?

practicality

The third basic issue in analyzing a question of policy: Will the speaker's plan solve the problem? Will it create new and more serious problems?

> Building a multilevel parking garage on campus would provide more student parking, but the cost would require a sharp increase in tuition.
>
> Switching to e-textbooks would save the school district money in the long run, but the initial investment would be costly at a time when the district's budget is already stretched thin.
>
> A national ID card might be an easy way for people to verify their identity for security purposes, but it could also infringe on civil liberties and give the government too much personal information about individuals.

These are significant concerns. Whenever you advocate a new policy, you must be prepared to show that it is workable. No matter how serious a problem may be, listeners usually want some assurance that a speaker's plan will actually solve the problem.[10]

One way to provide this assurance is to show that a plan similar to yours has been successfully implemented elsewhere. For example, Video 16.3 in the online Media Library for this chapter shows an excerpt from a student speech calling for tougher measures to reduce smoking in the speaker's state. As you view the video, notice how the speaker points to the success of a similar plan in California as evidence that it will work in her state.

connect

View this excerpt from "The Most Dangerous Habit" in the online Media Library for this chapter (Video 16.3).

If you oppose a shift in policy, one of your major arguments will be that the change is impractical—that it will create more problems than it can solve. For example, critics of a plan to send astronauts to Mars might say that it is highly risky and requires technology that does not currently exist. Others might argue that the cost of the mission would be better spent on any number of causes here on Earth. If listeners accept these arguments, they will probably decide that NASA should not continue working on sending astronauts to Mars.

How much of your speech should you devote to need, to plan, and to practicality? The answer depends on your topic and your audience. For example, if your audience is not aware of the health and environmental problems caused by antibacterial chemicals in household products, you will have to give much of your time to need before covering plan and practicality. On the other hand, if your listeners already know about the problems caused by antibacterial household products, you can quickly remind them of need and then devote most of your speech to plan and practicality.

ORGANIZING SPEECHES ON QUESTIONS OF POLICY

Effective organization is crucial when you speak on a question of policy. Although any of the basic patterns of organization explained in Chapter 9 can be used, four special patterns are especially valuable for policy speeches. They are problem-solution order, problem-cause-solution order, comparative advantages order, and Monroe's motivated sequence.

Problem-Solution Order

If you advocate a change in policy, your main points often will fall naturally into problem-solution order. In the first main point you demonstrate the need for a new policy by showing the extent and seriousness of the problem. In the second main point you explain your plan for solving the problem and show its practicality. For example:

problem-solution order

A method of organizing persuasive speeches in which the first main point deals with the existence of a problem and the second main point presents a solution to the problem.

Specific Purpose: To persuade my audience that the U.S. Congress should pass legislation curbing the spread of phony pharmaceuticals.

Central Idea: Because phony pharmaceuticals are a serious problem in the United States, Congress should pass legislation ensuring that the medications we buy are safe.

Main Points:

I. The spread of phony pharmaceuticals is a serious problem.
   A. Phony pharmaceuticals are one of the most profitable areas of criminal activity in the world.
   B. The spread of phony pharmaceuticals is producing serious health risks in the United States.

II. Solving the problem of phony pharmaceuticals requires action by the federal government.
   A. Congress should pass legislation targeting the spread of phony pharmaceuticals and imposing strict penalties for violators.
   B. Experts believe that such legislation will go a long way toward solving the problem.

connect

View an excerpt from "Phony Pharmaceuticals" in the online Media Library for this chapter (Video 16.4).

You can use the problem-solution format just as easily to organize a speech opposing a change in policy. In such a speech your job is to defend the current system and to attack your opponents' proposed policy. Thus in the first main point you might argue that there is *not* a need for change. In the second main point you might show that even if there were a serious problem, the suggested new policy would *not* solve it and would create serious problems of its own. For example:

Specific Purpose: To persuade my audience that the city council should not pass legislation merging the police and fire departments.

Central Idea: Merging the police and fire departments is neither necessary nor practical.

Main Points:

I. Merging the police and fire departments is not necessary.
   A. Under the current system, the police department has developed a reputation for excellence that has made it a model for departments in other cities,
   B. The fire department is equally well-respected for doing its job quickly and efficiently.

II. Besides being unnecessary, merging the police and fire departments is highly impractical.
   A. Rather than saving the city money, merging the departments would increase costs.
   B. Merging the departments would also harm morale and reduce the high level of performance we expect from our police force and firefighters.

PROBLEM-CAUSE-SOLUTION ORDER

problem-cause-solution order

A method of organizing persuasive speeches in which the first main point identifies a problem, the second main point analyzes the causes of the problem, and the third main point presents a solution to the problem.

For a variation on problem-solution order, you might arrange your speech in problem-cause-solution order. This produces a speech with three main points—the first identifying a problem, the second analyzing the causes of the problem, and the third presenting a solution to the problem. For example:

Specific Purpose: To persuade my audience that action is required to deal with the problem of childhood obesity.

Central Idea: Childhood obesity is a serious problem that can be controlled by changes in diet and exercise.

Main Points:

I. Childhood obesity is a major problem in the United States.
   A. Childhood obesity continues to grow at a rapid pace.
   B. Obesity is producing serious health problems among children.

II. There are two major causes of the increase in childhood obesity.
   A. The first cause is dietary.
   B. The second cause is physical inactivity.

III. Solving the problem requires dealing with both causes.
   A. Parents and schools must make sure that children are eating healthy foods.
   B. Parents and schools must also make sure that children get enough exercise.

connect

View an excerpt from "The Epidemic of Childhood Obesity" in the online Media Library for this chapter (Video 16.5).

Some teachers prefer this method of organization because it requires a speaker to identify the causes of the problem. This in turn makes it easier to check whether the proposed solution will get at the causes of the problem.

Comparative Advantages Order

comparative advantages order

A method of organizing persuasive speeches in which each main point explains why a speaker's solution to a problem is preferable to other proposed solutions.

When your audience already agrees that a problem exists, you can devote your speech to comparing the advantages and disadvantages of competing solutions. In such a situation, you might put your speech in comparative advantages order, devoting each main point to explaining why your solution is preferable to other proposed solutions.

Suppose you are speaking at a meeting of the city council about ways to alleviate traffic congestion in your city. Some citizens support the construction of a new highway. You, however, support a rapid bus system that can be built on already-existing roads. Using comparative advantages order, you compare the highway proposal with the bus-system proposal and show why the latter is a better choice. Your specific purpose, central idea, and main points might look like this:

Because it follows the process of human thinking, Monroe's motivated sequence is especially useful for persuasive speakers who seek immediate action from their listeners.

Specific Purpose: To persuade my audience that our city should build a rapid bus system instead of a new highway.

Central Idea: A rapid bus system will be cheaper and more effective than a new highway.

Main Points:

I. Research models show that we will save a million dollars if we build a rapid bus system instead of a new highway.

II. Research models also show that a rapid bus system will reduce traffic congestion more than a new highway.

Monroe's Motivated Sequence

Developed in the 1930s by Alan Monroe, a professor of speech at Purdue University, the motivated sequence is tailor-made for policy speeches that seek immediate action. The sequence has five steps that follow the psychology of persuasion:

1. *Attention.* First, you gain the attention of your audience by using one or more of the methods described in Chapter 10: relating to the audience, showing the importance of the topic, making a startling statement, arousing curiosity or suspense, posing a question, telling a dramatic story, or using visual aids.
2. *Need.* Next, you make the audience feel a need for change. You show there is a serious problem with the existing situation. It is important to state the need clearly and to illustrate it with strong supporting materials. By the end of this step, listeners should be so concerned about the problem that they are psychologically primed to hear your solution.
3. *Satisfaction.* Having aroused a sense of need, you satisfy it by providing a solution to the problem. You present your plan and show how it will work. Be sure to offer enough details about the plan to give listeners a clear understanding of it.

Monroe's motivated sequence

A method of organizing persuasive speeches that seek immediate action. The five steps of the motivated sequence are attention, need, satisfaction, visualization, and action.

4. *Visualization.* Having given your plan, you intensify desire for it by visualizing its benefits. The key to this step is using vivid imagery to show your listeners how *they* will profit from your policy. Make them *see* how much better conditions will be once your plan is adopted.
5. *Action.* Once the audience is convinced that your policy is beneficial, you are ready to call for action. Say exactly what you want the audience to do—and how to do it. Then conclude with a final stirring appeal that reinforces their commitment to act.

Many speakers prefer the motivated sequence because it is more detailed than problem-solution order. It follows the process of human thinking and leads the listener step by step to the desired action. One indication of its effectiveness is that it is widely used by people who make their living by persuasion—especially advertisers. The next time you watch television, pay close attention to the commercials. You will find that many of them follow the motivated sequence.

Try using the motivated sequence when you want to spur listeners to action. You should find it easy and effective, as did one student who used it in a speech urging classmates to work for passage of a local tenants' rights bill. Here are the highlights of his speech:

Attention:	Have you ever had cockroaches running through the cupboards in your apartment? Have you shivered in the cold because the furnace was broken? Or waited months for the security deposit you never got back even though you left your apartment as clean as when you moved in?
Need:	Throughout this city students and other tenants are being victimized by unresponsive and unethical landlords. Just last year more than 200 complaints were filed with the city housing department, but no action has been taken against the landlords.
Satisfaction:	These problems could be solved by passing a strong tenants' rights bill that defines the rights of tenants, specifies the obligations of landlords, and imposes strict penalties for violators.
Visualization:	Such bills have worked in a number of college communities across the nation. If one were passed here, you would no longer have to worry about substandard conditions in your apartment. Your landlord could not violate the terms of your lease or steal your security deposit.
Action:	A tenants' rights bill has been proposed to the city council. You can help get it passed by signing the petition I will pass around after my speech. I also urge you to circulate petitions among your friends and to support the bill when it is debated in the city council next week. If we all work together, we can get this bill through the council.

Monroe's motivated sequence is perfectly compatible with the standard method of outlining discussed in Chapter 11. The following outline shows how one speaker incorporated the sequence into a speech urging her classmates to change the way they use their cell phones (the full text is printed in the appendix that follows Chapter 19):

Specific Purpose: To persuade my audience to use their cell phones in a way that will protect their health.

Central Idea: You can avoid the long-term health risks of cell phone use by making some simple changes.

Introduction

Attention:

I. Your cell phone is your constant companion. You use it everywhere you go, day and night.

II. But what if your constant companion is potentially hazardous to your health?

III. After doing extensive research, I hope to persuade each of you to use your cell phone in a manner that will protect your health.

connect

View an excerpt from "The Dangers of Cell Phones" in the online Media Library for this chapter (Video 16.6).

Body

Need:

I. Although cell phones are safe in the short run, they may pose long-term health risks.
   - A. Using a cell phone exposes you to radiation that builds up over time.
   - B. Some scientists warn about the long-term dangers of cell phone use.
   - C. Even cell phone manufacturers caution against keeping phones too close to the body.

Satisfaction:

II. You can guard against these risks by making simple changes in the way you use your cell phone.
   - A. Above all, do not press your cell phone against your head while talking.
   - B. Get in the habit of using ear buds or your phone's internal speaker.

Using public speaking in your CAREER

After earning your teaching certificate, you landed a job in one of the best public school districts in the state. You've excelled in the classroom, and evaluations of your teaching are consistently outstanding.

But the newly announced state budget means drastic cuts for the district. Either 100 teachers will be laid off, or every teacher will have to accept a 10 percent pay cut. Because the newest teachers are the first to be fired, and you have been on the job for only three years, you know that the only way to keep your position is if all teachers agree to the pay cut. What's more, laying off 100 teachers will mean more students in each classroom, which will harm the quality of education.

In one week, the school superintendent will hold an open meeting for teachers to voice their opinions. You plan on arguing for the pay cut, but you're unsure how to organize your speech. Which of the following methods of organization will be most effective, and why: problem-solution, comparative advantages, Monroe's motivated sequence?

Visualization: III. These changes will help protect your health.
A. They are easy changes to make.
B. They will help you use your cell phone without long-term health risks.

Conclusion

Action: I. So I encourage each of you to make these changes starting today.
II. Make sure your constant companion is not endangering your health.

Try using the motivated sequence when you seek immediate action from your listeners. Over the years it has worked for countless speakers—and it can work for you as well.

Sample Speech with Commentary

connect

View "Changing Lives Through the Literacy Network" in the online Media Library for this chapter (Video 16.7).

The following persuasive speech deals with a question of policy and provides an excellent example of Monroe's motivated sequence. As you read the speech, notice how the speaker uses strong, well-chosen supporting materials as she moves through each step of the motivated sequence. The speech also shows how a speaker's delivery can enhance the impact of his or her ideas—as you can see by watching Video 16.7 in the online Media Library for this chapter.

Changing Lives Through the Literacy Network

COMMENTARY	SPEECH
The first step in Monroe's motivated sequence is gaining attention, which the speaker accomplishes with a vivid hypothetical example that she ties directly to her audience through the use of "you" and "your."	Imagine being dropped into a foreign country—a country where you can't read the street signs, can't order food from a menu, can't fill out a job application. You're surrounded by scribbles and squiggles that simply don't make sense. Now imagine that that country isn't a foreign one, but your own.
A real-life example shows that the opening hypothetical scenario is not far-fetched. Poignant and memorable, the example introduces Dwayne MacNamara, who will appear again later in the speech.	That's exactly what people like Dwayne MacNamara experience on a daily basis. A father of two daughters, Dwayne has struggled with reading and writing for years. These struggles made it difficult for him to find a job, to take care of his family, and to develop a positive self-image. "Not being able to read and write as well as other people," Dwayne says, "has taken a life-long toll on my confidence and my ability to make sound decisions."

Here the speaker reveals the topic of her speech and indicates that low literacy is a local, as well as a national, problem.

Dwayne is far from alone in dealing with these problems. Low literacy affects millions of adults throughout the United States, including right here in Madison and Dane County.

The speaker establishes her credibility by citing her personal experience with the Literacy Network. She ends the introduction by stating her central idea and previewing the body of her speech.

For the past year, I've been volunteering at the Literacy Network—a local, Madison-based, nonprofit organization that helps adults and families with reading, writing, and speaking skills. I've seen the problems people face because of low literacy, and I've also seen how improved literacy can change people's lives for the better. Today I'd like to encourage you to join me as a volunteer. But first let's look more closely at low adult literacy and the problems it can cause.

The speaker moves into the need step of Monroe's motivated sequence, in which she explains the problem of low adult literacy.

According to a 2012 report from the U.S. Department of Education and the National Research Council, more than 30 million adults in the United States lack basic literacy skills. Another 60 million have only basic skills, but little beyond that.

A combination of statistics and expert testimony documents the extent of low adult literacy. The speaker uses high-quality evidence and clearly cites her sources.

When you add these two groups together, 90 million people—more than 40 percent of the adult population—have trouble reading the newspaper, understanding instructions from a doctor, registering to vote, or reading a lease for a place to live. As the National Commission on Adult Literacy states, we face an "adult education crisis that permeates every aspect of American life."

This paragraph builds upon the previous one by showing the many challenges facing adults who have low literacy skills.

The problem is even worse when you consider the social consequences of low adult literacy. According to a report from the American Institutes for Research, 42 percent of people with less-than-basic literacy skills live in poverty. Adults with low literacy are less likely to participate in the workforce, to assist with their children's education, and to be involved in their community.

By moving from the national level to the local level, this paragraph shows how low adult literacy affects the immediate community.

Here in Madison we are not immune to these challenges. The Literacy Network estimates that 17,000 people in Dane County lack "the functional literacy skills needed to read a letter from their children's teacher, a label in a grocery store, or instructions from a doctor." Another 38,000 don't know English well enough to perform these tasks.

As in this case, testimony from a personal interview can be an excellent way to reinforce a speaker's ideas.

When I interviewed Jeff Burkhart, Executive Director of the Literacy Network, he told me that "even though we live in a university town, thousands of people still struggle with everyday literacy skills necessary for success."

The question at the start of this paragraph signals that the speaker is moving to the satisfaction section of her speech. Notice how clearly she explains the range of services provided by the Literacy Network.

So what can you and I do to help combat the problem of low adult literacy? One option is to volunteer at the Literacy Network. It offers a range of services that include basic skills of reading and writing, learning English as a second language, even math and health skills. Best of all, all these services are free. Individuals and families pay absolutely nothing to receive help.

The speaker encourages her classmates to join her as a volunteer at the Literacy Network. She provides options for her listeners by noting a number of ways in which they can contribute.

But the Literacy Network can only offer its services for free if it has enough volunteers—and that's where you come in. Whatever your skill set, the Literacy Network has a way for you to help. You can join me as a tutor and help improve people's writing, speaking, and reading skills. If tutoring doesn't sound right for you, you can help with data entry, fundraising, or scheduling. There are also positions for photographers and those with computer skills.

In this paragraph and the next, the speaker addresses the audience's possible hesitations about volunteering. By relating her own experiences as a new volunteer, she personalizes her ideas and gives them added credibility.

If you volunteer as a tutor, you don't need prior experience, teaching certification, or fluency in another language. You'll attend a training seminar at which the staff will show you exactly what to do. I have to admit: I was a little nervous during my first training seminar. But it calmed my nerves and helped me understand exactly what I was doing. Then, when I met my adult learner for the first time, I was ready to get started.

Whenever a speaker asks listeners to donate time to a cause, it is important to show how they can fit the volunteer activities into their schedules.

But, you may be asking, how much time does it take to be a literacy tutor? The usual commitment is two hours a week. It can be before class, after class, during lunch, on the weekends—whatever works best for you. You can even pick the place. I meet my learner in a study room at Memorial Library. It's a convenient spot for both of us.

Having explained her plan and its practicality, the speaker moves into the visualization section. Returning to the example of Dwayne MacNamara gives the speech a sense of unity and shows the concrete benefits provided by the Literacy Network.

Whether you volunteer as a tutor or in some other capacity, you *will* change the lives of people who have suffered for far too long. Remember Dwayne MacNamara, who I mentioned in my introduction? He lives here—in Madison. Because of the Literacy Network, he now works at a home-improvement store, where reading instructions and dealing with customers is essential.

An instance of peer testimony, the quotation from Dwayne MacNamara is particularly effective.

Dwayne is also able for the first time to help his kids with their homework. He even reads to them every night before bed. "The Literacy Network gave me the skills I needed to succeed," Dwayne says. "I have become more confident, and I am more motivated and excited to go forward with life."

As you can see from the video, the sincerity and directness of the speaker's delivery add to her persuasiveness.

Dwayne's experience is matched by many others. Here are some brochures you can take a look at after my speech. They are filled with success stories from people here in Madison whose lives have been changed through literacy.

The speaker moves into the action section. Once again she addresses her classmates directly as "you."

So I hope you will join me as a volunteer. You can help someone's life go from isolation and despair to a life of progress and promise.

The Literacy Network's motto provides a perfect vehicle for the speaker's closing appeal.

"Improving Lives Through Literacy"—that's the motto of the Literacy Network. It's a motto I've seen come to life over the past year. And it's a motto I hope you will see for yourself by becoming a volunteer. Thank you.

Summary

Persuasion is the process of creating, reinforcing, or changing people's beliefs or actions. When you speak to persuade, you act as an advocate. The ability to speak persuasively will benefit you in every part of your life, from personal relations to community activities to career aspirations.

How successful you are in any persuasive speech depends on how well you tailor your message to your listeners' values, attitudes, and beliefs. You should think of your speech as a mental dialogue with your audience. Identify your target audience, anticipate objections they may raise to your point of view, and answer those objections in your speech.

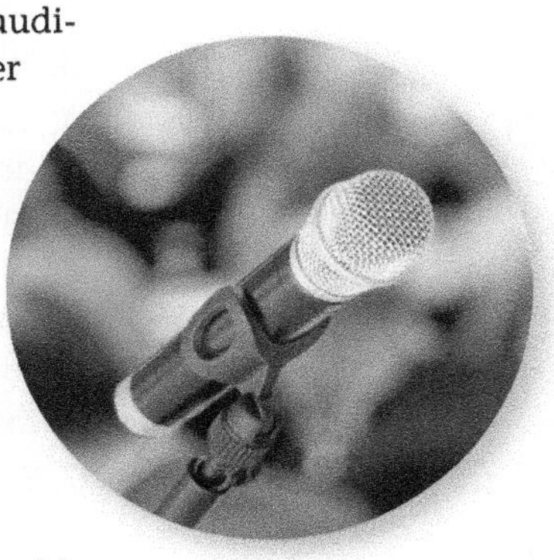

Persuasive speeches may center on questions of fact, value, or policy. When giving a persuasive speech about a question of fact, your role is akin to that of a lawyer in a courtroom trial. You will try to get your listeners to accept your view of the facts.

Questions of value involve a person's beliefs about what is right or wrong, good or bad, moral or immoral, ethical or unethical. When speaking about a question of value, you must justify your opinion by establishing standards for your value judgment. Speeches on questions of value do not argue directly for or against particular courses of action.

Once you go beyond arguing right or wrong to urging that something should or should not be done, you move to a question of policy. When you speak on a question of policy, your goal may be to evoke passive agreement or to spark immediate action. In either case, you will face three basic issues—need, plan, and practicality. How much of your speech you devote to each issue will depend on your topic and your audience.

There are several options for organizing speeches on questions of policy. If you advocate a change in policy, your main points will often fall naturally into problem-solution order or into problem-cause-solution order. If your audience already agrees that a problem exists, you may be able to use comparative advantages order. Whenever you seek immediate action from listeners, you should consider a more specialized organizational pattern known as Monroe's motivated sequence.

Regardless of your topic or method of organization, you need to make sure your goals are ethically sound and that you use ethical methods to persuade your audience.

Key Terms

persuasion (306)
mental dialogue with the audience (310)
target audience (310)
question of fact (311)
question of value (313)
question of policy (315)
speech to gain passive agreement (316)
speech to gain immediate action (316)
need (317)
burden of proof (317)
plan (317)
practicality (318)
problem-solution order (319)
problem-cause-solution order (320)
comparative advantages order (320)
Monroe's motivated sequence (321)

Review Questions

After reading this chapter, you should be able to answer the following questions:

1. What is the difference between an informative speech and a persuasive speech? Why is speaking to persuade more challenging than speaking to inform?
2. What does it mean to say that audiences engage in a mental dialogue with the speaker as they listen to a speech? What implications does this mental give-and-take hold for effective persuasive speaking?
3. What is the target audience for a persuasive speech?
4. What are questions of fact? How does a persuasive speech on a question of fact differ from an informative speech? Give an example of a specific purpose statement for a persuasive speech on a question of fact.
5. What are questions of value? Give an example of a specific purpose statement for a persuasive speech on a question of value.
6. What are questions of policy? Give an example of a specific purpose statement for a persuasive speech on a question of policy.
7. Explain the difference between passive agreement and immediate action as goals for persuasive speeches on questions of policy.
8. What are the three basic issues you must deal with when discussing a question of policy? What will determine the amount of attention you give to each of these issues in any particular speech?
9. What four methods of organization are used most often in persuasive speeches on questions of policy?
10. What are the five steps of Monroe's motivated sequence? Why is the motivated sequence especially useful in speeches that seek immediate action from listeners?

connect

For further review, go to the LearnSmart study module for this chapter.

Exercises for Critical Thinking

1. Look back at the story of Nicolás Navarro at the beginning of this chapter (page 305). Like Nicolás, most people do a certain amount of persuading every day in normal conversation. Keep a journal of your communication activities for an entire day, making special note of all instances in which you tried to persuade someone else to your point of view. Choose one of those instances and prepare a brief analysis of it.

   In your analysis, answer the following questions: (1) Who was the audience for your persuasive effort? (2) What were the "specific purpose" and the "central idea" of your persuasive message? (3) Did you rehearse your persuasive message ahead of time, or did it arise spontaneously from the situation? (4) Were you successful in achieving your specific purpose? (5) If you faced the same situation again, what strategic changes would you make in your persuasive effort?
2. Below are four specific purposes for persuasive speeches. In each case explain whether the speech associated with it concerns a question of fact, a question of value, or a question of policy. Then rewrite the specific purpose statement to

make it appropriate for a speech about one of the other two kinds of questions. For instance, if the original purpose statement is about a question of policy, write a new specific purpose statement that deals with the same topic as either a question of fact or a question of value.

Example:

Original statement: To persuade my audience that it is unfair for judges to favor natural parents over adoptive parents in child custody disputes. (question of value)

Rewritten statement: To persuade my audience that the courts should establish clear guidelines for settling disputes between adoptive parents and natural parents in child custody cases. (question of policy)

a. To persuade my audience that e-cigarettes are harmful to human health.

b. To persuade my audience that a national sales tax should be adopted to help reduce the national debt.

c. To persuade my audience that it is unethical for doctors to receive money from pharmaceutical companies to promote their products.

d. To persuade my audience to join Teach for America.

3. Choose a topic for a persuasive speech on a question of policy. Create two specific purpose statements about that topic—one for a speech to gain passive agreement, another for a speech to motivate immediate action. Once you have the specific purpose statements, explain how the speech seeking immediate action would differ in structure and persuasive appeals from the speech seeking passive agreement. Be specific.

4. Analyze "Phony Pharmaceuticals" in the appendix of sample speeches that follows Chapter 19. Because this is a speech on a question of policy, pay special attention to how the speaker deals with the basic issues of need, plan, and practicality. Does the speaker present a convincing case that a serious problem exists? Does she offer a clear plan to solve the problem? Does she demonstrate that the plan is practical?

5. Select a television commercial that is organized according to Monroe's motivated sequence. Prepare a brief analysis in which you (a) identify the target audience for the commercial and (b) describe each step in the motivated sequence as it appears in the commercial.

YES on

8

Methods of Persuasion

Building Credibility

Using Evidence

Reasoning

Appealing to Emotions

Sample Speech with Commentary

Persuasion is big business. Authors and consultants promise to teach you the one key secret to persuading people to do what you want. Dan Lok claims to reveal "forbidden psychological tactics" that will "give you an unfair advantage in dealing with people." Chris St. Hilaire offers "simple strategies to seduce audiences and win allies." Kevin Dutton claims to have discovered "a single, definitive formula" for "a mysterious, previously unidentified, superstrain of persuasion." These people charge thousands of dollars for their seminars and motivational speeches. Companies and individuals flock—and pay—to read and hear what they have to say.

It sounds good, but does anyone really have the "one key secret" to persuasion? Probably not. Persuasion is too complicated for that. Yet, as the number of books, seminars, and videos on the subject shows, there is a perpetual fascination with the strategies and tactics of effective persuasion.

What makes a speaker persuasive? Why do listeners accept one speaker's views and reject those of another? How can a speaker motivate listeners to act in support of a cause, a campaign, or a candidate?

People have been trying to answer these questions for thousands of years—from the ancient Greek philosopher Aristotle to modern-day communication researchers. Although many answers have been given, we can say that listeners will be persuaded by a speaker for one or more of four reasons:

Because they perceive the speaker as having high *credibility.*

Because they are won over by the speaker's *evidence.*

Because they are convinced by the speaker's *reasoning.*

Because their *emotions* are touched by the speaker's ideas or language.

In this chapter we will look at each of these. We will not discover any magical secrets that will make you an irresistible persuasive speaker. But if you learn the principles discussed in this chapter, you will greatly increase your odds of winning the minds and hearts of your listeners.

Building Credibility

Here are two sets of imaginary statements. Which one of each pair would you be more likely to believe?

The U.S. judicial system needs major organizational changes to deal with the growing number of court cases. (Sonia Sotomayor)

The U.S. judicial system can deal with the number of court cases without any organizational changes. (Aaron Rodgers)

Technology is changing professional football in ways that the average fan cannot see. (Aaron Rodgers)

Technology is not having a major impact on professional football. (Sonia Sotomayor)

ethos

The name used by Aristotle for what modern students of communication refer to as credibility.

Most likely you chose the first in each pair of statements. If so, you were probably influenced by your perception of the speaker. You are more likely to respect the judgment of Sotomayor, Associate Justice of the U.S. Supreme Court, when she speaks about the organization of the American judiciary. You are more likely to respect the judgment of Rodgers, quarterback of the Green Bay Packers, when he speaks about technology in professional football. Some instructors call this factor *source credibility.* Others refer to it as *ethos,* the name given by Aristotle.

FACTORS OF CREDIBILITY

Many things affect a speaker's credibility, including sociability, dynamism, physical attractiveness, and perceived similarity between speaker and audience. Above all, though, credibility is affected by two factors:

- *Competence*—how an audience regards a speaker's intelligence, expertise, and knowledge of the subject.
- *Character*—how an audience regards a speaker's sincerity, trustworthiness, and concern for the well-being of the audience.

The more favorably listeners view a speaker's competence and character, the more likely they are to accept what the speaker says. No doubt you are familiar with this from your own experience. Suppose you take a course in economics. The course is taught by a distinguished professor who has published widely in prestigious journals, who sits on a major international commission, and who has won several awards for outstanding research. In class, you hang on this professor's every word. One day the professor is absent; a colleague from the Economics Department—fully qualified but not as well known—comes to lecture instead. Possibly the fill-in instructor gives the same lecture the distinguished professor would have given, but you do not pay nearly as close attention. The other instructor does not have as high credibility as the professor.

credibility

The audience's perception of whether a speaker is qualified to speak on a given topic. The two major factors influencing a speaker's credibility are competence and character.

It is important to remember that credibility is an attitude. It exists not in the speaker, but in the mind of the audience. A speaker may have high credibility for one audience and low credibility for another. A speaker may also have high credibility on one topic and low credibility on another. Looking back to our imaginary statements, most people would more readily believe Aaron Rodgers speaking about professional football than Aaron Rodgers speaking about the organization of the U.S. judiciary.

TYPES OF CREDIBILITY

Not only can a speaker's credibility vary from audience to audience and topic to topic, but it can also change during the course of a speech—so much so that we can identify three types of credibility:

- *Initial credibility*—the credibility of the speaker before she or he starts to speak.
- *Derived credibility*—the credibility of the speaker produced by everything she or he says and does during the speech itself.
- *Terminal credibility*—the credibility of the speaker at the end of the speech.[1]

initial credibility

The credibility of a speaker before she or he starts to speak.

derived credibility

The credibility of a speaker produced by everything she or he says and does during the speech.

terminal credibility

The credibility of a speaker at the end of the speech.

All three are dynamic. High initial credibility is a great advantage for any speaker, but it can be destroyed during a speech, resulting in low terminal credibility. The reverse can also occur, as in the following example:

> Amit Patel is the information technology manager for a nonprofit research foundation. Soon after taking the job, he installed a new content management system for the company's Web site. He assumed there would be some glitches, but they turned out to be much worse than anything he had imagined. It took nine months to get the system working properly.
>
> A year later, the foundation decided to purchase new tablets that would allow employees to interact more efficiently with data on the internal network. When Amit discussed the tablets at a weekly staff meeting, he had low initial credibility. Everyone remembered the content management system, and they did not want to go through the same problems again.
>
> Aware of his low initial credibility, Amit began by reminding everyone that he hoped to make their jobs easier. He then acknowledged that he had told them the same thing about the content management system—an admission that drew a laugh and helped everyone relax. Finally, he explained that he had checked with other nonprofits that had adopted the same tablets he was purchasing, and they had all told him that the tablets worked flawlessly.

> By the time Amit finished, most staff members were eager to start using their tablets. He had achieved high terminal credibility.

In every speech you give you will have some degree of initial credibility, which will be strengthened or weakened by your message and how you deliver it. And your terminal credibility from one speech will affect your initial credibility for the next one. If your audience sees you as sincere and competent, they will be much more receptive to your ideas.

ENHANCING YOUR CREDIBILITY

How can you build your credibility in your speeches? At one level, the answer is frustratingly general. Since everything you say and do in a speech will affect your credibility, you should say and do *everything* in a way that will make you appear capable and trustworthy. In other words—give a brilliant speech and you will achieve high credibility!

The advice is sound, but not all that helpful. There are, however, some specific ways you can boost your credibility while speaking. They include explaining your competence, establishing common ground with the audience, and speaking with genuine conviction.

Explain Your Competence

One way to enhance your credibility is to advertise your expertise on the speech topic. Did you investigate the topic thoroughly? Then say so. Do you have experience that gives you special knowledge or insight? Again, say so.

Here is how two students revealed their qualifications. The first stressed her study and research:

connect

View these excerpts from "Bursting the Antibacterial Bubble" and "Keeping the Safety Net for Those Who Need It" in the online Media Library for this chapter (Video 17.1).

> Before I studied antibacterial products in my public-health class, I always used antibacterial soaps and antibacterial all-surface cleaner for my apartment. I also know from my class survey that 70 percent of you use antibacterial soaps, cleaners, or other products. But after learning about the subject in class and reading research studies for this speech, I'm here to tell you that, try as we might, we cannot build a bubble between ourselves and germs with antibacterial products and that these products actually create more problems than they solve.

The second student emphasized her background and personal experience:

> Most of us have no idea what it means to be poor and hungry. But before returning to school last year, I spent three years working at local assistance centers. I can't tell you everything I have seen. But on the basis of what I can tell you, I hope you will agree with me that government help for the poor and needy must be maintained.

Both speakers greatly increased their persuasiveness by establishing their credibility.

Establish Common Ground with Your Audience

Another way to bolster your credibility is to establish common ground with your audience. You do not persuade listeners by assaulting their values and rejecting their opinions. As the old saying goes, "You catch more flies with

A speaker's credibility has a powerful impact on how her or his speech is received. One way to boost your credibility is to deliver your speeches expressively and with strong eye contact.

honey than with vinegar." The same is true of persuasion. Show respect for your listeners. You can make your speech more appealing by identifying your ideas with those of your audience—by showing how your point of view is consistent with what they believe.[2]

Creating common ground is especially important at the start of a persuasive speech. Begin by identifying with your listeners. Show that you share their values, attitudes, and experiences. Get them nodding their heads in agreement, and they will be much more receptive to your ultimate proposal. Here is how a businesswoman from Massachusetts, hoping to sell her product to an audience in Colorado, began her persuasive speech:

creating common ground

A technique in which a speaker connects himself or herself with the values, attitudes, or experiences of the audience.

> I have never been in Colorado before, but I really looked forward to making this trip. A lot of my ancestors left Massachusetts and came to Colorado nearly 150 years ago. Sometimes I have wondered why they did it. They came in covered wagons, carrying all their possessions, and many of them died on the journey. The ones who got through raised their houses and raised their families. Now that I've seen Colorado, I understand why they tried so hard!

The audience laughed and applauded, and the speaker was off to a good start.

Now look at a different approach, used in a classroom speech favoring a tuition increase at the speaker's school—an unpopular point of view with his classmates. He began by saying:

connect

View this excerpt from "Let's Protect the Quality of Our Education" in the online Media Library for this chapter (Video 17.2).

> As we all know, there are many differences among the people in this class. But regardless of age, major, background, or goals, we all share one thing in common—we're all concerned about the quality of education at this school. And that quality is clearly in danger.
>
> The economic crisis has hit every aspect of life, and education is no exception. Budgets are shrinking, faculty salaries are falling, student services are

disappearing, and we are being crowded out of classes we need to take. Whether we like it or not, we have a problem—a problem that affects each of us.

There are no easy answers, but one thing that will help solve the problem is an increase in tuition. I don't like it any more than you do, but sometimes we have to do what is necessary to protect the quality of our education.

By stressing common perceptions of the problem, the student hoped to get off on the right foot with his audience. Once that was done, he moved gradually to his more controversial ideas.

Deliver Your Speeches Fluently, Expressively, and with Conviction

There is a great deal of research to show that a speaker's credibility is strongly affected by his or her delivery. Moderately fast speakers, for example, are usually seen as more intelligent and confident than slower speakers. So too are speakers who use vocal variety to communicate their ideas in a lively, animated way. On the other hand, speakers who consistently lose their place, hesitate frequently, or pepper their talk with "uh," "er," and "um" are seen as less competent than speakers who are poised and dynamic.[3]

All of this argues for practicing your persuasive speech fully ahead of time so you can deliver it fluently and expressively. In addition to being better prepared, you will take a major step toward enhancing your credibility. (Review Chapter 13 if you have questions about speech delivery.)

Speaking techniques aside, the most important way to strengthen your credibility is to deliver your speeches with genuine conviction. President Harry Truman once said that in speaking, "sincerity, honesty, and a straightforward manner are more important than special talent or polish." If you wish to convince others, you must first convince yourself. If you want others to believe and care about your ideas, you must believe and care about them yourself. Your spirit, enthusiasm, and conviction will carry over to your listeners.

Using Evidence

Evidence consists of supporting materials—examples, statistics, testimony—used to prove or disprove something. As we saw in Chapter 8, most people are skeptical. They are suspicious of unsupported generalizations. They want speakers to justify their claims. If you hope to be persuasive, you must support your views with evidence. Whenever you say something that is open to question, you should give evidence to prove you are right.

evidence

Supporting materials used to prove or disprove something.

Evidence is particularly important in classroom speeches because few students are recognized as experts on their speech topics. Research has shown that speakers with very high initial credibility do not need to use as much evidence as do speakers with lower credibility. For most speakers, though, strong evidence is absolutely necessary. It can enhance your credibility, increase both the immediate and long-term persuasiveness of your message, and help "inoculate" listeners against counterpersuasion.[4]

Evidence is also crucial whenever your target audience opposes your point of view. As we saw in Chapter 16, listeners in such a situation will mentally argue with you—asking questions, raising objections, and creating counter-arguments to "answer" what you say. The success of your speech will depend partly on how well you anticipate these internal responses and give evidence to refute them.

You may want to review Chapter 8, which shows how to use supporting materials. The following case study illustrates how they work as evidence in a persuasive speech.

HOW EVIDENCE WORKS: A CASE STUDY

Let's say one of your classmates is talking about shortcomings in the U.S. mental health system. Instead of just telling you what she thinks, the speaker offers strong evidence to prove her point. Notice how she carries on a mental dialogue with her listeners. She imagines what they might be thinking, anticipates their questions and objections, and gives evidence to answer the questions and resolve the objections.

She begins this way:

> Right now in our city, there is a homeless man muttering to himself on a street corner. An elderly woman living with too many cats. A teenager cutting her arms and legs. Some call them crazy. But to me, these are people who need help—help that they're not receiving because of our nation's inadequate mental-health services.

How do you react? If you already know about the deficiencies in mental-health services, you probably nod your head in agreement. But what if you don't know? Or what if you're skeptical? Perhaps you think taxpayer dollars could be better spent elsewhere. If so, a few anecdotes probably won't persuade you. Mentally you say to the speaker, "These are sad stories, but maybe they're isolated cases. Do we really have a national problem?"

Anticipating just such a response, the speaker gives evidence to support her point:

> According to a recent story on *CNN.com*, the number of state-run psychiatric beds across America has decreased by 14 percent during the past five years. More shockingly, since 1960 that number has fallen by a whopping 92 percent.

"Okay, that's a big decline," you may think. "But people with mental-health issues receive care in other ways. The number of psychiatric beds doesn't tell the whole story." The speaker answers:

> What happens to the people who can't receive treatment at a state-run facility? According to Bernard Harcourt, a criminology professor at the University of Chicago, many end up behind bars. Fifty years ago, there were almost 1.1 million people in mental-health facilities, compared with 270,000 people in prison. Today, there are only 150,000 people in mental-health facilities and 2 million in prison. As the mental-health population has declined, the prison population has skyrocketed.

"That's an interesting correlation," you say to yourself. "But is that the extent of the problem?" Keeping one step ahead of you, the speaker continues:

> Nor is the mental-health crisis isolated to our prisons. Consider the following statistics from the National Alliance on Mental Illness. Untreated mental illnesses

> cost the United States almost $200 billion a year in lost productivity. Adults living with serious, but treatable, mental illness die an average of 25 years earlier than the rest of the population. And veterans who experience mental health issues are committing suicide at alarming rates—an average of 22 every single day of the year.

"I didn't know that," you say to yourself. "Is there anything else?"

> One last point. *Time* magazine reports that more and more children are not getting the mental-health care they need. There are currently 7,500 psychiatrists serving children and adolescents. To meet demand, however, we need more than 20,000 psychiatrists. On top of everything else, we are putting our children at risk.

Now are you convinced? Chances are you will at least think about the lack of mental-health care as a serious problem. You may even decide that increasing funding for mental-health services would be a good investment of tax dollars. If so, you will have changed your mind in part because the speaker supported each of her claims with evidence.

TIPS FOR USING EVIDENCE

Any of the supporting materials discussed in Chapter 8—examples, statistics, testimony—can work as evidence in a persuasive speech. As we saw in that chapter, there are guidelines for using each kind of supporting material regardless of the kind of speech you are giving. Here we look at four special tips for using evidence in a persuasive speech.

Use Specific Evidence

No matter what kind of evidence you employ—statistics, examples, or testimony—it will be more persuasive if you state it in specific rather than general terms.[5] In the speech about mental illness, for example, the speaker did not say, "Lack of adequate mental-health care costs the U.S. economy lots of money." That would have left the audience wondering how much "lots" amounts to. By saying, "untreated mental illnesses cost the United States almost $200 billion a year in lost productivity," the speaker made her point much more persuasively. She also enhanced her credibility by showing that she had a firm grasp of the facts.

Use Novel Evidence

Evidence is more likely to be persuasive if it is new to the audience.[6] You will gain little by citing facts and figures that are already well known to your listeners. If they have not persuaded your listeners already, they will not do so now. You must go beyond what the audience already knows and present striking new evidence that will get them to say, "Hmmm, I didn't know *that.* Maybe I should rethink the issue." Finding such evidence usually requires hard digging and resourceful research, but the rewards are worth the effort.

Use Evidence from Credible Sources

Listeners find evidence from competent, credible sources more persuasive than evidence from less qualified sources.[7] Above all, listeners are suspicious of evidence from sources that appear to be biased or self-interested. In assessing

Persuasive speeches need strong evidence to convince skeptical listeners. Research shows that evidence will be most convincing when it is stated in specific rather than general terms.

the current state of airline safety, for example, they are more likely to be persuaded by testimony from impartial aviation experts than from the president of American Airlines. If you wish to be persuasive, rely on evidence from objective, nonpartisan sources.

Make Clear the Point of Your Evidence

When speaking to persuade, you use evidence to prove a point. Yet you would be surprised how many novice speakers present their evidence without making clear the point it is supposed to prove. A number of studies have shown that you cannot count on listeners to draw, on their own, the conclusion you want them to reach.[8] When using evidence, be sure listeners understand the point you are trying to make.

Notice, for example, how the speaker in Video 17.3 in the online Media Library for this chapter drives home the point of his evidence about the rate of motorcycle fatalities in comparison to automobile fatalities:

> According to the Governors Highway Safety Association, last year there were more than 5,000 motorcycle deaths in the United States. That's a jump of 9 percent from the previous year. If 5,000 people dead doesn't sound like a lot, consider this: Over the past 15 years, motorcycle deaths have doubled, while automobile deaths have dropped by 23 percent. Here in Wisconsin alone, 114 people died last year. That's a 34 percent increase from the year before.
>
> Clearly, we can do more to solve the problem. Here in Wisconsin, there's an easy solution: We can save lives simply by requiring that all motorcyclists wear a helmet.

connect

View this excerpt from "Saving Lives with Motorcycle Helmets" in the online Media Library for this chapter (Video 17.3).

Evidence is one element of what Aristotle referred to as *logos*—the logical appeal of a speaker. The other major element of logos is reasoning, which works in combination with evidence to help make a speaker's claims persuasive.

logos

The name used by Aristotle for the logical appeal of a speaker. The two major elements of logos are evidence and reasoning.

checklist

Evidence

YES	NO	
☐	☐	1. Are all my major claims supported by evidence?
☐	☐	2. Do I use sufficient evidence to convince my audience of my claims?
☐	☐	3. Is my evidence stated in specific rather than general terms?
☐	☐	4. Do I use evidence that is new to my audience?
☐	☐	5. Is my evidence from credible, unbiased sources?
☐	☐	6. Do I identify the sources of my evidence?
☐	☐	7. Is my evidence clearly linked to each point that it is meant to prove?
☐	☐	8. Do I provide evidence to answer possible objections the audience may have to my position?

Reasoning

The story is told about Hack Wilson, a hard-hitting outfielder for the Brooklyn Dodgers baseball team in the 1930s.[9] Wilson was a great player, but he had a fondness for the good life. His drinking exploits were legendary. He was known to spend the entire night on the town, stagger into the team's hotel at the break of dawn, grab a couple hours sleep, and get to the ballpark just in time for the afternoon game.

This greatly distressed Max Carey, Wilson's manager. At the next team meeting, Carey spent much time explaining the evils of drink. To prove his point, he stood beside a table on which he had placed two glasses and a plate of live angleworms. One glass was filled with water, the other with gin—Wilson's favorite beverage. With a flourish Carey dropped a worm into the glass of water. It wriggled happily. Next Carey plunged the same worm into the gin. It promptly stiffened and expired.

A murmur ran through the room, and some players were obviously impressed. But not Wilson. He didn't even seem interested. Carey waited a little, hoping for some delayed reaction from his wayward slugger. When none came, he prodded, "Do you follow my reasoning, Wilson?"

"Sure, skipper," answered Wilson. "It proves that if you drink gin, you'll never get worms!"

And what does this story prove? No matter how strong your evidence, you will not be persuasive unless listeners grasp your reasoning.

Reasoning is the process of drawing a conclusion based on evidence. Sometimes we reason well—as when we conclude that ice particles forming

Reasoning is an important part of persuasive speaking. In a legal trial, for example, neither the prosecution nor the defense is likely to sway the jury unless their reasoning is clear and convincing.

on the trees may mean the roads will be slippery. Other times we reason less effectively—as when we conclude that spilling salt will bring bad luck. Most superstitions are actually no more than instances of faulty reasoning.

Reasoning in public speaking is an extension of reasoning in other aspects of life. As a public speaker, you have two major concerns with respect to reasoning. First, you must make sure your own reasoning is sound. Second, you must try to get listeners to agree with your reasoning. Let us look, then, at four basic methods of reasoning and how to use them in your speeches.

reasoning

The process of drawing a conclusion on the basis of evidence.

REASONING FROM SPECIFIC INSTANCES

When you reason from specific instances, you progress from a number of particular facts to a general conclusion.[10] For example:

reasoning from specific instances

Reasoning that moves from particular facts to a general conclusion.

Fact 1: My physical education course last term was easy.

Fact 2: My roommate's physical education course was easy.

Fact 3: My brother's physical education course was easy.

Conclusion: Physical education courses are easy.

As this example suggests, we use reasoning from specific instances daily, although we probably don't realize it. Think for a moment of all the general conclusions that arise in conversation: Politicians are corrupt. Professors are bookish. Dorm food is awful. Where do such conclusions come from? They come from observing particular politicians, professors, dormitories, and so on.

The same thing happens in public speaking. The speaker who concludes that unethical banking practices are common in the United States because several major banks have been guilty of fraud in recent years is reasoning from specific instances. So is the speaker who argues that anti-Semitism is increasing on college campuses because there have been a number of attacks on Jewish students and symbols at schools across the nation.

Such conclusions are never foolproof. No matter how many specific instances you give (and you can give only a few in a speech), it is always possible that an exception exists. Throughout the ages people observed countless white swans in Europe without seeing any of a different color. It seemed an undeniable fact that all swans were white. Then, in the 19th century, black swans were discovered in Australia![11]

When you reason from specific instances, beware of jumping to conclusions on the basis of insufficient evidence. Make sure your sample of specific instances is large enough to justify your conclusion.

Also make sure the instances you present are fair, unbiased, and representative. (Are three physical education courses *enough* to conclude that physical education courses in general are easy? Are the three courses *typical* of most physical education courses?)

Finally, reinforce your argument with statistics or testimony. Because you can never give enough specific instances in a speech to make your conclusion irrefutable, you should supplement them with testimony or statistics demonstrating that the instances are representative.

REASONING FROM PRINCIPLE

Reasoning from principle is the opposite of reasoning from specific instances. It moves from the general to the specific.[12] When you reason from principle, you progress from a general principle to a specific conclusion. We are all familiar with this kind of reasoning from statements such as the following:

1. All people are mortal.
2. Socrates is a person.
3. Therefore, Socrates is mortal.

This is a classic example of reasoning from principle. You begin with a general statement ("All people are mortal"), move to a minor premise ("Socrates is a person"), and end with a specific conclusion ("Socrates is mortal").

reasoning from principle

Reasoning that moves from a general principle to a specific conclusion.

Speakers often use reasoning from principle when trying to persuade an audience. One of the clearest examples from American history is Susan B. Anthony's famous speech "Is It a Crime for a U.S. Citizen to Vote?" Delivered on numerous occasions in 1872 and 1873, at a time when women were legally barred from voting, Anthony's speech reasoned along the following lines:

1. The United States Constitution guarantees all U.S. citizens the right to vote.
2. Women are U.S. citizens.
3. Therefore, the United States Constitution guarantees women the right to vote.

This argument progresses from a general principle ("The United States Constitution guarantees all U.S. citizens the right to vote") through a minor premise ("Women are U.S. citizens") to a conclusion ("Therefore, the United States Constitution guarantees women the right to vote").

When you use reasoning from principle in a speech, pay special attention to your general principle. Will listeners accept it without evidence? If not, give evidence to support it before moving to your minor premise. You may also need to support your minor premise with evidence. When both the general principle and the minor premise are soundly based, your audience will be much more likely to accept your conclusion.

CAUSAL REASONING

There is a patch of ice on the sidewalk. You slip, fall, and break your arm. You reason as follows: "*Because* that patch of ice was there, I fell and broke my arm." This is an example of causal reasoning, in which someone tries to establish the relationship between causes and effects.

causal reasoning

Reasoning that seeks to establish the relationship between causes and effects.

As with reasoning from specific instances, we use causal reasoning daily. Something happens and we ask what caused it to happen. We want to know the causes of chronic fatigue syndrome, of the football team's latest defeat, of our roommate's peculiar habits. We also wonder about effects. We speculate about the consequences of chronic fatigue syndrome, of the star quarterback's leg injury, of telling our roommate that a change is needed.

As any scientist (or detective) will tell you, causal reasoning can be tricky. The relationship between causes and effects is not always clear. For example, the fact that one event happens after another does not mean that the first is the cause of the second. The closeness in time of the two events may be entirely coincidental. If a black cat crosses your path and five minutes later you fall and break your arm, you needn't blame your accident on the poor cat.

You also need to beware of assuming that events have only one cause. In fact, most events have several causes. What causes the economy to boom or bust? Interest rates? Gas prices? Tax policy? Labor costs? Consumer confidence? World affairs? *All* these factors—and others—affect the economy. When you use causal reasoning, be wary of the temptation to attribute complex events to single causes.

ANALOGICAL REASONING

When arguing from analogy, a speaker compares two similar cases and infers that what is true for one case is also true for the other: For example:

analogical reasoning

Reasoning in which a speaker compares two similar cases and infers that what is true for the first case is also true for the second.

> If you're good at tennis, you will probably be good at Ping-Pong.

Although playing Ping-Pong is not exactly the same as playing tennis, the two are close enough that the speaker is on firm ground in concluding that being skilled at one increases the odds of being skilled at the other.

Analogical reasoning is used frequently in persuasive speeches—especially when the speaker is dealing with a question of policy. When arguing for a new policy, you should find out whether it has been tried elsewhere. You may be able to claim that your policy will work because it has worked in like circumstances. Here is how one speaker used reasoning from analogy to support his claim that controlling handguns will reduce violent crime in the United States:

> Will my policy work? The experience of foreign countries suggests it will. In England, guns are tightly regulated; even the police are unarmed, and the murder rate is trivial by American standards. Japan has even fewer guns than England, and its crime rate is lower than England's. On the basis of these comparisons, we can conclude that restricting the ownership of guns will reduce crime and murder rates in America.

By the same token, if you argue against a change in policy, you should check whether the proposed policy—or something like it—has been implemented elsewhere. Here, too, you may be able to support your case by reasoning from analogy—as did one speaker who opposed gun control:

> Advocates of gun control point to foreign countries such as England and Japan to prove their case. But the key to low personal violence in these and other countries is the peaceful character of the people, not gun control laws. Switzerland, for example, has a militia system; more than 1 million automatic rifles and military pistols are sitting at this moment in Swiss homes. Yet Switzerland's murder rate is only 8 percent of ours. In other words, cultural factors are more important than gun control when it comes to violent crime.

As these examples illustrate, argument from analogy can be used on both sides of an issue. You are more likely to persuade your audience if the analogy shows a truly parallel situation.

FALLACIES

fallacy

An error in reasoning.

A fallacy is an error in reasoning. As a speaker, you need to avoid fallacies in your speeches. As a listener, you need to be alert to fallacies in the speeches you hear.

Logicians have identified more than 125 different fallacies. Here we look at 10 that you should guard against.

Hasty Generalization

hasty generalization

A fallacy in which a speaker jumps to a general conclusion on the basis of insufficient evidence.

Hasty generalization is the most common fallacy in reasoning from specific instances. It occurs when a speaker jumps to a conclusion on the basis of too few cases or on the basis of atypical cases. For example:

> Throughout American history, military leaders have always made excellent presidents. Look at the examples of George Washington, Andrew Jackson, and Dwight Eisenhower.

Washington, Jackson, and Eisenhower are widely regarded as outstanding chief executives, but are these examples enough to conclude that military leaders *always* make excellent presidents? In fact, they are not. James Buchanan and Ulysses S. Grant were both highly decorated military leaders during the 19th century, but they are usually rated among the nation's worst presidents. An accurate statement would be:

> Throughout American history, military leaders have sometimes made excellent presidents—as with Washington, Jackson, and Eisenhower.

This statement is factually correct and avoids the fallacy of hasty generalization.

False Cause

false cause

A fallacy in which a speaker mistakenly assumes that because one event follows another, the first event is the cause of the second.

The fallacy of false cause is often known by its Latin name, *post hoc, ergo propter hoc,* which means "after this, therefore because of this." In other words, the fact that one event occurs after another does not mean that the first is the cause of the second. The closeness in time of the two events may be entirely coincidental—as in this case:

In addition to using evidence to support their ideas, effective persuasive speakers rely on research to help them avoid fallacies that may undermine their credibility and persuasiveness.

> When a team from the NFC wins the Super Bowl, economic growth during the next year is stronger than when a team from the AFC wins the Super Bowl. Therefore, if we want economic growth, we should root for a team from the NFC to win this year's Super Bowl.

There may be a slight correlation between economic growth and which conference wins the Super Bowl, but there is no *causal* connection between the two events. Whether the American economy rises or falls is not dependent on the outcome of the Super Bowl.

Invalid Analogy

As we saw on 343–344, when reasoning from analogy, a speaker concludes that what is true in one case is also true in another. An invalid analogy occurs when the two cases being compared are not essentially alike. For example:

invalid analogy

An analogy in which the two cases being compared are not essentially alike.

> Employees are like nails. Just as nails must be hit on the head to get them to work, so must employees.

This statement is obviously fallacious. No one in his or her right mind can seriously think that employees, which are human beings, can be compared with inanimate objects such as nails.

But what about the following statement:

> In Great Britain, the general election campaign for prime minister lasts less than three weeks. Surely we can do the same with the U.S. presidential election.

At first glance, this analogy may seem perfectly sound. But are the British and American political systems enough alike to warrant the conclusion? Not really. The United States is much larger than Great Britain and its party system operates much differently. As a result, the factors that allow Great Britain to conduct campaigns for prime minister in less than three weeks are not present in the United States. The analogy is not valid.

As this example suggests, determining whether an analogy is valid or invalid is not always easy, but doing so is important for speakers and listeners alike.

Bandwagon

bandwagon

A fallacy which assumes that because something is popular, it is therefore good, correct, or desirable.

How often have you heard someone say, "It's a great idea—everyone agrees with it"? This is a classic example of the bandwagon fallacy, which assumes that because something is popular, it is therefore good, correct, or desirable.

Much advertising is based on the bandwagon fallacy. The fact that more people use Tylenol than Advil does not prove that Tylenol is a better painkiller. Tylenol's popularity could be due to clever marketing. The question of which product does a better job reducing pain is a medical issue that has nothing to do with popularity.

The bandwagon fallacy is also evident in political speeches. Consider the following statement:

> The governor must be correct in his approach to social policy; after all, the polls show that 60 percent of the people support him.

This statement is fallacious because popular opinion cannot be taken as proof that an idea is right or wrong. Remember, "everyone" used to believe that the world is flat and that space flight is impossible.

Red Herring

red herring

A fallacy that introduces an irrelevant issue to divert attention from the subject under discussion.

The name of this fallacy comes from an old trick used by farmers in England to keep fox hunters and their hounds from galloping through the crops. By dragging a smoked herring with a strong odor along the edge of their fields, the farmers could throw the dogs off track by destroying the scent of the fox.

A speaker who uses a red herring introduces an irrelevant issue in order to divert attention from the subject under discussion. For instance:

> How dare my opponents accuse me of political corruption at a time when we are working to improve the quality of life for all people in the United States.

What does the speaker's concern about the quality of life in the United States have to do with whether he or she is guilty of political corruption? Nothing! It is a red herring used to divert attention away from the real issue.

Ad Hominem

ad hominem

A fallacy that attacks the person rather than dealing with the real issue in dispute.

Latin for "against the man," *ad hominem* refers to the fallacy of attacking the person rather than dealing with the real issue in dispute. For instance:

> The head of the commerce commission has a number of interesting economic proposals, but let's not forget that she comes from a very wealthy family.

By impugning the commissioner's family background rather than dealing with the substance of her economic proposals, the speaker is engaging in an *ad hominem* attack.

Sometimes, of course, a person's character or integrity can be a legitimate issue—as in the case of a police chief who violates the law or a corporate president who swindles stockholders. In such cases, a speaker might well raise questions about the person without being guilty of the *ad hominem* fallacy.

Either-Or

Sometimes referred to as a false dilemma, the either-or fallacy forces listeners to choose between two alternatives when more than two alternatives exist. For example:

> The government must either raise taxes or eliminate services for the poor.

This statement oversimplifies a complex issue by reducing it to a simple either-or choice. Is it true that the *only* choices are to raise taxes or to eliminate services for the poor? A careful listener might ask, "What about cutting the administrative cost of government or eliminating pork-barrel projects instead?"

You will be more persuasive as a speaker and more perceptive as a listener if you are alert to the either-or fallacy.

either-or

A fallacy that forces listeners to choose between two alternatives when more than two alternatives exist.

Slippery Slope

The slippery slope fallacy takes its name from the image of a boulder rolling uncontrollably down a steep hill. Once the boulder gets started, it can't be stopped until it reaches the bottom.

A speaker who commits the slippery slope fallacy assumes that taking a first step will lead inevitably to a second step and so on down the slope to disaster—as in the following example:

> Now that the TSA is allowed to use full body scanners and invasive pat-downs before letting us through security, it's only a matter of time before they strip-search every man, woman, and child who wants to fly on a plane.

If a speaker claims that taking a first step will lead inevitably to a series of disastrous later steps, he or she needs to provide evidence or reasoning to support the claim. To assume that all the later steps will occur without proving that they will is to commit the slippery slope fallacy.

slippery slope

A fallacy which assumes that taking a first step will lead to subsequent steps that cannot be prevented.

Appeal to Tradition

Appeal to tradition is fallacious when it assumes that something old is *automatically* better than something new. For example:

> I don't see any reason to abolish the electoral college. It has been around since the adoption of the U.S. Constitution in 1787, and we should keep it as long as the United States continues to exist.

There are good arguments on both sides of the debate over abolishing the electoral college. However, to conclude that the electoral college should be kept forever solely because it has always been a part of the U.S. Constitution commits the fallacy of appeal to tradition.

Just because a practice, an institution, or an idea is old does not automatically make it better. Its value should be based on its contributions to society, not on its age. If tradition were the sole measure of value, we would still have slavery, women would not be able to vote, and people would undergo surgery without anesthesia.

appeal to tradition

A fallacy which assumes that something old is automatically better than something new.

Using public speaking in your CAREER

As the service manager for a local home improvement company, you have been pleased to see your company expand its size and scope, but you don't want that growth to come at the expense of customer service. In particular, you're worried about losing touch with one of the company's key demographics—women, who make up 55 percent of your customer base. To prevent this from happening, you have developed a plan for a range of personalized services targeted at women, including one-on-one teaching of do-it-yourself skills and free in-home consultations.

When you present your plan at a meeting of the company's management team, you listen as one executive argues in opposition. Among his points are the following: (1) If your plan is adopted, customers will expect more and more special services and eventually will demand free installation of flooring and carpeting; (2) Because a majority of the management team opposes your plan, it must not be a good idea; (3) One of your competitors tried a customer service plan specifically for women, but it did not succeed; therefore, your plan is doomed to failure.

In your response to the executive, you will point out the fallacy in each of his points. What are those fallacies?

Appeal to Novelty

appeal to novelty

A fallacy which assumes that something new is automatically better than something old.

The fallacy of appeal to novelty is the opposite of appeal to tradition. Appeal to novelty assumes that because something is new, it is therefore superior to something that is older. For example:

> Our church should adopt the 2011 New International Version of the Bible because it is 400 years newer than the King James Version.

The fact that the New International Version of the Bible is newer than the King James Version (completed in 1611), does not *automatically* make it better. There are many reasons why a church might prefer the New International Version, but the speaker should *explain* those reasons, rather than assuming that one version is better than another simply because it is new.

Advertisers often commit the fallacy of appeal to novelty. They tout their latest products as "new and improved," yet we know from experience that new does not always mean improved. As always, we need to look carefully at the claim and make sure it is based on sound reasoning.[13]

Appealing to Emotions

Effective persuasion often requires emotional appeal. As the Roman rhetorician Quintilian stated, "It is feeling and force of imagination that make us eloquent."[14] By adding "feeling" and the "force of imagination" to your logical arguments, you can become a more compelling persuasive speaker.

WHAT ARE EMOTIONAL APPEALS?

Emotional appeals—what Aristotle referred to as *pathos*—are intended to make listeners feel sad, angry, guilty, afraid, happy, proud, sympathetic, reverent, or the like. These are often appropriate reactions when the question is one of value or policy. As George Campbell wrote in his *Philosophy of Rhetoric,* "When persuasion is the end, passion also must be engaged."[15]

pathos

The name used by Aristotle for what modern students of communication refer to as emotional appeal.

Below is a list of some of the emotions evoked most often by public speakers. Following each emotion are a few examples of subjects that might stir that emotion:

- *Fear*—of serious illness, of natural disasters, of sexual assault, of personal rejection, of economic hardship.
- *Compassion*—for war refugees, for battered women, for neglected animals, for starving children, for victims of AIDS.
- *Pride*—in one's country, in one's family, in one's school, in one's ethnic heritage, in one's personal accomplishments.
- *Anger*—at terrorists and their supporters, at business leaders who act unethically, at members of Congress who abuse the public trust, at landlords who exploit student tenants, at vandals and thieves.
- *Guilt*—about not helping people less fortunate than ourselves, about not considering the rights of others, about not doing one's best.
- *Reverence*—for an admired person, for traditions and institutions, for one's deity.

There are many other emotions and many other subjects that might stir them. However, this brief sample should give you an idea of the kinds of emotional appeals you might use to enhance the message of your persuasive speech.

Emotional appeals often make a persuasive speech more compelling. Such appeals should always be used ethically and should not be substituted for facts and logic.

GENERATING EMOTIONAL APPEAL

Use Emotional Language

As we saw in Chapter 12, one way to generate emotional appeal is to use emotion-laden words. Here, for instance, is part of the conclusion from a student speech about the challenges and rewards of working as a volunteer with Teach for America:

> The promise of America sparkles in the eyes of every child. Their dreams are the glittering dreams of America. When those dreams are dashed, when innocent hopes are betrayed, so are the dreams and hopes of the entire nation. It is our duty—to me, it is a sacred duty—to give all children the chance to learn and grow, to share equally in the American dream of freedom, justice, and opportunity.

The underlined words and phrases have strong emotional power, and in this case they produced the desired effect. Be aware, however, that packing too many emotionally charged words into one part of a speech can call attention to the emotional language itself and undermine its impact. The emotion rests in your audience, not in your words. Even the coldest facts can touch off an emotional response if they strike the right chords in a listener.

Develop Vivid Examples

Often a better approach than relying on emotionally charged language is to let emotional appeal grow naturally out of the content of your speech. The most effective way to do this is with vivid, richly textured examples that pull listeners into the speech.

Here is how one speaker used a vivid example for emotional appeal. She was speaking about the malaria epidemic in Africa. Here is what she might have said, stripping the content of emotional appeal:

> Malaria is one of the biggest problems facing Africa. Many die from it every day. If the rest of the world doesn't help, the malaria epidemic will only get worse.

What she actually said went something like this:

> Nathan was only five years old when the fever struck him. At first, no one knew what was wrong. No one knew that parasites inside his body had infected his red blood cells. No one knew those cells were clumping together, choking the flow of blood through his body and damaging his vital organs. No one knew his kidneys would soon fail and seizures would begin. No one knew he would wind up in a coma.
>
> The parasites in Nathan's body came from a mosquito bite, a bite that gave him malaria. And Nathan is not alone. The World Health Organization tells us the horrible truth: In Africa, a child dies from malaria every 30 seconds.

connect

View this excerpt from "The Tragedy of Malaria" in the online Media Library for this chapter (Video 17.4).

People who listen to a speech like that will not soon forget it. They may well be moved to action—as the speaker intends. The first speech, however, is not nearly as compelling. Listeners may well nod their heads, think to themselves "good idea"—and then forget about it. The story of Nathan and his tragic fate gives the second speech emotional impact and brings it home to listeners in personal terms.

Speak with Sincerity and Conviction

Ronald Reagan was one of the most effective speakers in U.S. history. Even people who disagreed with his political views often found him irresistible. Why? Partly because he seemed to speak with great sincerity and conviction.

What was true for Reagan is true for you as well. The strongest source of emotional power is your conviction and sincerity. All your emotion-laden words and examples are but empty trappings unless *you* feel the emotion yourself. And if you do, your emotion will communicate itself to the audience through everything you say and do—not only through your words, but also through your tone of voice, rate of speech, gestures, and facial expressions.

ETHICS AND EMOTIONAL APPEAL

Much has been written about the ethics of emotional appeal in speechmaking. Some people have taken the extreme position that ethical speakers should avoid emotional appeal entirely. To support this view, they point to speakers who have used emotional appeal to fan the flames of hatred, bigotry, and fanaticism.

There is no question that emotional appeals can be abused by unscrupulous speakers for detestable causes. But emotional appeals can also be wielded by honorable speakers for noble causes—by Winston Churchill to rouse the world against Adolf Hitler and the forces of Nazism, by Martin Luther King to call for racial justice. Few people would question the ethics of emotional appeal in these instances.

Nor is it always possible to draw a sharp line between reason and emotional appeal. Think back to the story of Nathan, the five-year-old boy who was infected with malaria. The story certainly has strong emotional appeal. But is there anything unreasonable about it? Or is it irrational for listeners to respond to it by donating to anti-malarial causes? By the same token, is it illogical to be compassionate for victims of natural disasters? Angered by corporate wrongdoing? Fearful about cutbacks in student aid? Reason and emotion often work hand in hand.

Emotional language and vivid examples can help generate emotional appeal, but neither will be effective unless the speaker talks with genuine sincerity and conviction.

One key to using emotional appeal ethically is to make sure it is appropriate to the speech topic. If you want to move listeners to act on a question of policy, emotional appeals are not only legitimate but perhaps necessary. If you want listeners to do something as a result of your speech, you will probably need to appeal to their hearts as well as to their heads.

On the other hand, emotional appeals are usually inappropriate in a persuasive speech on a question of fact. Here you should deal only in specific information and logic. Suppose someone charges your state governor with illegal campaign activities. If you respond by saying "I'm sure the charge is false because I have always admired the governor," or "I'm sure the charge is true because I have always disliked the governor," then you are guilty of applying emotional criteria to a purely factual question.

Even when trying to move listeners to action, you should never substitute emotional appeals for evidence and reasoning. You should *always* build your persuasive speech on a firm foundation of facts and logic. This is important not just for ethical reasons, but for practical ones as well. Unless you prove your case, careful listeners will not be stirred by your emotional appeals. You need to build a good case based on reason *and* kindle the emotions of your audience.[16]

When you use emotional appeal, keep in mind the guidelines for ethical speechmaking discussed in Chapter 2. Make sure your goals are ethically sound, that you are honest in what you say, and that you avoid name-calling and other forms of abusive language. In using emotional appeal, as in other respects, your classroom speeches will offer a good testing ground for questions of ethical responsibility.

Sample Speech with Commentary

connect

View "The Living-Wage Solution" in the online Media Library for this chapter (Video 17.5).

The following persuasive speech on a question of policy is organized in problem-solution order. As you read the speech, notice how it employs the methods of persuasion discussed in this chapter. Pay special attention to the speaker's evidence, which she uses not only to establish the existence of a serious problem but also to explain her plan and to document its practicality.

In addition, the speech shows how visual aids can be used in a persuasive presentation to help an audience keep track of complex data and arguments. You can view it in the online Media Library for this chapter.

The Living-Wage Solution

COMMENTARY

The speaker opens with an extended example that gains attention and draws the audience into the speech.

SPEECH

José Morales was sleeping on cardboard boxes in a garage in Compton, California. Before the sun came up, he would walk to a nearby bus stop, where he would ride the bus for two hours to Los Angeles International Airport, where he worked as a janitor. On two occasions, he was mugged while waiting for the bus. Working 40 hours a week for minimum wage, this was the best he could do.

The speaker completes her opening story and identifies the topic of her speech.

But then José's situation improved drastically. As Robert Pollin, an economist at the University of Massachusetts, reports, José received health insurance and a 36 percent raise. He had enough money to rent his own apartment and to buy a car. It all happened because José started to receive the living wage.

In this paragraph, the speaker defines the living wage and contrasts it with the minimum wage. As you can see on the video, she uses PowerPoint to help clarify her points.

What is the living wage, you ask? Well, it's not the same as the minimum wage. The minimum wage is set by Congress and is the same in every part of the country. The living wage goes beyond the minimum wage. As the *Wall Street Journal* reported in August 2013, the living wage is tied to the local cost of living and can vary from location to location. Its purpose is to help workers and their families meet the most basic standard of living, even when that standard of living is higher than the minimum wage.

Here the speaker establishes her credibility by noting that her conclusions are supported by "numerous economists and public-policy researchers."

I first heard about the living wage last semester in my econ class. After researching it for this speech, I've come to the same conclusion as numerous economists and public-policy researchers. The living wage can help the working poor without adversely affecting businesses or the health of the economy.

The speaker ends her introduction with a concise statement of her central idea and a preview of the main points she will discuss in the body.

That's why we need to pass federal legislation mandating a living wage—a wage that can help people secure the basic necessities of life. So let's first look at the difficulties faced by the working poor, and then we'll look at the living-wage solution.

This speech is organized in problem-solution order. Here the speaker starts the problem main point by documenting the number of working poor in the United States. She cites a combination of statistics and uses PowerPoint to help listeners follow along as she moves from figure to figure.

Poverty remains a significant problem in the United States in part because wages have not kept up with the cost of living. According to a recent study by the Bureau of Labor Statistics, more than 46 million Americans live in poverty. Of these 46 million, 10 million are referred to as the "working poor": people who are employed at least 27 weeks a year and who are still stuck in poverty. Of these 10 million people, half—5 million—are employed full time. They work 40 hours a week, 52 weeks a year, but they still can't make ends meet.

The speaker explains why the current minimum wage is inadequate to keep a family above the poverty line.

How can that be? It happens in part because of the federal minimum wage. Since 2009, the minimum wage has been $7.25 an hour. If you calculate that, someone working full time would earn just over $15,000 a year. For an individual, that's just above the poverty line. The problem comes when there are two-, three-, or four-person households—as with a single mother trying to squeak by. It's almost impossible to raise a family on $15,000 a year.

Pointing to the ineptitude of Congress helps the audience understand why the minimum wage lags behind the cost of living.

Another problem is that the federal minimum wage doesn't change until Congress changes it—and we all know how long it can take for Congress to do anything. In fact, it took Congress more than 10 years to raise the minimum wage from its previous $5.25 to its current rate of $7.25. As a result, millions of workers were still earning in 2008 what they had earned in 1998.

The speaker ends her first main point with expert testimony that sums up the problem and emphasizes the need for action.

The result was "a lost decade for wage growth," according to *The State of Working America*, published in 2012 by Cornell University Press. The same book predicts another lost decade if we don't take action soon.

A question leads into the solution main point, in which the speaker lays out a plan, shows its practicality, and responds to potential objections.

So what can we do? How can we help make sure that people who work full time earn enough money to lift themselves and their families above the poverty level? One way is to implement a federally mandated living wage.

The speaker provides background on living wage plans in the United States. Such plans, she notes, currently cover only 1 percent of workers—which is why a national living wage law is needed to cover everyone who works full time.

The first city in America to institute a living wage was Baltimore, in 1994. Since then, the living-wage movement has spread to more than 140 jurisdictions. However, as David Neumark, Matthew Thompson, and Leslie Koyle reported in a 2012 issue of the *Journal of Labor Policy*, most living-wage laws cover only people who work for companies with government contracts. At best only 1 percent of workers in a city receive the living wage. It's time to cover everyone who works full time—and to do so with a national living-wage law.

The speaker's plan consists of two parts. Here she discusses the living-wage calculator.

Here's how such a law would work. First, we would calculate the living wage for every county in the United States. To do that, we'd use the living-wage calculator created by Amy Glasmeier, a professor of Urban Studies and Planning at MIT.

The speaker does an excellent job of explaining complex ideas clearly and concisely. Once again, she uses visual aids to highlight key points.

Based on this calculator, the living wage in Chicago, my hometown, for this year would be $10.48 per hour. In Dallas, it would be $9.29. In New York, it would be $12.75. As you can see, there is large variation in the cost of living across different parts of the country. A national living wage would account for these variations.

The second part of the speaker's plan ties the living wage to the cost of living.

Second, we would tie the living wage to the Consumer Price Index. The Consumer Price Index tracks the price of goods and services in different parts of the country. As the Consumer Price Index increases, the living wage would increase at the same rate.

As you can see from the video, the speaker communicates with excellent vocal variety and strong eye contact.

In Chicago, the Consumer Price Index rose by 2 percent last year. The living wage in that city would then go from $10.48 an hour to $10.69 an hour. And it would cover everyone who works full time, whether they work for the government or in the private sector. In this way, we can ensure that wages for everyone keep up with the cost of living.

Responding to potential objections, which the speaker does in this and the following paragraph, is a crucial part of persuasive speaking. Like the rest of the speech, this section is crisply organized and uses signposts to help the audience keep track of the speaker's ideas.

As you might expect, there is opposition to instituting a living-wage policy. Those who oppose the living wage offer two main arguments. First, they argue that the living wage would be too costly for businesses. But that's not what Jeff Thompson and Jeff Chapman, researchers at the Economic Policy Institute, found. After surveying existing living-wage laws, they found that the increased cost of wages is offset by higher productivity and lower employee turnover. Happier workers mean stronger businesses.

Here, as elsewhere, the speaker supports her argument with expert testimony. Notice how clearly she identifies her source and states his qualifications. This is a fine example of how to work oral citations into a speech.

The second argument of critics is that the living wage will lead to fewer jobs. But again the research doesn't bear this out. A 2011 study in *Economic Development Quarterly* by T. William Lester, a professor at the University of North Carolina, found that living-wage laws do not have a large negative impact on employment. In a 2012 study, Lester, who specializes in labor economics, found that living-wage laws can actually "create jobs of higher quality." In addition to being good for workers, a living-wage law can benefit businesses and the economy in general.

The speaker signals the beginning of her conclusion and restates her central idea.

In conclusion, the time has come to pay American workers a wage that will keep up with the cost of living. We need a federally mandated living wage. In a time of massive corporate profits and skyrocketing executive pay, those at the bottom of society deserve to advance along with those at the top.

Returning to the example cited in the introduction gives the speech a sense of psychological unity. The quotation from José Morales adds emotional appeal and leads into the strong closing line.

Those like José Morales, who I mentioned at the start of my speech, deserve a better future. "Everyone thinks that working here at the airport we must earn a lot of money," Morales says. "It's not true, but at least now with the living wage we can hold our heads up high." And that's something everyone working a full-time job should be able to say.

Summary

Listeners accept a speaker's ideas for one or more of four reasons—because they perceive the speaker as having high credibility, because they are won over by the speaker's evidence, because they are convinced by the speaker's reasoning, or because they are moved by the speaker's emotional appeals.

Credibility is affected by many factors, but the two most important are competence and character. The more favorably listeners view a speaker's competence and character, the more likely they are to accept her or his ideas. Although credibility is partly a matter of reputation, you can enhance your credibility during a speech by establishing common ground with your listeners, by letting them know why you are qualified to speak on the topic, and by presenting your ideas fluently and expressively.

If you hope to be persuasive, you must also support your views with evidence—examples, statistics, and testimony. Regardless of what kind of evidence you use, it will be more persuasive if it is new to the audience, stated in specific rather than general terms, and from credible sources. Your evidence will also be more persuasive if you state explicitly the point it is supposed to prove.

No matter how strong your evidence, you will not be persuasive unless listeners agree with your reasoning. In reasoning from specific instances, you move from a number of particular facts to a general conclusion. Reasoning from principle is the reverse—you move from a general principle to a particular conclusion. When you use causal reasoning, you try to establish a relationship between causes and effects. In analogical reasoning, you compare two cases and infer that what is true for one is also true for the other.

Whatever kind of reasoning you use, avoid fallacies such as hasty generalization, false cause, invalid analogy, appeal to tradition, and appeal to novelty. You should also be on guard against the red herring, slippery slope, bandwagon, *ad hominem,* and either-or fallacies.

Finally, you can persuade your listeners by appealing to their emotions. One way to generate emotional appeal is by using emotion-laden language. Another is to develop vivid, richly textured examples. Neither, however, will be effective unless you feel the emotion yourself and communicate it by speaking with sincerity and conviction.

As with other methods of persuasion, your use of emotional appeal should be guided by a firm ethical rudder. Although emotional appeals are usually inappropriate in speeches on questions of fact, they are legitimate—and often necessary—in speeches that seek immediate action on questions of policy. Even when trying to move listeners to action, however, you should never substitute emotional appeals for evidence and reasoning.

Key Terms

ethos (332)
credibility (333)
initial credibility (333)
derived credibility (333)
terminal credibility (333)
creating common ground (335)
evidence (336)
logos (339)
reasoning (341)
reasoning from specific instances (341)
reasoning from principle (342)
causal reasoning (343)
analogical reasoning (343)
fallacy (344)
hasty generalization (344)
false cause (344)
invalid analogy (345)
bandwagon (346)
red herring (346)
ad hominem (346)
either-or (347)
slippery slope (347)
appeal to tradition (347)
appeal to novelty (348)
pathos (349)

Review Questions

After reading this chapter, you should be able to answer the following questions:

1. What is credibility? What two factors exert the most influence on an audience's perception of a speaker's credibility?
2. What are the differences among initial credibility, derived credibility, and terminal credibility?
3. What are three ways you can enhance your credibility during your speeches?
4. What is evidence? Why do persuasive speakers need to use evidence?
5. What are four tips for using evidence effectively in a persuasive speech?
6. What is reasoning from specific instances? Why is it important to supplement reasoning from specific instances with testimony or statistics?
7. What is reasoning from principle? How is it different from reasoning from specific instances?
8. What is causal reasoning? Why is the relationship between causes and effects not always clear?
9. What is analogical reasoning? Why is analogical reasoning frequently used in persuasive speeches on questions of policy?
10. What are the ten logical fallacies discussed in this chapter?
11. What is the role of emotional appeal in persuasive speaking? Identify three methods you can use to generate emotional appeal in your speeches.

connect

For further review, go to the LearnSmart study module for this chapter.

Exercises for Critical Thinking

1. Research has shown that a speaker's initial credibility can have great impact on how the speaker's ideas are received by listeners. Research has also shown that a speaker's credibility will vary from topic to topic and audience to audience. In the left-hand column below is a list of well-known public figures. In the right-hand column is a list of potential speech topics. Assume that each speaker will be addressing your speech class.

   For each speaker, identify the topic in the right-hand column on which she or he would have the highest initial credibility for your class. Then explain how the speaker's initial credibility might be affected if the speaker were discussing the topic in the right-hand column directly across from her or his name.

Speaker	**Topic**
Mark Zuckerberg	The Art of Making Movies
Carrie Underwood	Life in the White House
Louis C. K.	The Future of Social Media
Michelle Obama	Trends in Country Music
Quentin Tarantino	The Challenges of Stand-Up Comedy

2. Identify the kind of reasoning used in each of the following statements. What weaknesses, if any, can you find in the reasoning of each?
   a. The U.S. Constitution prohibits cruel and unusual punishment. Life sentencing for juvenile offenders is cruel and unusual punishment. Therefore, life sentencing for juvenile offenders is contrary to the U.S. Constitution.
   b. We can see from its work all around the world that Women for Women International is a worthy charitable organization. It has helped women in Rwanda operate sewing machines and make clothing. It has given women in Kosovo the skills to operate businesses in their communities. It has shown women in the Democratic Republic of Congo how to create and market ceramics.
   c. According to a study by the National Institutes of Health, children with gluten sensitivity have a three times greater risk of developing scoliosis than do children without gluten sensitivity. We can see, then, that gluten sensitivity is the cause of scoliosis.
   d. Almost every industrialized nation in the world except for the United States has a national curriculum and national tests to help ensure that schools throughout the country are meeting high standards of education. If such a system can work elsewhere, it can work in the United States.
3. Over the years there has been much debate about the role of emotional appeal in public speaking. Do you believe it is ethical for public speakers to use emotional appeals when seeking to persuade an audience? Do you feel there are certain kinds of emotions to which an ethical speaker should not appeal? Why or why not? Be prepared to explain your ideas in class.
4. Analyze the sample speech with commentary at the end of this chapter ("The Living-Wage Solution," pages 352–355). Pay special attention to the speaker's credibility, evidence, reasoning, and emotional appeal. View the video of the speech in the online Media Library for this chapter so you can also assess the speaker's delivery and use of visual aids.

This class is just the beginning of your public speaking career.

CHAPTER 9

SPEAKING BEYOND THE CLASSROOM

Objectives

www.mhhe.com/brydon7e

After reading this chapter and reviewing the online learning resources at www.mhhe.com/brydon7e, you should be able to:

- Present a speech of introduction.
- Present or accept an award.
- Make a speech of commemoration.
- Make a speech to entertain.
- Make a wedding toast.
- Present an elevator pitch.
- Handle a question-and-answer session.
- Lead or participate in a small group discussion.
- Recognize symptoms of groupthink and take measures to avoid it.
- Effectively participate in panel discussions in a small group.
- Recognize the potential benefits of a career in public speaking.

Key Concepts

agenda
elevator pitch
eulogy
group
groupthink
panel discussion
speech of acceptance
speech of commemoration
speech of introduction
speech of recognition
speech to entertain

"You've been giving your attention to a turkey stuffed with sage; you are now about to consider a sage stuffed with turkey."

—WILLIAM MAXWELL EVARTS (1818–1901)
American statesman, speaking after a Thanksgiving dinner[1]

Dragon's Den requires contestants to make a pitch to venture capitalists to get their projects funded.

Have you ever seen an episode of *Dragon's Den*? First broadcast in the United Kingdom, there is now a U.S. version of this TV reality show dedicated to the big dreams of inventors and entrepreneurs alike. Participants selected for the show are given the opportunity to "pitch" their concept or product to a panel of venture capitalists in the hope of obtaining the funding necessary to take it to the next level.

Dragon's Den showcases a type of public speaking that was once largely confined to Hollywood. You pitched a concept for a film or TV show to people with the power to "green light" the concept to begin the process of making it a reality. Today, however, mastery of the art of the pitch is necessary to anyone who hopes to see an idea take wing, whether it's an internal proposal for a new version of a company's smart phone, a plan to market the phone, or the methodology necessary to measure customer satisfaction with the phone following its launch.

Like everything else, the transaction between speaker and audience is evolving. Although we feel safe in saying that public speaking will remain a primary medium through which we carry out some of our culture's most important customs and rituals, it would be dishonest for us to say that the lessons and skills that we've shared in the past 15 chapters will never need to be modified and adapted to rhetorical situations we haven't anticipated.

Our purpose in this last chapter is twofold. First, we want to emphasize the fact that this book and the course in which you are enrolled have begun the process of preparing you to meet predictable challenges you'll face when required to speak during times of joy and personal satisfaction, as well as times of duress and even grief. Second, we want to demonstrate that the same skills that will help you meet these conventional challenges can be generalized well beyond their original scope, whether you need an effective "elevator pitch" or need to lead a team at work.

SPEAKING OF . . .

The Wedding Toast

Whereas 40 percent of people express fears about presenting a public speech, 97 percent report that they are fearful over the prospect of being asked to give a wedding toast. One potential consequence of this fact is that unrehearsed and poorly thought-out wedding toasts have become the rule rather than the exception. Wedding planner Deborah McCoy describes some of them in her book *The World's Most Unforgettable Weddings.* They range from simply incoherent toasts by maids of honor, to raunchy and obscenity-laced stories about the bachelor party by best men.

Simply put, there is no excuse for dishonoring a bride and groom with a terrible toast. And this is especially true of a best man or maid/matron of honor. The idea is to honor the couple—not get a laugh, or worse, at their expense.

Here are some tips for making an appropriately memorable wedding toast:

1. Consult with the couple about what they expect from you.
2. Learn about who will be in attendance and take into account their diversity in age, education, and experience.
3. Talk to the wedding planner if it's an option.
4. Make it short, sweet, and memorable for the right reasons.
5. Prepare, including finding an appropriate story, anecdote, or quote that celebrates the event.
6. Rehearse.
7. Hold off on the champagne until after you've given the toast.
8. Speak clearly and loudly enough for all to hear.
9. Face the bride and groom, but don't turn your back on guests.
10. Ask the guests to join "with you" in your toast.

Source: J. Freedom du Lac, "Burnt Toasts: Bad Taste Seems to Be Rigueur at Many Weddings," *Sacramento Bee,* June 17, 2003, E1–2.

One of the most common speeches we will give is the wedding toast.

Rituals and Special Occasions

No matter how much the world changes and the tools with which we communicate evolve, certain rituals and customs regarding speaking public are not about to suddenly disappear from the rhetorical landscape. With the possible of exception of a speech in which you are *expected* to entertain an audience, there are rituals and special occasions for public speaking you cannot altogether dodge. They range from the deceptively simple and short art of proposing an apropos toast to the much more challenging task of eulogizing someone whose life made yours more meaningful. With respect to the former, we offer some helpful tips in the box "Speaking of . . . The Wedding Toast."

As we have repeatedly emphasized throughout this book, the chances of any speech succeeding begins with an analysis of the rhetorical situation. This is doubly so, however, in the case of rituals and special occasions, whether your purpose is to honor newlyweds with a toast, introduce a guest speaker or honoree, graciously accept an award, or thank a group of people who have gathered to honor your own achievements. Consider the seemingly simple task of a short speech in which you have been asked to introduce a featured guest at work, a service club such as the Rotary, or a representative from the national college fraternity or sorority with which you are affiliated.

Speech of Introduction

speech of introduction
A speech that briefly sets the stage for an upcoming speaker.

A **speech of introduction** should briefly set the stage for an upcoming speaker or a featured guest. Typically you and the audience know the purpose of the occasion. Where people drop the ball in such situations involves their commitment to learn enough in advance about the background of the speaker or guest to make a proper introduction. Speeches of introduction are designed to meet two objectives. The first is to enlist the audience's attention and interest, and the second is to reinforce or induce the audience's perceptions of the speaker or guest's credibility. You cannot achieve either of these without knowing something about the person's biography. As a result, it is common for this person or the one who extended the invitation to provide you in advance with background information, such as a brief biographical sketch. Such sketches provide highlights about the person you can then use to enlist your audience's interest and establish the speaker or guest's credentials.

Time and again, we've seen this information ignored by otherwise competent and responsible people tasked with an introduction. In more than a few cases, in fact, the speaker admits a lack of preparation, telling the audience he or she didn't get a chance to become familiar with the biography of the person about to be introduced. So the speaker ends up fumbling through the introduction by reading the biographical sketch for the first time. This is, quite simply, inexcusable. What's more, it embarrasses all parties involved, beginning with the introducer. The key, then, is preparation and practice when tasked with a speech of introduction. Begin by familiarizing yourself with the person's biographical sketch well in advance of the event. If you haven't been provided with one, make a point of getting one. Learn the highlights of the sketch well enough it deliver the introduction extemporaneously–and deliver it like you mean it!

Tips and Tactics

Guidelines for a Speech of Introduction

- *Be brief.* The audience came to hear the speaker, not the introducer. A one- or two-minute introduction is sufficient for most speech situations. For a particularly lengthy or formal speech situation, the introduction might be longer, but in no case should it exceed about 10 percent of the speaker's time (six minutes out of an hour, for example).
- *Don't steal the speaker's thunder.* Although you want to prepare the audience for what is to come by focusing their attention on the topic, you should not discuss the substance of the speech topic. Again, the audience wants to hear the speaker's views on the topic, not yours. Your job is to create an appetite for the upcoming main course, not fill up the audience with hors d'oeuvres.

- *Be prepared: Work with the speaker in advance.* It is best to talk to the speaker or a representative about your role as introducer. Are there specific points to be stressed? Is there anything the speaker wants to avoid? Some speakers may even want to preview your introductory remarks or may provide written suggestions for you.

Speech of Recognition

The elements of a good speech of introduction also apply to speeches of recognition. A **speech of recognition** presents an award honoring an individual. Although audience members frequently know something about the person being recognized, this isn't always the case. Thus, you may need to connect the narrative of the honoree's life, including the purpose for the award, to the lives of audience members. To do so, you must make sure that you are not only well acquainted with the honoree, but also sufficiently knowledgeable about the audience's composition that you can predict how this mutual familiarity can best be communicated to connect the two.

speech of recognition A speech presenting an award honoring an individual.

Speech of Acceptance

There are rituals and occasions where we are the object of attention and must find a way to respond that is both gracious and appropriate to the situation. According to most of the sports writers and broadcasters who listened to Michael Jordan's acceptance speech at his induction to the National Basketball Association Hall of Fame, the game's greatest player fell short on both counts. As one writer put it, "This wasn't a Hall of Fame induction speech, but a bully tripping nerds with lunch trays in the school cafeteria. He had a responsibility to his standing in history, to players past and present, and he let everyone down."[2]

A **speech of acceptance** expresses thanks to the people responsible for presenting it, as well as those who helped the honoree achieve the very thing that led to the award–for example, friends and family or coworkers and teammates. In many cultures, calling attention to ourselves is considered to be in bad taste, even though the research on nonverbal communication suggests that spontaneous expressions of pride may not be conscious. Many of us have been taught this norm. Even so, there are times in our lives when we cannot help being the center of attention. One of them is when we are singled out publicly for some recognition or award. For some, this becomes a dilemma. On one hand, they know they need to accept the recognition or award in a fashion that recognizes and pays tribute to those responsible. On the other hand, they don't want to appear as if they expected the recognition or award and prepared their remarks well in advance of the event. All too often, therefore, they do not prepare or rehearse their response and end up appearing humble but tongue-tied. Most audiences would prefer to hear someone accept recognition in a fashion that is both gracious and articulate, even if it was obviously prepared in advance. Being well spoken does not mean that we are self-absorbed or glib.

speech of acceptance A speech expressing thanks for an award or honor.

A good speech of acceptance should serve four functions. First, it should be either brief or within the time constraints imposed by the situation, as when you are one of several people being recognized. Second, it should be genuine and heartfelt. Audience members can typically tell by the speaker's nonverbal behavior whether expressions of gratitude are sincere. Third, it should reciprocate the recognition by praising the people or group who have singled you out. Fourth, it should engender liking. People like people who like them. It's well worth the effort to make audience members feel liked and attractive.

Rather than rehash everything we've said about the characteristics of an effective speech, simply review and put to good use what you've already learned about the speech transaction: Open with impact, connect the occasion to the needs of your audience, use content that is appropriate to the occasion in your message, and close your speech so that you leave your audience with an impression that is favorable and memorable.

Speech of Commemoration

speech of commemoration
A speech that calls attention to the stature of the person or people being honored, or emphasizes the significance of an occasion.

eulogy
A kind of commemorative speech about someone who has died that is usually given shortly after his or her death.

A **speech of commemoration** is slightly different from one of recognition. Very often it centers on an event of cultural significance, such as a turning point in the nation's history or an episode of collective sacrifice. Famous examples well worth revisiting online include the written accounts of Lincoln's Gettysburg Address and video of Ronald Reagan's speech commemorating the 50th anniversary of D-Day, the day when U.S. soldiers stormed the beaches of Normandy to begin the liberation of France from Nazi Germany during World War II.

The fact that few of us are likely to find ourselves speaking from the same platform as Lincoln or Reagan doesn't mean that we will never find ourselves in the position of commemorating an event or a life. Adult children are expected to speak in commemoration of their parents' 50th wedding anniversary, just as parents are expected to speak in commemoration of their grown children's wedding.

The speech of commemoration that we often dread, but that in some respects is one of the most important we will ever make, is a **eulogy,** typically

Senator John McCain is joined by other former POWs as he prepares to deliver a eulogy for retired Vice Admiral William P. Lawrence, who was also a POW in Vietnam.

delivered shortly after a person's death. The eulogy is a ritual as old as recorded time itself and an important custom in most cultures. Writing and delivering a eulogy can be trying. It also can prove an uplifting and empowering narrative for the living. For example, when Earl Spencer eulogized his sister, Diana, Princess of Wales, he spoke lovingly of her as "the very essence of compassion, of duty, of style, of beauty. All over the world she was a symbol of selfless humanity, a standard-bearer for the rights of the downtrodden, a very British girl who transcended nationality, someone with a natural nobility who was classless, who proved in the last year that she needed no royal title to continue to generate her particular brand of magic."[3]

Speech to Entertain

Jon Stewart at the 2006 Academy Awards.

When the great British actor Donald Wolfit lay on his deathbed, he was reputedly told by a young actor, "Sir Donald, after a life so filled with success and fame, dying must be hard." His reply has become famous: "Dying is easy . . . Comedy is hard."[4] True or false, it's hard to argue with the admonition. It is not easy to be funny, one of the chief functions expected of a speech to entertain. Sometimes called "after dinner speaking" because it's frequently delivered following a meal, a speech to entertain is more than just a string of jokes or a comedy monologue. A **speech to entertain** makes its point through the use of humor. Because not everyone is capable of being funny, self-awareness may be the most important criterion to consider.

Before you even think about this type of speech, answer this: Do you think you're funny? Better yet: Do you have good reason to believe that people in general think you can be funny? Assuming the answer is yes to the last question, a speech to entertain needs to meet the criteria all effective speeches must meet, beginning with the fact that it should reflect the situation and the audience.

speech to entertain
A speech that makes its point through the use of humor.

Subjects

Every year the Washington Press Corps hosts a dinner for the president of the United States. Every year the organizers invite a personality to present an after dinner speech. Examples include Don Imus during the Clinton administration, Stephen Colbert during the Bush administration, and most recently Wanda Sykes, who spoke at the first event honoring president Obama.

It probably comes as no great shock to you that at each of the preceding occasions the speakers managed to offend someone in the audience. Don Imus didn't make a friend of president Clinton, because his speech contained numerous and thinly veiled references to Clinton's affair with White House intern Monica Lewinsky. Although Stephen Colbert's satire was more cerebral, his skewering of president Bush's intelligence failed to enamor him with Republicans in the audience. And Wanda Sykes's speech, which for the first time introduced racial humor, managed to upset both black and white audience members.

You need to pay attention to the topic you select for a speech intended to entertain. The topics that work best are also the ones you have a great deal of experience with, including some notion about how you can appropriately relate this experience to your audience. Keynote speakers at the National Convention of Alcoholics Anonymous, for example, can predict with some certainty that self-effacing humor about the stupid things they did while under the influence will resonate with their audience. Could the same be said, however, if they were speaking at the National Convention of Mothers Against Drunk Driving? A little common sense goes a long away in determining topics that are fair game or taboo relative to the situation and makeup of the audience.

Organization

Typically a speech to entertain needn't rigidly conform to any of the specific patterns of organization introduced in Chapter 9. If there is a preferred organizational pattern for speeches meant to entertain, it is the narrative. Storytelling, as many gifted and highly paid professional speakers demonstrate, is ideally suited to entertaining an audience. With its familiar beginning, middle, and end, both speaker and audience know which direction the speech is headed.

As we also pointed out in Chapter 14, narratives have the potential to transport audience members to the events the story describes. The reason the stories Chris Rock shares work so well is because audience members can see themselves in the scenarios he describes, whether they focus on parenting, lovers' quarrels, or the absurd events of everyday life. The same can be said of many other comedic storytellers, including Jeff Foxworthy. Foxworthy's trademark setup ("You might be a Redneck . . .") works so well because we either know someone who fits the description supplied or find elements of ourselves in it.

Sources of Humor

What we find funny may be at odds with what you find funny. Humor that is obvious to one person, moreover, may go unnoticed by another. For example, a recent study of college students who described themselves as conservatives, found that these students thought Stephen Colbert's comments were meant to be taken seriously.[5] So we are not about to tell you how to be funny in terms of the content you select or the style in which it is delivered. The following is a list of traditional sources of humor that some, but not all, people have drawn from in the attempt to entertain.[6]

- *Exaggeration.* Will Ferrell and Adam Sandler have made a living off exaggeration. In their character sketches, such as Ferrell's portrayal of stock car driver Ricky Bobby or Sandler's hockey-stick-wielding golfer Happy Gilmore, both go way over the top to make a point.
- *Incongruity.* Two objects that under normal circumstances would never be connected are incongruous. For example, pairing Jim Carey with the

normally serious Jeff Daniels in the movie *Dumb and Dumber* was, in and of itself, incongruous. The oddity of casting them together made the film funnier than it might have been had Carey been paired with another actor known for physical comedy.

- *Attacking authority.* Making fun of authority figures is a staple of humor. Matt Stone and Trey Parker have gotten rich off making parents, teachers, self-important movie stars, religion, politicians, talk show hosts, and the federal government look ridiculous. But in addition to making us laugh in this respect, their attacks on authority figures also make a point about hypocrisy. The same can be said for *Family Guy* creator Seth McFarlane, *Beavis and Butthead*'s Mike Judd, and the Godfather to all animated TV satire, *The Simpsons'* Matt Groening.
- *Sarcasm.* Used skillfully, sarcasm is another traditional source of humor (particularly when directed against sources of authority). David Spade, Dennis Leary, and Lewis Black all use sarcasm to great effect. So does Bill Maher. The downside to sarcasm is that many people just don't get it, confusing it with mean-spirited nastiness. This is especially so if audience members believe the sarcasm is unfairly directed at a person they potentially find sympathetic. Thus, it can easily backfire, in particular with less than sophisticated audiences.
- *Irony.* In Mike Judd's film *Idiocracy,* the narrative is set up with a simple premise: Smart people produce fewer children than dumb ones, both now and in the future. The irony is found in the future Judd depicts, where the dumbing-down of the population has created a trash-filled landscape and led to the election of the Ultimate Fighting champion as president of the United States.
- *Self-deprecating humor.* Few sources of humor are as safe or as appreciated by an audience as the fun we poke at ourselves. Self-deprecating humor not only negates the risk of audience alienation associated with sarcasm and attacks on authority figures, it can make the famous and highly accomplished appear downright ordinary. When actors George Clooney and Brad Pitt allow themselves to be portrayed as dorks in a Coen Brothers' film, they endear themselves to their audience. A good example of the power of self-deprecating humor was put on display by Hall of Fame quarterback Terry Bradshaw at a speech in Sacramento, California. Bradshaw was appearing at a forum for business leaders and found himself in the company of, among other luminaries, Colin Powell. Bradshaw remarked to the audience as he opened his speech, "I have no clue about why I was invited to speak here today. I made my living by putting my hands under another man's butt."[7]
- *Delivery.* Humor is driven by a combination of content and delivery. For instance, two people can tell an identical joke, and only one will lead an audience to laugh. A deadpan delivery may work for one speaker but prove disastrous for another. There is, in other words, no single style for delivering a speech intended to entertain people. If you have evidence that you can pull off what may be the most difficult of all types of speeches to deliver, the chances are your style only needs to be refined rather than made over.

Transferring Your Skill Set to Other Settings

The elevated status of public speaking in ancient civilizations has had an undeniable effect on the study of the speech transaction ever since. As a consequence, those of us who study and teach public speaking all too often confine both what we think about the subject and the examples that follow to life's largest rhetorical arenas–for instance, politics. We've tried to avoid leaving you with the impression that models of effective speaking can be found only in these largest of life's arenas. Still, we want to try one more time to show you how common and important the skill set we've focused on is in everyday rhetorical venues.

The Elevator Pitch

Much as e-mail changed both the way we communicate and the language used to construct messages, the effects of text messaging on communication and language may be even greater. While the debate on the nature of these effects is just beginning, the effect of text messaging on the pace and duration of the communication transactions between people is undeniable in at least one respect: They start and end in a hurry.

The trend for saying what you need to say in the least amount of time possible is nowhere more evident than in the elevator pitch, a form of public speaking that derives its name from the average time it takes to get on and off a mechanical elevator. In about 300 or fewer words, the ideal **elevator pitch** takes 30 seconds to provide an audience with a broad overview of a concept, product, or practice. It evolved during the dot.com frenzy as a means for angel investors and venture capitalists to hear as many proposals in the shortest time possible so that they could distill the ones they perceived as having the greatest promise. For good or bad, it has become the standard speech format in many industries, most notably information technology.

> **elevator pitch**
> A thirty-second to 3-minute speech designed to introduce and enlist interest in a concept, product, or practice.

Thankfully, the 30-second format has been modified to accommodate the fact that it is nearly impossible to do justice to a worthwhile proposal in less than a minute. Imagine, for example, the delegates assembled in Philadelphia at the Continental Congress in July 1776 telling Thomas Jefferson that he had 30 seconds to explain the Declaration of Independence, or Franklin Delano Roosevelt telling Einstein that he had 30 seconds to explain nuclear fission and its implications for the outcome of World War II.

One-, two-, and three-minute elevator pitches share elements in common, including six basic questions that they need to answer:

1. What is the concept, product, or service?
2. What is the need the concept, product, or service satisfies?
3. What is the revenue model?
4. Who are the people on the team?
5. Who are the competitors?
6. What are the differentiators that give you a competitive advantage?

The key to an effective elevator speech is to be brief, but thorough enough to ensure that the essence and significance of the concept, product, or practice gets through to the listener. Every sentence uttered must both be high in impact and connected to the self-interest of each audience member.

The goal of an elevator pitch is to enlist enough interest to get you to the next level of the process. Usually this means audience members have questions they want to ask you in the effort to better understand the concept, product, or service. As anyone who has watched an episode of *Dragon's Den* will tell you, audience members also may ask questions that challenge your assumptions about the very worth of the concept, product, or service you propose.

Controversial filmmaker Michael Moore takes audience questions.

Courtesy of The Orion

Handling the Q & A

Many speeches, not just successful elevator pitches, are followed by question-and-answer sessions. Here are some basic guidelines for handling the question-and-answer period following a speech:[8]

- *If this hasn't been prearranged, announce at the outset that you will take questions at the end of your speech.* Unless you have no choice, under no circumstances take questions during the speech, as it will cause you to lose control of the situation. When audience members know they will have the opportunity to ask questions at the end of the speech, they will be able to think about them as you speak.
- *Know far more about the substance of your speech than what you specifically share in the speech itself.* You need to know more than you cover in the speech if you are to take questions. If you expect a hostile audience, it is a good idea to anticipate their toughest questions and prepare answers in advance.
- *Restate questions if they cannot be heard by all or strike you as unclear.* If you are speaking with a microphone, someone asking a question from the audience probably cannot be heard. Restating the question not only allows everyone to hear what was asked, it also allows you time to think of an answer. If a question is wordy, hostile, or imprecise, try to rephrase it in a way that neutralizes some of the problems with the question.
- *Answer questions directly with facts to back up your answers.* This requires you to be fully prepared. However, if you don't know the answer, just say so. You can always promise to obtain the facts and get back to the questioner at a later date. It is better to admit you don't know an answer than to be proved wrong because you tried to bluff your way through an answer.
- *Depending on the circumstances, take questions from different audience members.* Don't let yourself get into a debate or an argument with one audience member. Insist that everyone who has a question gets a chance to ask it before you return to a previous questioner. Choose questioners from different parts of the room so that everyone feels he or she will get a chance.

- *Be brief.* Answer questions as succinctly as possible and move on to the next question. Overly long answers bore the audience and frustrate others who want to ask questions.
- *If appropriate and in your control, announce when you are near the end of the Q&A.* When you sense the audience growing restless, the questions have become repetitive, or you are near the end of your allotted time, simply announce that you can take only one or two more questions.
- *If given the opportunity at the end of the Q&A, restate the focus of your speech and summarize its essential points.* This is your chance to get in the last word and remind the audience of the basic theme of your speech. Depending on the situation, you may want to make yourself available for informal discussion after the speech.

Small Groups

group
Three or more individuals who are aware of each other's presence, share a purpose for the group's formation, and engage in communication transactions.

Facets of the skill set that makes one an effective public speaker can be transferred to the inevitable task-oriented groups and teams you may be a member of or lead both now and in the future. A **group** normally consists of three or more individuals who are aware of each other's presence, share a purpose for the group's formation, and engage in communication transactions.

What's good about groups also can be what is bad about them. For example, when groups are assigned a collective task, the hope is that the group will manage it more effectively than any single group member could working alone. What frequently happens in practice, however, is that individual group members

Small group meetings are common in all walks of life.

use this fact to excuse themselves from taking personal responsibility for undesirable group outcomes, such as failing to solve a problem given to the group. As you probably know from your own experience with school-related group work, one or two group members can end up carrying the entire load group members were supposed to share.

Given this caveat, the skill set needed to construct and deliver a good speech has significant carryover to the skill set group members need to solve problems, achieve goals, and share the results of their deliberations when required to do so. Examples of the most important skills in this overall set are the abilities to critically think, understand the situation as well as the constraints that characterize it, and understand the cultural, demographic, and individual differences among group members. Groups also must know how to conduct the research important to an assigned task, and be able to support the decisions made to complete the task.

Leading a Task-Oriented Group

With the exception of loosely defined social groups, leaderless groups are virtually nonexistent in business, education, and government. Leaders may be designated by a manager or they can emerge from the group. Regardless, a leader in name only is no leader at all.

Although leadership styles may vary, leaders are expected to empower group members intellectually and move them along procedurally. Meeting the first expectancy is what truly separates an effective from an ineffective leader. Roles can be assigned and responsibilities distributed to group members, but that doesn't necessarily mean that they will embrace either. To gain group members' compliance, the leader of a group must be perceived as competent and trustworthy, the operational definition of source credibility, a term discussed in Chapter 14.

It's also the leader's job to systematically move the group from point A to point B, including developing an agenda, keeping face-to-face discussions on track, asking probing questions, summarizing progress, and transitioning from one agenda to the next. The leader usually calls the next face-to-face meeting and also connects the assignments and responsibilities of group members during the interim to the agenda of the next meeting. Finally, all group members share a responsibility for avoiding the folly of groupthink.

Developing an Agenda

A group without an agenda is one that will fail, fall short, or take twice as long to meet its responsibilities. The **agenda** defines the purpose and direction the group takes for a single meeting as well as for an entire project. It may involve defining a problem, mapping out the steps necessary to solve it, and establishing the criteria that will be used in weighing possible solutions. Yet it also can be as simple as mapping out the sequence of topics that the group needs to discuss in a single meeting. Regardless of its scope, however, a sound agenda is a reflection of the critical thought that a group brings to bear on a problem, and it is every bit as important to a group's success as sound organization is to a speech's success. What's more, a sound agenda can be, and often is, based on some of the same patterns for organizing a speech we introduced in Chapter 9.

agenda
Something that defines the purpose and direction a group takes for a single meeting as well as for an entire project.

Keeping Groups on Task

What transpires when group members meet face-to-face is a direct consequence of what took place when they last met and the task-oriented work that occurred in between. When group members fail to complete their assignments or do so halfheartedly, the quality of face-to-face interaction will suffer proportionately. In the "real world," it is the leader's duty to keep group members on task between and during face-to-face meetings. Anyone who has ever wasted time being party to a group that is unprepared to work face-to-face at a scheduled meeting will thank the true leader who, rather than muddling through the allotted meeting time, brings the real issue to the surface then and there.

Probing Questions

There are many types of questions leaders can and should use to probe the intellectual contributions group members bring to the table. Four of the most important are questions asking for information, interpretation, suggestions, and procedure. A *question of information,* for example, could ask group members to report on the research they were assigned at the last meeting. *Questions of interpretation* seek clarification. They probe respondents to expand on the results of their research, including gray areas that may have been uncovered. Because a leader's influence emanates from perceptions of credibility, it's always a good idea to ask for leaders to enlist the input of the group. For example, leaders can ask for *suggestions* about where to turn next or how to fill in holes that remain in the group's investigation of the problem. Unless group members also believe that such solicitations will be taken seriously, a leader is better off not asking for the group's input. Finally, *procedural questions* can serve multiple purposes. Asking a group whether it's time to move on, for instance, is both a question and a suggestion in cases where the group has bogged down or a single group member simply refuses to let go of an issue the rest of the group has moved past.

Summarizing and Transitioning to Other Points

As we pointed out regarding your speeches, summaries and transitional devices such as signposts are highly functional. At some point it will become apparent that the group is moving in a specific direction. Although not everyone may agree on every point, as the leader you can try to summarize those points on which everyone agrees, thus defining which issues need further exploration. By the same token, as a leader you are obligated to make sure that a group has reached consensus and that all viewpoints have been sufficiently aired and debated. For example, think how differently things might have turned out had president Lyndon Johnson paid serious attention to the dissenters in his cabinet when he committed hundreds of thousands of U.S. troops to what Secretary of Defense Robert McNamara later admitted was an unwinnable war in Vietnam fought over false assumptions.[9]

Setting the Agenda for the Next Meeting

Assuming the group's task has not been completed, the next action is to agree on a time and place for the next meeting, group member tasks that need to be completed, tasks necessary to the agenda, and items for the next meeting. This should be done deliberately and without haste, even when people clearly show signs indicating they are ready to leave the meeting.

Avoiding Groupthink

Whether you lead a group or take your membership in a group seriously, we would be remiss if we didn't alert you to the fact that even the most well-intended groups are susceptible to the folly and fallout from **groupthink**.[10] In a very real sense, groupthink is the result of unsound reasoning and most often occurs in highly cohesive groups.

groupthink
A mode of thinking where highly cohesive group members become so insulated from outside criticism and so convinced of their own moral superiority, they lose their capacity to think critically.

Groupthink is characterized by eight symptoms that alone and in combination erode the ability of group members to reason critically:

1. The illusion of invulnerability.
2. Unquestioned belief in the group's moral superiority.
3. Collective rationalizations.
4. Stereotypical and condescending views of people outside the group.
5. Pressure to conform.
6. Self-censorship.
7. The illusion of consensus.
8. "Mind-guards" who protect the leader from dissenting points of view.

Examples of powerful groups exhibiting these symptoms that should have been painfully obvious are historically significant. Victims of groupthink include the closest advisors to numerous presidents, the top directors of important governmental agencies, and the chief officers of powerful international corporations. Consider the following examples of historically significant groups that fell victim to groupthink. NASA's launch of the doomed space shuttle *Challenger* occurred despite the best advice of the engineers who created the space shuttle's solid booster rockets not to launch the *Challenger*. The spectacular failure to first prevent and then contain the Deep Water Horizon oil spill was a result of a series of faulty decisions by BP and its subcontractors. Finally, consider the top advisors in the Bush administration who told the president that Iraq would be economically self-sufficient within a year after the overthrow of Saddam Hussein. These and many other examples are well-documented cases of ignoring critics and hunkering down as a group–classic symptoms of groupthink with tragic consequences.

Given just how susceptible to groupthink the movers and shakers in the world have proven to be, it's safe to assume that the groups we either lead or participate in are not immune to the phenomenon. It's in our self-interest, therefore, to look at the tips and tactics that should help us avoid groupthink.

Tips and Tactics

Guidelines for Avoiding Groupthink

- Play the role of devil's advocate and encourage others to do so.
- If you lead the group and members feel beholden to you, probe them for ideas but don't prejudice the group with your views.
- Bring in outside experts to voice opposite points of view.

- Have an outside and completely independent group work on the problem.
- Reward rather than discourage dissent.
- Don't fall prey to impulsive decisions hastily implemented.

Panel Discussions

panel discussion
An extemporaneous group discussion held for the benefit of an audience.

A **panel discussion** is an extemporaneous group discussion held for the benefit of an audience. In a panel discussion, as in a speech, it is important that the group has a clear outline of the topics to be covered, and that members are adequately prepared. The advantage of a panel discussion is that it is a blend of preparation and spontaneity. Members should feel free to comment on one another's points, ask questions, and openly discuss points throughout the presentation.

Bill Main is a Certified Speaking Professional who earns between $6,500 to $9,500 for speaking engagements. He has clients throughout the nation and is considered to be in the top 3 percent of professional speakers.
George Rogers

A panel discussion requires a leader to act as the *moderator* of the presentation. The moderator calls on members and keeps the discussion on track. Members who want to comment on another member's statement should wait to be recognized by the moderator. A panel discussion is more formal than a normal private group discussion.

Most panel discussions also provide an opportunity for audience members to ask questions. This can occur as the group moves through its outline or can be held as a *forum* period at the end of the panel presentation.

The outline for a panel discussion is similar to that of a speech; however, some modifications need to be made. Here is an example of a panel discussion outline on the topic of secondhand smoke:

I. Introduction of topic and group members.
II. Is secondhand tobacco smoke harmful?
III. What is being done to limit exposure to secondhand smoke?
IV. What is causing these efforts to fall short?
V. Recommendations for new regulations on smoking in public places.

Ideally, each member should be able to offer comments on each of these topics, rather than having one member prepared on each topic. A panel discussion should be a true discussion, not a series of individual presentations.

Public Speaking as a Career

There is one other type of true public speaking that we decided was best left to the close of this chapter and our book: the type for which you get paid. For example, if you took the time to visit the National Platform Speaker Association, you would open yourself to a world of possibility hidden from most people. Every year corporate America, as well as the hundreds of national and regional associations that represent nearly every career path conceivable, spend millions of dollars on speakers tasked with informing and entertaining employees and

IN THEIR OWN WORDS

SPEAKING TO IMPACT!

by Rick Rigsby, PhD

Dr. Rick Rigsby

Dr. Rick Rigsby is president and CEO of Rick Rigsby Communications and founder of Rick Rigsby Ministries. With over 200 engagements annually, Dr. Rigsby presents to diverse audiences ranging from Fortune 500 corporations to churches around the world. He is a featured speaker at the Promise Keepers national events and speaks at chapel services for numerous teams in the National Football League. A former award-winning communication professor at Texas A&M University, Dr. Rigsby continues to serve as chaplain for the Aggies football team. We asked him to discuss how his training and experience as a public speaker have impacted his life:

The ability to speak passionately, powerfully, and persuasively will inspire people and offer you opportunities for a lifetime. My professional success is contingent on the ability to speak with precision, power, and authority. And so is yours!

As a motivational speaker, I must be my very best every time I take the stage. I cannot afford to be average or kind of good. I must be inspiring, motivating, provocative, knowledgeable, moving, and credible. In other words, I must make an IMPACT . . . and not just an impression.

I learned the value of rhetoric at an early age, realizing that through the use of language, tone, timing, and intent, I could summon the power to make people laugh, cry, or think. Moving from the streets of the San Francisco Bay Area to the college classroom, I learned formally about the rich tradition of rhetoric. I fell in love with the process of communication and the potential to influence lives through the power of the spoken word.

My education would serve me well—first during an exhilarating career as a television news reporter in Northern California. Eventually, I would attend graduate school earning a master's degree from my alma mater, California State University, Chico, followed by time at the University of Oregon where I earned a doctorate. I spent two decades teaching college students the power of communication and how the spoken word works to establish and maintain every contour of life.

As president of my own professional speaking organization, I use every communication lesson learned to insure that I am at the top of my game. With over two hundred engagements a year, and a stable of speakers that I am responsible for training, it is critical that I model the art of effective communication. Such an accomplishment would not be possible without my teachers—from Socrates, Plato, and Aristotle in Greece to Brydon and Scott at Chico State!

During a 30-year career built on the study and practice of oratory, I know how to use words to decrease my distance from my audience—thus creating a more intimate environment more conducive to listening and learning. I know how to be rhetorically bilingual—how to speak to both the head and the heart. Most of all I know how to engage audience members—whether 50 or 5000!

The art of persuasion is a learned behavior. If you are willing to learn, prepare your presentations, and practice your craft . . . you may find yourself one day standing in front of thousands and making millions! Are you ready? Well, what are you waiting for? Continue reading and discover how you can learn to move mountains . . . by making an impact with words!!!!

association members. Some of the people paid to speak are famous, as a consequence of their role in life and achievements, but the chances are good that a majority of these speakers are people who are completely unfamiliar to you. One of them is Dr. Rick Rigsby, featured in the box "In Their Own Words: Speaking to Impact!"

A Parting Thought

Not long ago we attended an event where distinguished alumni spoke to undergraduates at a career forum. They represented a wide spectrum of positions in business, civil service, education, engineering, entertainment, and science. Although we expected the few who had graduated with degrees in communication to talk about the role of public speaking in their success, we were most gratified by the fact that so many others echoed what they had to say. They were unanimous in letting students know that whatever their plans following graduation, they shouldn't pass on the opportunity to take a class in public speaking.

These alumni reinforced something we have learned from our experience. Sooner or later, successful college graduates move beyond the narrow confines of the professional path for which they were initially trained. The salesperson becomes the sales manager; the computer engineer becomes the CEO; the TV writer becomes an officer in the writers' guild; and the ecologist becomes a lobbyist. Chief among the responsibilities that both precede and follow such turning points is skill in the art and science of public speaking–making the necessary connection between one and many.

OLC www.mhhe.com/brydon7e

To evaluate your understanding of this chapter, visit our Online Learning Center Web site for quizzes and other chapter study aids.

Summary

Rituals and special occasions give rise to different types of speeches, including:

- Speeches of introduction
- Speeches of recognition
- Speeches of acceptance
- Speeches of commemoration
- Speeches to entertain

The skill set you develop as a public speaker in its most conventional sense, easily transfers to less conventional settings and even small group communication and panel discussions.

An increasingly common but unconventional type of public speaking is called the elevator pitch, which is usually between 30 seconds to a few minutes in length and is dedicated to proposing a concept, product or service.

Successful elevator pitches as well as other types of speeches can lead to a question and answer session that requires extra preparation from a speaker.

Group leaders and members frequently rely on many of the same intellectual tools and skills as public speakers. Among the tasks of group leaders and members are:

- Developing an agenda
- Keeping the group on task
- Asking probing questions
- Setting the agenda for the next meeting
- Avoiding groupthink.

Panel discussions, which are similar to both groups and speeches, also involve elements of the speech transaction, including the need to base research on an analysis of the situation and audience, organized messages, effective delivery and sound reasoning.

Careers in public speaking can be both satisfying and lucrative.

Check Your Understanding: Exercises and Activities

1. Your best friend is getting married, and you will be asked to say a few words at the wedding. Prepare your toast. Do the same thing for a wedding anniversary, a baptism, and a bar or bat mitzvah.
2. Think of a special award for one of your classmates. Write a speech of recognition for presenting the award.
3. Track down several quotations and anecdotes that are general enough to be used as an opening or a closing for a speech of acceptance or a speech of recognition. There are numerous Web sites devoted to finding quotations. One of our favorites is www.brainyquote.com/. In addition, there are numerous print sources you can turn to. For example:

   Clifton Fadiman, ed., *The Little Brown Book of Anecdotes* (Boston: Little, Brown, 1985).

   Edmund Fuller, ed., *2,500 Anecdotes for All Occasions* (New York: Avenel Books, 1980).

   James B. Simpson, ed., *Simpson's Contemporary Quotations: The Most Notable Quotes Since 1950* (Boston: Houghton Mifflin, 1988).
4. A speech of nomination can make or break the nominee's chances for being elected to office. Speeches of nomination are more common than you may think. Social clubs such as fraternities and sororities, business and professional associations such as the Soroptomists, Rotary, or local Bar are all examples. On a separate sheet of paper, list and explain what you think are the essential characteristics of a speech of nomination. Then see if you can find a published example of a speech of nomination that conforms to your criteria. Mark the conforming examples on a copy of the speech with a highlighter and share your analysis with classmates.

Notes

1. Edmund Fuller, ed., *2,500 Anecdotes for All Occasions* (New York: Avenel Books, 1980), 135.
2. Adrian Wojnarowski, "Jordan's Night to Remember Turns Petty," *Yahoo Sports,* 12 September 2009. [Retrieved from http://sports.yahoo.com/nba/news?slug=aw-jordanhall091209&prov=yhoo&type=lgns.]

3. "I Stand Before You . . . ," *Newsweek,* 15 September 1997, 24.

4. Rabbi Yaakov Asher Sinclair, "The Last Laugh," *Ohrnet,* 2002. [Retrieved from http://ohr.edu/ohrnet/5762/shmos/teruma.pdf.]

5. Heather L. LaMarre, Kristen D. Landreville, and Michael A. Beam, "The Irony of Satire: Political Ideology and the Motivation to See What You Want to See in The Colbert Report," *International Journal of Press/Politics,* 14, no. 9 (2002): 212–31. [Retrieved from http://hij.sagepub.com/cgi/content/abstract/14/2/212.]

6. Adapted from Jack Perella and Steven R. Brydon, "Speaking to Entertain," in *Intercollegiate Forensics: A Participant's Handbook,* ed. T. C. Winebrenner, 42–46. © 1992 Northern California Forensics Association.

7. Sam Stanton, "Clinton Remains Topic A at Cal Expo Speechathon," *Sacramento Bee,* 10 October 1998, A23.

8. Some of these guidelines are based on a pamphlet by Robert Haakensan, *How to Handle the Q&A* (Philadelphia: Smith Kline & French Laboratories, Department of Public Relations, n.d.).

9. *The Fog of War,* director Errol Morris with Robert S. McNamara, Sony Pictures Classics, 2003.

10. Irving R. Janis, *Groupthink,* 2nd. ed. (Boston: Houghton-Mifflin, 1983).

10

Delivery

If you were to record one of Ellen DeGeneres's comedy routines, memorize it word for word, and stand up before your friends to recite it, would you get the same response DeGeneres does? Not very likely. And why not? Because you would not *deliver* the jokes as DeGeneres does. Of course, the jokes are basically funny. But Ellen DeGeneres brings something extra to the jokes—her manner of presentation, her vocal inflections, her perfectly timed pauses, her facial expressions, her gestures. All these are part of an expert delivery. It would take you years of practice—as it took DeGeneres—to duplicate her results.

No one expects your speech class to transform you into a multimillion-dollar talk show host. Still, this example demonstrates how important delivery can be to any public speaking situation. Even a mediocre speech will be more effective if it is presented well, whereas a wonderfully written speech can be ruined by poor delivery.

This does not mean dazzling delivery will turn a mindless string of nonsense into a triumphant oration. You cannot make a good speech without having something to say. But having something to say is not enough. You must also know *how* to say it.

nonverbal communication

Communication based on a person's use of voice and body, rather than on the use of words.

Speech delivery is a matter of *nonverbal communication.* It is based on how you use your voice and body to convey the message expressed by your words. There is a great deal of research showing that the impact of a speaker's words is powerfully influenced by his or her nonverbal communication. In this chapter, we will explain how you can use nonverbal communication to deliver your speeches effectively and to increase the impact of your verbal message.

What Is Good Delivery?

Wendell Phillips was a leader in the movement to abolish slavery in the United States during the 1800s. Some people considered him the greatest speaker of his time. The following story suggests one reason why:

> Shortly before the Civil War an Andover student, learning that Phillips was to lecture in Boston, made a 22-mile pilgrimage on foot to hear him. At first the trip seemed hardly worthwhile, for the student discovered that Phillips was not an orator in the grand manner, but spoke in an almost conversational style. He stood on the platform, one hand lightly resting on a table, talked for what seemed to be about 20 minutes, concluded, and sat down. When the student looked at his watch, he found to his astonishment that he had been listening for an hour and a half![1]

Good delivery does not call attention to itself. It conveys the speaker's ideas clearly, interestingly, and without distracting the audience. Most audiences prefer delivery that combines a certain degree of formality with the best attributes of good conversation—directness, spontaneity, animation, vocal and facial expressiveness, and a lively sense of communication.

Speech delivery is an art, not a science. What works for one speaker may fail for another. And what succeeds with today's audience may not with tomorrow's. You cannot become a skilled speaker just by following a set of rules in a textbook. In the long run, there is no substitute for experience. But take heart! A textbook *can* give you basic pointers to get you started in the right direction.

When you plan your first speech (or your second or third), you should concentrate on such basics as speaking intelligibly, avoiding distracting mannerisms, and establishing eye contact with your listeners. Once you get these elements under control and begin to feel fairly comfortable in front of an audience, you can work on polishing your delivery to enhance the impact of your ideas. Eventually, you may find yourself able to control the timing, rhythm, and momentum of a speech as skillfully as a conductor controls an orchestra.

Methods of Delivery

There are four basic methods of delivering a speech: (1) reading verbatim from a manuscript, (2) reciting a memorized text, (3) speaking impromptu, and (4) speaking extemporaneously. Let us look at each.

READING FROM A MANUSCRIPT

Certain speeches *must* be delivered word for word, according to a meticulously prepared manuscript. Examples include a Pope's religious proclamation, an engineer's report to a professional meeting, or a President's message to Congress. In such situations, absolute accuracy is essential. Every word of the speech will be analyzed by the press, by colleagues, perhaps by enemies. In the case of the President, a misstated phrase could cause an international incident.

manuscript speech

A speech that is written out word for word and read to the audience.

Although it looks easy, delivering a speech from manuscript requires great skill. Some people do it well. Their words "come alive as if coined on the spot."[2] Others ruin it every time. Instead of sounding vibrant and conversational, they come across as wooden and artificial. They falter over words, pause in the wrong places, read too quickly or too slowly, speak in a monotone, and march through the speech without even glancing at their audience. In short, they come across as *reading to* their listeners, rather than *talking with* them.

If you are in a situation where you must speak from a manuscript, practice aloud to make sure the speech sounds natural. Work on establishing eye contact with your listeners. Be certain the final manuscript is legible at a glance. Above all, reach out to your audience with the same directness and sincerity that you would if you were speaking extemporaneously.

RECITING FROM MEMORY

Among the feats of the legendary orators, none leaves us more in awe than their practice of presenting even the longest and most complex speeches entirely from memory. Nowadays it is no longer customary to memorize any but the shortest of speeches—toasts, congratulatory remarks, acceptance speeches, introductions, and the like.

If you are giving a speech of this kind and want to memorize it, by all means do so. However, be sure to memorize it so thoroughly that you will be able to concentrate on communicating with the audience, not on trying to remember the words. Speakers who gaze at the ceiling or stare out the window trying to recall what they have memorized are no better off than those who read dully from a manuscript.

SPEAKING IMPROMPTU

An impromptu speech is delivered with little or no immediate preparation. Few people choose to speak impromptu, but sometimes it cannot be avoided. In fact, many of the speeches you give in life will be impromptu. You might be called on suddenly to "say a few words" or, in the course of a class discussion, business meeting, or committee report, want to respond to a previous speaker.

impromptu speech

A speech delivered with little or no immediate preparation.

When such situations arise, don't panic. No one expects you to deliver a perfect speech on the spur of the moment. If you are in a meeting or discussion, pay close attention to what the other speakers say. Take notes of major points with which you agree or disagree. In the process, you will automatically begin to formulate what you will say when it is your turn to speak.

Whenever you are responding to a previous speaker, try to present your speech in four simple steps: First, state the point you are answering. Second, state the point you wish to make. Third, support your point with appropriate statistics, examples, or testimony. Fourth, summarize your point. This four-step method will help you organize your thoughts quickly and clearly.

If time allows, sketch a quick outline of your remarks on a piece of paper before you rise to speak. This will help you remember what you want to say and will keep you from rambling.

If the situation calls for you to speak from a lectern, walk to it calmly, take a deep breath or two (not a visible gasp), establish eye contact with your audience, and begin speaking. No matter how nervous you are inside, do your best to look calm and assured on the outside.

Once you begin speaking, maintain eye contact with the audience. Help the audience keep track of your ideas with signposts such as "My first point is . . . ; second, we can see that . . . ; in conclusion, I would like to say. . . ." By stating your points clearly and concisely, you will come across as organized and confident.

As with other kinds of public speaking, the best way to become a better impromptu speaker is to practice. You can do this on your own. Simply choose a topic on which you are already well informed, and give a one- or two-minute impromptu talk on some aspect of that topic. Any topic will do, no matter how serious or frivolous it may be. You don't even need an audience—you can speak to an empty room. Better yet, record the speech and play it back to hear how you sound. The purpose is to gain experience in pulling your ideas together quickly and stating them succinctly.

SPEAKING EXTEMPORANEOUSLY

In popular usage, "extemporaneous" means the same as "impromptu." But technically the two are different. Unlike an impromptu speech, which is delivered off-the-cuff, an extemporaneous speech is carefully prepared and practiced in advance. In presenting the speech, the extemporaneous speaker uses only a brief set of notes or a speaking outline to jog the memory (see Chapter 11). The exact wording is chosen at the moment of delivery.

extemporaneous speech

A carefully prepared and rehearsed speech that is presented from a brief set of notes.

This is not as hard as it sounds. Once you have your outline (or notes) and know what topics you are going to cover and in what order, you can begin to practice the speech. Every time you run through it, the wording will be slightly different. As you practice the speech over and over, the best way to present each part will emerge and stick in your mind.

The extemporaneous method has several advantages. It gives more precise control over thought and language than does impromptu speaking; it offers greater spontaneity and directness than does speaking from memory or from a full manuscript; and it is adaptable to a wide range of situations. It also encourages the conversational quality audiences look for in speech delivery.

conversational quality

Presenting a speech so it sounds spontaneous no matter how many times it has been rehearsed.

"Conversational quality" means that no matter how many times a speech has been rehearsed, it still *sounds* spontaneous. When you speak extemporaneously—and have prepared properly—you have full control over your ideas, yet you are not tied to a manuscript. You are free to establish strong eye contact, to gesture naturally, and to concentrate on talking *with* the audience rather than declaiming *to* them.

For an example of extemporaneous delivery, look at Video 13.1 in the online Media Library for this chapter. The student is demonstrating how to breathe when doing yoga. She clearly has rehearsed a great deal, and she

Whether talking extemporaneously or from a manuscript, a speaker needs to gesture naturally, establish eye contact with the audience, and establish a strong communicative bond with listeners.

knows what she wants to say, but she has not memorized the speech. She has a brief set of speaking notes in case she needs them, but she is not tied to the notes. Rather, she selects her words as she goes along, maintains strong eye contact with the audience, and has excellent conversational quality.

Like thousands of previous students, you can become adept at speaking extemporaneously by the end of the term. As one student commented in looking back at his class: "At the start, I never thought I'd be able to give my speeches without a ton of notes, but I'm amazed at how much progress I've made. It's one of the most valuable things I learned in the entire class."

Most experienced speakers prefer the extemporaneous method, and most teachers emphasize it. Later in this chapter (pages 251–252), we'll look at a step-by-step program for practicing your extemporaneous delivery.

connect

View an excerpt from "Yoga: Uniting Mind, Body, and Spirit" in the online Media Library for this chapter (Video 13.1).

The Speaker's Voice

What kind of voice do you have? Is it rich and resonant like Morgan Freeman's? Soft and alluring like Scarlett Johansson's? Loud and irritating like Dick Vitale's? Whatever the characteristics of your voice, you can be sure it is unique. Because no two people are exactly the same physically, no two people have identical voices.

A golden voice is certainly an asset for a public speaker, but some of the most famous speakers in history have had undistinguished voices. Abraham Lincoln had a harsh and penetrating voice; Winston Churchill suffered from a slight lisp and an awkward stammer. Like them, you can overcome natural disadvantages and use your voice to the best effect. Lincoln and Churchill learned to *control* their voices. You can do the same thing.

The aspects of voice you should work to control are volume, pitch, rate, pauses, vocal variety, pronunciation, articulation, and dialect.

VOLUME

volume

The loudness or softness of the speaker's voice.

At one time, a powerful voice was essential for an orator. Today, electronic amplification allows even a soft-spoken person to be heard in any setting. But in the classroom you will speak without a microphone. When you do, be sure to adjust your voice to the acoustics of the room, the size of the audience, and the level of background noise. If you speak too loudly, your listeners will think you boorish. If you speak too softly, they will not understand you.

Remember that your own voice always sounds louder to you than to a listener. Soon after beginning your speech, glance at the people farthest away from you. If they look puzzled, are leaning forward in their seats, or are otherwise straining to hear, you need to talk louder.

PITCH

pitch

The highness or lowness of the speaker's voice.

inflections

Changes in the pitch or tone of a speaker's voice.

monotone

A constant pitch or tone of voice.

Pitch is the highness or lowness of a speaker's voice. The faster sound waves vibrate, the higher their pitch; the slower they vibrate, the lower their pitch.

Changes in pitch are known as *inflections.* Inflection is what makes the difference between the "Aha!" triumphantly exclaimed by Sherlock Holmes upon discovering a seemingly decisive clue and the "Aha" he mutters when he learns the clue is not decisive after all. If you were to read the preceding sentence aloud, your voice would probably go up in pitch on the first "Aha" and down on the second.

In ordinary conversation, we instinctively use inflections to convey meaning and emotion. People who do not are said to speak in a *monotone,* a trait whose only known benefit is to cure insomnia in one's listeners.

Although few people speak in an absolute monotone, with no variation whatever in pitch, many fall into repetitious pitch patterns that are just as hypnotic. You can guard against this by recording your speeches as you practice them. If all your sentences end on the same inflection—either upward or downward—work on varying your pitch patterns to fit the meaning of your words.

RATE

rate

The speed at which a person speaks.

Rate refers to the speed at which a person talks. People in the United States usually speak at a rate between 120 and 150 words per minute, but there is no uniform rate for effective speechmaking. Franklin Roosevelt spoke at 110 words per minute, John Kennedy at 180. Martin Luther King opened his "I Have a Dream" speech at 92 words per minute and finished it at 145. The best rate of speech depends on several things—the vocal attributes of the speaker, the mood she or he is trying to create, the composition of the audience, and the nature of the occasion.

Two obvious faults to avoid are speaking so slowly that your listeners become bored or so quickly that they lose track of your ideas. Novice speakers are particularly prone to racing through their speeches at a frantic rate. Fortunately, this is usually an easy habit to break, as is the less common one of crawling through one's speech at a snail's pace.

The key in both cases is becoming aware of the problem and concentrating on solving it. Use a recording device to check how fast you speak. Pay special attention to rate when practicing your speech. Finally, be sure to include reminders about delivery on your speaking outline so you won't forget to make the adjustments when you give your speech in class.

PAUSES

Learning how and when to pause is a major challenge for most beginning speakers. Even a moment of silence can seem like an eternity. As you gain more poise and confidence, however, you will discover how useful the pause can be. It can signal the end of a thought unit, give an idea time to sink in, and lend dramatic impact to a statement. "The right word may be effective," said Mark Twain, "but no word was ever as effective as a rightly timed pause."

pause

A momentary break in the vocal delivery of a speech.

Developing a keen sense of timing is partly a matter of common sense, partly a matter of experience. You will not always get your pauses just right at first, but keep trying. Listen to accomplished speakers to see how they use pauses to modulate the rate and rhythm of their messages. Work on pauses when you practice your speeches.

Make sure you pause at the end of thought units and not in the middle. Otherwise, you may distract listeners from your ideas. Most important, do not fill the silence with "uh," "er," or "um." These *vocalized pauses* can create negative perceptions about a speaker's intelligence and often make a speaker appear deceptive.[3]

vocalized pause

A pause that occurs when a speaker fills the silence between words with vocalizations such as "uh," "er," and "um."

VOCAL VARIETY

Just as variety is the spice of life, so is it the spice of public speaking. A flat, listless, unchanging voice is as deadly to speechmaking as a flat, listless, unchanging routine is to daily life. When giving a speech, you should strive for vocal variety—changes in rate, pitch, and volume that will give your voice interest and expressiveness.

vocal variety

Changes in a speaker's rate, pitch, and volume that give the voice variety and expressiveness.

For an excellent example of vocal variety, look at Video 13.2 in the online Media Library for this chapter. The speaker, Sajjid Zahir Chinoy, was born and raised in Bombay, India, before coming to the United States to attend college at the University of Richmond. At the end of his senior year, Chinoy was selected as the student commencement speaker in a campus-wide competition. He spoke of the warm reception he received at Richmond and of how cultural differences can be overcome by attempting to understand other people.

The best rate of speech depends partly on the mood a speaker wants to create. To communicate the splendor of a rainbow over Victoria Falls, you would probably speak at a slower-than-normal rate.

At the end of his speech, Chinoy received thunderous applause—partly because of what he said, but also because of how he said it. Addressing the audience of 3,000 people without notes, he spoke extemporaneously with strong eye contact and excellent vocal variety. The speech was so inspiring that the main speaker, Harvard psychiatrist Robert Coles, began his presentation by paying tribute to Chinoy. "I've been to a number of commencements," said Coles, "but I've never heard a speech quite like that!"

connect

View an excerpt from "Questions of Culture" in the online Media Library for this chapter (Video 13.2).

How can you develop a lively, expressive voice? Above all, by approaching every speech as Chinoy approached his—as an opportunity to share with your listeners ideas that are important to you. Your sense of conviction and your desire to communicate will give your voice the same spark it has in spontaneous conversation.

PRONUNCIATION

We all mispronounce words now and again. Here, for example, are four words with which you are probably familiar. Say each one aloud.

pronunciation

The accepted standard of sound and rhythm for words in a given language.

genuine	arctic
err	nuclear

Very likely you made a mistake on at least one, for they are among the most frequently mispronounced words in the English language. Let's see:

Word	Common Error	Correct Pronunciation
genuine	gen-u-wine	gen-u-win
arctic	ar-tic	arc-tic
nuclear	nu-cu-lar	nu-cle-ar
err	air	ur

Every word leads a triple life: it is read, written, and spoken. Most people recognize and understand many more words in reading than they use in ordinary writing, and about three times as many as occur in spontaneous speech.[4] This is why we occasionally stumble when speaking words that are part of our reading or writing vocabularies. In other cases, we may mispronounce the most commonplace words out of habit.

The problem is that we usually don't *know* when we are mispronouncing a word. If we are lucky, we learn the right pronunciation by hearing someone else say the word properly or by having someone gently correct us in private. If we are unlucky, we mispronounce the word in front of a roomful of people, who may raise their eyebrows, groan, or laugh.

All of this argues for practicing your speech in front of as many trusted friends and relatives as you can corner. If you have any doubts about the proper pronunciation of certain words, be sure to check a dictionary.

ARTICULATION

Articulation and pronunciation are not identical. Sloppy articulation is the failure to form particular speech sounds crisply and distinctly. It is one of several causes of mispronunciation, but you can articulate a word sharply and still mispronounce it. For example, if you say the "s" in "Illinois" or the "p" in "pneumonia," you are making a mistake in pronunciation, regardless of how precisely you articulate the sounds.

Among college students, poor articulation is more common than ignorance of correct pronunciation. We know that "let me" is not "lemme," that "going to" is not "gonna," that "did you" is not "didja," yet we persist in articulating these words improperly. Here are some other common errors in articulation you should work to avoid:

articulation

The physical production of particular speech sounds.

Word	Misarticulation
ought to	otta
didn't	dint
don't know	dunno
have to	hafta
want to	wanna
will you	wilya

If you have sloppy articulation, work on identifying and eliminating your most common errors. Like other bad habits, careless articulation can be broken only by persistent effort—but the results are well worth it. As Shakespeare advised, "Mend your speech a little, lest you may mar your fortunes."

DIALECT

Most languages have dialects, each with a distinctive accent, grammar, and vocabulary. Dialects are usually based on regional or ethnic speech patterns. The United States has four major regional dialects—Eastern, New England, Southern, and General American. We also have multiple ethnic dialects. As the nation has become more diverse culturally, it has also become more diverse linguistically.[5]

dialect

A variety of a language distinguished by variations of accent, grammar, or vocabulary.

Linguists have concluded that no dialect is inherently better or worse than another. Dialects are not linguistic badges of superiority or inferiority. They are usually shaped by our regional or ethnic background, and every dialect is "right" for the community of people who use it.

When is a given dialect appropriate in public speaking? The answer depends above all on the composition of your audience. Heavy use of any dialect—regional or ethnic—can be troublesome when the audience does not share that dialect. In such a situation, the dialect may cause listeners to make negative judgments about the speaker's personality, intelligence, and competence. This is why professional speakers have been known to invest large amounts of time (and money) to master the General American dialect used by most television news broadcasters.

Does this mean you must talk like a television news broadcaster if you want to be successful in your speeches? Not at all. Regional or ethnic dialects do not pose a problem as long as the audience is familiar with them and finds them appropriate. When speaking in the North, for example, a southern politician may avoid regional dialect. But when addressing audiences in the South, the same politician may intentionally include regional dialect as a way of creating common ground with listeners.

Although not strictly speaking a matter of dialect, the proficiency of non-native speakers of English often arises in the speech classroom. Fortunately, teachers and students alike usually go out of their way to be helpful and encouraging to international students and others for whom English is not the primary language. Over the years, many non-native speakers of English have found speech class a supportive environment in which to improve their proficiency in spoken English.[6]

The Speaker's Body

Imagine yourself at a party. During the evening you form impressions about the people around you. Jonte seems relaxed and even-tempered, Nicole tense and irritable. Kyndra seems open and straightforward, Sun-Hi hostile and evasive. Amin seems happy to see you; Seth definitely is not.

How do you reach these conclusions? To a surprising extent, you reach them not on the basis of what people say with words, but because of what they say with their posture, gestures, eyes, and facial expressions. Suppose you are sitting next to Amin, and he says, "This is a great party. I'm really glad to be here with you." However, his body is turned slightly away from you, and he keeps looking at someone across the room. Despite what he says, you know he is *not* glad to be there with you.

Much the same thing happens in speechmaking. Posture, facial expression, gestures, eye contact—all affect the way listeners respond to a speaker. How we use these and other body motions to communicate is the subject of a fascinating area of study called kinesics. One of its founders, Ray Birdwhistell, estimated that more than 700,000 physical signals can be sent through bodily movement. Studies have shown that these signals have a significant impact on the meaning communicated by speakers.

kinesics

The study of body motions as a systematic mode of communication.

Research has also lent support to what the Greek historian Herodotus observed more than 2,400 years ago: "People trust their ears less than their eyes." When a speaker's body language is inconsistent with his or her words, listeners may well believe the body language rather than the words.[7] Here are the major aspects of physical action that will affect the outcome of your speeches.

PERSONAL APPEARANCE

If you were Lady Gaga, you could show up to make an MTV Music Video Award presentation speech wearing a bizarre creation that left little to the imagination. If you were Albert Einstein, you could show up to address an international science conference wearing wrinkled trousers, a sweater, and tennis shoes. While the members of your audience would certainly comment on your attire, your reputation would not be harmed. In fact, it might be enhanced. You would be one of the few, the very few, who live outside the rules, who are expected to be unusual.

Now imagine what would happen if the president of a corporation showed up to address a stockholders' meeting attired like Lady Gaga, or if the President of the United States spoke on national television wearing wrinkled clothes and tennis shoes. Both presidents would soon be looking for work. Barring the occasional eccentric, every speaker is expected by her

Good speakers use a lively voice to bring their ideas to life. They also use gestures, eye contact, and facial expressions to create a bond with their audience.

or his audience to exhibit a personal appearance in keeping with the occasion of the speech.

Many studies have confirmed that personal appearance plays an important role in speechmaking.[8] Listeners always see you before they hear you. Just as you adapt your language to the audience and the occasion, so should you dress and groom appropriately. Although the force of your speech can sometimes overcome a poor impression created by personal appearance, the odds are against it. Regardless of the speaking situation, you should try to evoke a favorable first impression.

MOVEMENT

Novice speakers are often unsure about what to do with their body while giving a speech. Some pace back and forth across the podium, shift their weight from one foot to the other, fidget with their notes, or jingle coins in their pockets. Still others turn into statues, standing rigid and expressionless from beginning to end.

Such quirks usually stem from nervousness. If you are prone to distracting mannerisms, your teacher will identify them so you can work on controlling them. With a little concentration, these mannerisms should disappear as you become more comfortable speaking in front of an audience.

As important as how you act during the speech is what you do just *before* you begin and *after* you finish. As you rise to speak, try to appear calm, poised, and confident, despite the butterflies in your stomach. When you reach the lectern, don't lean on it, and don't rush into your speech. Give yourself time to get set. Arrange your notes just the way you want them. Stand quietly as you wait to make sure the audience is paying attention. Establish eye contact with your listeners. Then—and only then—should you start to talk.

When you reach the end of your speech, maintain eye contact for a few moments after you stop talking. This will give your closing line time to sink in. Unless you are staying at the lectern to answer questions, collect your notes and return to your seat. As you do so, maintain your cool, collected demeanor. Whatever you do, don't start to gather your notes before you have finished talking, and don't cap off your speech with a huge sigh of relief or some remark like, "Whew! Am I glad that's over!"

When practicing your speeches, spend a little time rehearsing how you will behave at the beginning and at the end. It is one of the easiest—and one of the most effective—things you can do to improve your image with an audience.

GESTURES

gestures

Motions of a speaker's hands or arms during a speech.

Few aspects of delivery cause students more anguish than deciding what to do with their hands. "Should I clasp them behind my back? Let them hang at my sides? Rest them on the lectern? And what about gesturing? When should I do that—and how?" Even people who use their hands expressively in everyday conversation seem to regard them as awkward appendages when speaking before an audience.

Over the years, more nonsense has been written about gesturing than any other aspect of speech delivery. Adroit gestures *can* add to the impact of a speech; but effective speakers do not need a vast repertoire of gestures. Some accomplished speakers gesture frequently, others hardly at all. The primary rule is this: Whatever gestures you make should not distract from your message. They should *appear* natural and spontaneous, help clarify or reinforce your ideas, and be suited to the audience and occasion. For a good example, look at Video 13.3 in the online Media Library for this chapter.

connect

View an excerpt from "Third-Culture Kid" in the online Media Library for this chapter (Video 13.3).

Gesturing tends to work itself out as you acquire experience and confidence. For now, make sure your hands do not upstage your ideas. Avoid flailing them about, wringing them together, or toying with your rings. Once you have eliminated these distractions, forget about your hands. Think about communicating with your listeners, and your gestures will take care of themselves—just as they do in conversation.

EYE CONTACT

The eyes have been called "the windows of the soul." We look to them to help gauge a speaker's truthfulness, intelligence, attitudes, and feelings.

eye contact

Direct visual contact with the eyes of another person.

Although patterns of eye contact in everyday conversation vary from culture to culture, there is wide agreement across cultures on the importance of eye contact in public speaking. In most circumstances, one of the quickest ways to establish a communicative bond with your listeners is to look at them personally and pleasantly. Avoiding their gaze is one of the surest ways to lose them.

Speakers in the United States who fail to establish eye contact are perceived as tentative or ill at ease and may be seen as insincere or dishonest. It is no wonder, then, that teachers urge students to look at the audience 80 to 90 percent of the time they are talking. You may find this disconcerting at first. But after one or two speeches, you should be able to meet the gaze of your audience fairly comfortably.

It isn't enough just to look at your listeners; *how* you look at them also counts. Beware of the tendency to gaze intently at one part of the audience while ignoring the rest. In speech class, some students look only at the section of the room where the teacher is sitting. Others avoid looking anywhere near the teacher and focus on one or two sympathetic friends. You should try to establish eye contact with your whole audience.

When addressing a small audience such as your class, you can usually look briefly from one person to another. For a larger group, you can scan the

Research shows that eye contact is one of the most important elements in speech delivery. No matter what the situation, you want your eyes to convey confidence, sincerity, and conviction.

audience rather than try to engage the eyes of each person individually. No matter what the size of your audience, you want your eyes to convey confidence, sincerity, and conviction.

Look at Video 13.4 in the online Media Library for this chapter to see a fine example of eye contact. The speaker is telling her classmates how they can become volunteers for the Special Olympics. Notice how she uses her eyes to connect with her listeners at a personal level. This is the kind of strong communication you should strive for in your speeches.[9]

connect

View an excerpt from "Making a Difference Through the Special Olympics" in the online Media Library for this chapter (Video 13.4).

Practicing Delivery

Popular wisdom promises that practice makes perfect. This is true, but only if we practice properly. You will do little to improve your speech delivery unless you practice the right things in the right ways. Here is a five-step method that has worked well for many students:

1. Go through your preparation outline *aloud* to check how what you have written translates into spoken discourse. Is it too long? Too short? Are the main points clear when you speak them? Are the supporting materials distinct, convincing, interesting? Do the introduction and conclusion come across well? As you answer these questions, revise the speech as needed.
2. Prepare your speaking outline. In doing so, be sure to follow the guidelines in Chapter 11. Use the same visual framework as in the preparation outline. Make sure the speaking outline is easy to read at a glance. Give yourself cues on the outline for delivering the speech.

3. Practice the speech aloud several times using only the speaking outline. Be sure to "talk through" all examples and to recite in full all quotations and statistics. If your speech includes visual aids, use them as you practice. The first couple of times, you will probably forget something or make a mistake, but don't worry. Keep going and complete the speech as well as you can. Concentrate on gaining control of the *ideas;* don't try to learn the speech word for word. After a few tries you should be able to get through the speech extemporaneously with surprising ease.
4. Now begin to polish and refine your delivery. Practice the speech in front of a mirror to check for eye contact and distracting mannerisms. Record the speech to gauge volume, pitch, rate, pauses, and vocal variety. Most important, try it out on friends, roommates, family members—anyone who will listen and give you an honest appraisal. Because your speech is designed for people rather than for mirrors or recorders, you need to find out ahead of time how it goes over with people.
5. Finally, give your speech a dress rehearsal under conditions as close as possible to those you will face in class. Some students like to try the speech a couple times in an empty classroom the day before the speech is due. No matter where you hold your last practice session, you should leave it feeling confident and looking forward to speaking in your class.

If this or any practice method is to work, you must start early. Don't wait until the night before your speech to begin working on delivery. A single practice session—no matter how long—is rarely enough. Allow yourself *at least* a couple of days, preferably more, to gain command of the speech and its presentation.

Answering Audience Questions

If you have ever watched a press conference or heard a speaker answer questions after a talk, you know the question-and-answer session can make or break a presentation. A speaker who handles questions well can strengthen the impact of his or her speech. On the other hand, a speaker who evades questions or shows annoyance will almost certainly create the opposite effect.

The question-and-answer session is a common part of public speaking, whether the occasion is a press conference, business presentation, public hearing, or classroom assignment. An answer to a question is often the final word an audience hears and is likely to leave a lasting impression.

PREPARING FOR THE QUESTION-AND-ANSWER SESSION

The first step to doing well in a Q&A session is to take it as seriously as the speech itself. The two major steps in preparing are working out answers to possible questions and practicing the delivery of those answers.

Formulate Answers to Possible Questions

Once you know that your presentation will include questions from the audience, you should be thinking about possible questions even as you are writing your speech. If you practice your speech in front of friends, family, or coworkers, ask them to jot down questions. Keep track of all the questions and formulate answers. Write your answers in full to make sure you have thought them through completely.

If you are giving a persuasive speech, be sure to work out answers to objections the audience may have to your proposal. No matter how careful you are to deal with those objections in your speech, you can be sure they will come up in the Q&A session.

If you are speaking on a topic with technical aspects, be ready to answer specialized inquiries about them, as well as questions that seek clarification, in nontechnical terms. You might even prepare a handout that you can distribute afterward for people who want more information.

Practice the Delivery of Your Answers

You would not present a speech to a room full of people without rehearsing. Neither should you go into a Q&A session without practicing the delivery of your answers.

One possibility is to have a friend or colleague listen to your presentation, ask questions, and critique your answers. This method is used by political candidates and business leaders before debates or press conferences. Another possibility is to record your answers to anticipated questions, play them back, and revise them until they are just right.

As you rehearse, work on making your answers brief and to the point. Many simple questions can be answered in 30 seconds, and even complex ones should usually be answered in a minute or two. If you practice answering questions beforehand, you will find it much easier to keep to these time limits.

Of course, there is no way to predict every question you will receive. But if you go into the Q&A period fully prepared, you will be able to adapt to whatever occurs.

MANAGING THE QUESTION-AND-ANSWER SESSION

If you have ever watched a skillful speaker field inquiries from the audience, you know there is an art to managing a question-and-answer session. Entire books have been written on this subject, but the following suggestions will help get you started on the right foot.

Using public speaking in your CAREER

Utilizing your business degree and computer savvy, you have made a success of the online marketing company you started after graduating from college. Now in its third year, the company has prepared a proposal to design the e-commerce site for a major sporting goods retailer. In your 30-minute presentation to the retailer's management team, you will review the homepage designs, site maps, and security protocols.

You notice on the agenda that another 30 minutes has been allotted after your presentation for questions and answers. Knowing from your previous experience with clients how important the Q&A session can be, you want to be sure you are ready for it. What steps will you take to prepare?

Approach Questions with a Positive Attitude

A positive attitude will help you answer questions graciously and respectfully. Try to view questions from the audience as signs of genuine interest and a desire to learn more about your subject. If someone asks about a point that seems clear to you, don't respond by saying, "I discussed that at the beginning of my talk," or "The answer seems obvious." Instead, use moments like these to reiterate or expand upon your ideas.

A speaker who adopts a sharp or defensive tone while answering questions will alienate many people in the audience. Even if you are asked a hostile question, keep your cool. Avoid the temptation to answer defensively, sarcastically, or argumentatively. Most people in the audience will respect you for trying to avoid a quarrel.

Listen Carefully

It's hard to answer a question well if you don't listen carefully to it. Give the questioner your full attention. When faced with an unclear or unwieldy question, try to rephrase it by saying something like, "If I understand your question, it seems to me that you are asking. . . ." Another option is simply to ask the audience member to repeat the question. Most people will restate it more succinctly and clearly.

Direct Answers to the Entire Audience

When you are being asked a question, look at the questioner. Direct your answer, however, to the entire audience. Make occasional eye contact with the questioner as you answer, but speak primarily to the audience as a whole. If you speak just to the questioner, the rest of your audience may drift off.

When speaking to a large audience, repeat or paraphrase each question after it is asked. This involves the entire audience and ensures that they know the question. In addition, repeating or paraphrasing the question gives you a moment to frame an answer before you respond.

Be Honest and Straightforward

If you don't know the answer to a question, say so. Don't apologize, don't evade, and most important, don't try to bluff. Do, however, let the questioner know that you take the question seriously. Offer to check into the answer as soon as possible after the speech. If a more knowledgeable person is at hand, ask if she or he knows the answer.

Stay on Track

It's easy to get diverted or lose control of time in a lively Q&A session. Unless there is a moderator, the speaker is responsible for keeping things on track. Allow one follow-up question from each person, and don't let yourself be dragged into a personal debate with any questioner. If someone attempts to ask more than two questions, respond graciously yet firmly by saying, "This is an interesting line of questioning, but we need to give other people a chance to ask questions."

Sometimes, a listener will launch into an extended monologue instead of posing a question. When this happens, you can retain control of the situation by saying something like, "Those are very interesting ideas, but do you have a specific question I can answer?" If the person persists, offer to talk individually with him or her after the session.

Question-and-answer sessions are an important part of public speaking around the globe. Here Spanish delegates talk with reporters in Dublin, Ireland, about the 2014 European Parliament elections.

On some occasions, the length of the question-and-answer session is predetermined. On other occasions, it's up to the speaker. Make sure you allow enough time to get through issues of major importance, but don't let things drag on after the momentum of the session has started winding down. As the end approaches, offer to respond to another question or two. Then wrap things up by thanking the audience for its time and attention.[10]

Presenting Your Speech Online

The head of a small tech start-up, Matthew Rhee was excited about his presentation later that morning. He was going to speak to librarians around the state about new online catalogue software he was developing. The software promised to simplify the process of searching, finding, and even previewing library books from computers and mobile devices.

Matthew was particularly excited because he could talk without leaving his apartment. His potential clients would log in to a virtual meeting room, and he would speak from his computer to people in a half-dozen cities. Having made a couple of successful speeches to in-person audiences, he was confident about the outcome. He ran through his planned remarks a couple of times, but he didn't make any special adjustments for the online speaking situation.

Unfortunately, things did not go as smoothly as Matthew had expected. Because his computer was facing a window behind him, the audience had a hard time seeing his face. But they could see the clutter on his desk and the plain white t-shirt he was wearing—neither of which did much for his credibility. Nor did he help himself by slouching in his chair and drinking coffee as he spoke. By the end of the presentation, many of Matthew's listeners had either zoned out or had started checking their email.

online speech

A speech that has been created specifically for an audience that will view it online and in real time.

Like Matthew, many people underestimate the difficulty of presenting a speech online. An online speech is not simply a speech to an in-person audience that has been uploaded on YouTube or a campus server. An online speech, as defined here, is one that has been created specifically for an audience that will view it online and in real time, often using software designed for that purpose. Such a speech requires all the skills of speech preparation and delivery discussed throughout this book, but it also poses special challenges unique to the online environment.

Whether or not you give an online presentation in your speech class, there is a good chance that, like Matthew, you will one day find yourself speaking via the Internet to an audience that is spread across multiple locations. You may need to give a brief speech of self-introduction during an online job interview. You may be required, as part of your job, to present an online training session or to speak with potential clients about a service or a product. You may address a meeting of the school board or the city zoning commission from a remote location.

Some 12 million Web meetings take place in the United States every day, plus millions more around the world. As with other aspects of public speaking, there is no substitute for experience when it comes to giving speeches online. The following eight points, however, will help you get started in the right direction.

UNDERSTAND THE SPECIAL NATURE OF THE ONLINE ENVIRONMENT

When you deliver a traditional in-person speech, you're in the same room as your audience. You can see how many people are present. You can look them in the eye to keep them engaged. You have multiple forms of feedback to assess how fully they are paying attention and how well they are grasping your message.

In the online environment, you have a fundamentally different relationship with your audience. Because you are not in the same room with them, gauging their response can be difficult. Even if your software allows you to see the audience, you can't make direct eye contact with them. You might not know if they begin staring out the window, checking Facebook, or reading the news online.

The first step to a successful online speech is realizing that the online environment will transform almost every aspect of your presentation—including technology, the visual environment, nonverbal communication, pacing, Q&A, rehearsal, and adapting to unforeseen contingencies. We'll look at each of these in turn.

KNOW YOUR TECHNOLOGY

There are a number of software programs designed for online presentations—WebEx, GoToMeeting, Adobe Connect, Google Hangouts, and Cisco TelePresence, to name a few of the most popular. Beyond the basic function of allowing you to speak to people in remote locations, these programs have different features that may be more or less applicable to your presentation. Some programs allow you to combine audio and video with visual aids. Some allow you to see, hear, and chat with your audience. Some let you share documents and collaborate in real time. As a speaker,

Whether presenting online or to an in-person audience, you should rehearse under conditions as close as possible as to those you will face during the speech. Thorough preparation will increase your skill and confidence.

it is imperative that you know the capabilities and limitations of the software you'll be using.

Because some software programs are quite complex, you may be able to find someone who can help manage the technological side of your presentation. This is not always possible, but many businesses, universities, and nonprofit organizations have an IT person who is prepared to assist. This person may also have special equipment that will improve the video and audio quality of your speech.

CONTROL THE VISUAL ENVIRONMENT

The Internet is often informal. We Skype with family members, post photos of our social lives to Instagram, and watch cat videos on YouTube. Your online speech, however, should *not* be informal. It should be as polished and professional as an in-person speech. This requires, among other things, controlling the visual environment so it works *for* you rather than against you.

Pay attention to lighting. You don't want the room to seem too dark; neither do you want so much light that it washes you out. You can usually gauge what the audience will see on their screens through the video preview window—sometimes called "participant view"—that is included in most software programs.

When previewing yourself, check your distance from the webcam. If you sit too far away, you'll seem small and removed from your listeners. If you sit too close, you'll look like a selfie. If you aim the camera too low, you'll have a disproportionate amount of blank space above your head. A good rule of thumb is to sit two to three feet from the webcam so you fill most of the frame and the audience can see you from the chest up (look at Figure 13.1 on the next page).[11]

FIGURE 13.1

Another way to control the visual environment is to clean up what's around you. Get rid of clutter—cups, dishes, pens, paper, erasers, staplers—anything that can distract the audience's attention.

Finally, controlling the visual environment means taking your personal appearance seriously. Dress for your online speech as if you were delivering an in-person speech. The more professional you look on screen, the more professional you will feel when presenting—and the more professional you will appear to your audience.

ADAPT YOUR NONVERBAL COMMUNICATION

Your nonverbal communication is magnified dramatically when you speak via a camera of any kind. Gestures, facial expressions, eye movements—all become more noticeable, and potentially distracting.

This is something newscasters have long known. Their on-camera tricks can be useful for your online presentation. Because much of your speech will involve sitting in front of the webcam, your posture will need to be straight, but not rigid. The goal is to appear professional, relaxed, and confident.

Well-planned and deliberate hand gestures are also important. If your hands are too close to the camera, they'll draw attention to themselves. Too many hand movements can make you seem nervous and fidgety. Concentrate on using gestures that are natural but controlled. As one expert in online presentations explains, "The more defined your hands appear, the more defined your message will appear to your audience."[12]

Also be mindful of your eyes. As experienced online presenters know, the camera will heighten every eye movement. Avoid looking up or down, and make sure your eyes do not dart back and forth. Learning to speak to a camera is an acquired skill. Look into the camera as naturally as you can and imagine yourself establishing eye contact with an audience right in front of you. This will help your eye movements seem deliberate, controlled, and confident.

ADJUST YOUR PACING FOR THE ONLINE ENVIRONMENT

As speech consultant Cynthia Clay explains, online audiences have more ways to tune out than do in-person listeners, and the temptation to multitask is often irresistible.[13] Phones, coworkers, what's happening outside the window—all will be competing with you for attention. The pacing of your speech can help keep the audience focused on you instead of on the temptations around them.

One way to adjust the pacing of your speech for the online environment is to alter what appears on the audience's screen. Your listeners aren't likely to pay attention for long if they see only your talking head for 10 minutes. Try to incorporate visual aids into your presentation (see Chapter 14 for a full discussion of visual aids). Altering what's on screen can help keep your speech fresh and engaging.

Effective pacing also requires that you pay close attention to time constraints. Ask the person who invites you to speak how long your presentation should be. Make sure you meet or beat that length.

Regardless of the length of your speech, try to keep it moving at a brisk pace. People are accustomed to a crisp tempo when watching videos of almost any kind. Make sure you explain your ideas fully enough that the audience understands your message, but doesn't get bogged down in digressions or unnecessary details.

MANAGE Q&A FOR THE ONLINE ENVIRONMENT

Earlier in this chapter, we looked at how to handle question-and-answer sessions in traditional speech settings. Everything discussed there remains true in the online environment. But there is one additional factor you will need to consider—whether to invite questions as the speech proceeds or to keep them for the end.

Some experienced speakers like to encourage questions during the presentation because it can help keep the audience involved. The downside of this approach is that it can easily throw the speech off track. One audience member might have a laundry list of questions that will consume your time and encourage other listeners to direct their attention elsewhere.

For first-time online speakers, the best bet is usually to save Q&A for the end of the speech. This will allow you to communicate your message in an orderly fashion *and* to answer whatever questions your listeners may have.

REHEARSE FOR THE ONLINE ENVIRONMENT

Many people assume that an online speech requires less rehearsal than an in-person speech. In fact, it usually requires more.

There are two general stages to rehearsing an online speech. First, as with an in-person speech, you should try to practice in front of family, friends, or coworkers. They can give you feedback on such things as the structure of your speech, the clarity of your ideas, the tone of your voice, the pacing of your remarks, and so forth. Once you have these matters under control, you are ready to move to the second stage of rehearsal.

In this stage, you need to focus specifically on adapting your delivery for the online environment. Practice with the computer and software you will use on the day of your speech. Make sure you know all the computer commands and can execute them flawlessly. Practice with your visual aids so you

checklist

Presenting an Online Speech

YES	NO	
☐	☐	1. Have I considered the special nature of the online speech environment?
☐	☐	2. Do I understand the capabilities and limitations of my presentation software?
☐	☐	3. Do I control the visual environment of my presentation so it will work to my advantage?
☐	☐	4. Have I adapted my nonverbal communication so it will be effective when viewed online?
☐	☐	5. Will the pacing of my speech keep the audience focused on my message?
☐	☐	6. Have I considered how best to handle questions and answers?
☐	☐	7. Have I taken all the steps necessary to rehearse my speech for online presentation?
☐	☐	8. Do I have a backup plan in case I run into technical problems?

can integrate them seamlessly into your speech. Do everything you can to control the technical side of your presentation.

Because your audience will view the speech on either a computer screen or a projection screen, it is imperative that you rehearse with this in mind. Once you have mastered the technology and practiced in front of a live audience, deliver the speech into your webcam, record it, and play it back. Some online presentation software has a recording function built into the program.

Watching the video of your speech will help you frame the shot, hear your voice, gauge your eye contact, check your gestures, and see yourself through your audience's eyes. Make the necessary adjustments and record the speech again until you're happy with the final result.

HAVE A BACKUP PLAN

Have you ever run into problems logging on to a Web site? Encountered server errors? Waited impatiently for a video to buffer? All these things—and others—can play havoc with an online presentation. No matter how much time speakers invest in mastering the technology at their end, they can still be undermined by technological glitches at the audience's end.

This is why experts recommend that you *always* have a backup plan in case the technology fails. That plan might be to distribute an outline of your speech via email. It might be to move the speech to an audio-only conference call. It might even be to reschedule the speech once the technical problems are resolved. Because we have all been sabotaged by technology at one time or another, audiences usually have sympathy for a speaker who encounters such problems. Having a backup plan will make you look conscientious and considerate.

Summary

Speech delivery is a matter of nonverbal communication. It is based on how you use your voice and body to convey the message expressed by your words. Rather than calling attention to itself, effective delivery conveys the speaker's ideas clearly, engagingly, and without distracting the audience.

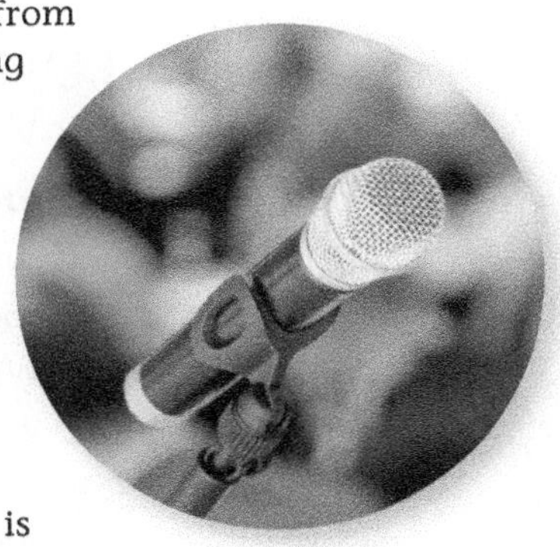

There are four basic methods of delivering a speech: reading verbatim from a manuscript, reciting a memorized text, speaking impromptu, and speaking extemporaneously. When speaking extemporaneously, you will have a brief set of notes or a speaking outline and will choose the exact wording of your speech at the moment of delivery.

To use your voice effectively you should work on controlling your volume, pitch, rate, pauses, vocal variety, pronunciation, articulation, and dialect. Volume is the relative loudness of your voice, and pitch is the relative highness or lowness. Rate refers to the speed at which you talk. Pauses, when carefully timed, can add punch to your speech, but you should avoid vocalized pauses ("er," "um," and the like).

Vocal variety refers to changes in volume, pitch, rate, and pauses, and is crucial to making your voice lively and animated. You also need correct pronunciation and distinct articulation. Avoid heavy use of dialect in situations where the audience does not share the dialect or will find it inappropriate.

Posture, personal appearance, facial expression, gestures, and eye contact also affect the way listeners respond to speakers. Dress and groom appropriately, use gestures and bodily movement to enhance your message, and make eye contact with your listeners.

You should practice all these aspects of delivery along with the words of your speech. Start your practice sessions early so you will have plenty of time to gain command of the speech and its presentation.

If your speech includes a question-and-answer session, anticipate the most likely questions, prepare answers to them, and practice delivering those answers. During the Q&A period, listen carefully to the questions, approach them positively, and respond to them briefly, graciously, and straightforwardly. Direct your answers to the full audience, rather than to the questioner alone, and make sure to end the session in a timely fashion.

If you are delivering a speech online, you will have to take a number of special steps. They include understanding the nature of the online environment, knowing the capabilities and limitations of your presentation software, controlling the visual environment, and adapting your pacing and nonverbal communication. You will also need to rehearse specifically for online presentation, decide how to handle Q&A, and develop a backup plan in case the technology fails you.

Key Terms

nonverbal communication (240)
manuscript speech (241)
impromptu speech (241)
extemporaneous speech (242)
conversational quality (242)
volume (244)
pitch (244)
inflections (244)
monotone (244)
rate (244)
pause (245)
vocalized pause (245)
vocal variety (245)
pronunciation (246)
articulation (247)
dialect (247)
kinesics (248)
gestures (250)
eye contact (250)
online speech (256)

Review Questions

After reading this chapter, you should be able to answer the following questions:

1. What is nonverbal communication? Why is it important to effective public speaking?
2. What are the elements of good speech delivery?
3. What are the four methods of speech delivery?
4. What are the eight aspects of voice usage you should concentrate on in your speeches?
5. What are four aspects of bodily action you should concentrate on in your speeches?
6. What are the five steps you should follow when practicing your speech delivery?
7. What steps should you take when preparing for a question-and-answer session? What should you concentrate on when responding to questions during the session?
8. What eight steps should you take if you are faced with presenting an online speech?

connect

For further review, go to the LearnSmart study module for this chapter.

Exercises for Critical Thinking

1. An excellent way to improve your vocal variety is to read aloud selections from poetry that require emphasis and feeling. Choose one of your favorite poems that falls into this category, or find one by leafing through a poetry anthology.

   Practice reading the selection aloud. As you read, use your voice to make the poem come alive. Vary your volume, rate, and pitch. Find the appropriate places for pauses. Underline the key words or phrases you think should be stressed. Modulate your tone of voice; use inflections for emphasis and meaning.

For this to work, you must overcome your fear of sounding affected or "dramatic." Most beginning speakers do better if they exaggerate changes in volume, rate, pitch, and expression. This will make you more aware of the ways you can use your voice to express a wide range of moods and meanings. Besides, what sounds overly "dramatic" to you usually does not sound that way to an audience. By adding luster, warmth, and enthusiasm to your voice, you will go a long way toward capturing and keeping the interest of your listeners.

If possible, practice reading the selection into a digital recorder. Listen to the playback. If you are not satisfied with what you hear, practice the selection some more and record it again.

2. Watch a 10-minute segment of a television drama with the sound turned off. What do the characters say with their dress, gestures, facial expressions, and the like? Do the same with a television comedy. How do the nonverbal messages in the two shows differ? Be prepared to report your observations in class.

3. Attend a speech on campus. You may choose either a presentation by a guest speaker from outside your school or a class session by a professor who has a reputation as a good lecturer. Prepare a brief report on the speaker's delivery.

   In your report, first analyze the speaker's volume, pitch, rate, pauses, vocal variety, pronunciation, and articulation. Then evaluate the speaker's personal appearance, bodily action, gestures, and eye contact. Explain how the speaker's delivery added to or detracted from what the speaker said. Finally, note at least two techniques of delivery used by the speaker that you might want to try in your next speech.

Speeches for Analysis and Discussion
Appendix

MEDICAL ROBOTS: FROM SCIENCE FICTION TO SCIENCE FACT

One of the toughest tasks for an informative speaker, inside the classroom or out, is exploring a technical topic with a general audience. The speaker must find a way to communicate complex ideas so they will be clear and meaningful to people who are not specialists in the subject—and who may know very little about it in advance of the speech. Like many things, this looks easy when done well. But in fact it takes a great deal of thought, planning, and creativity.

All of these elements can be seen in the following classroom speech on medical robots. It is skillfully organized, contains well-chosen supporting materials, and is expressed in everyday language that is appropriate for a non-technical audience. The speaker's communication is also enhanced by his dynamic delivery and superb visual aids. Most notable is his creative use of PowerPoint in paragraph 5 to visualize for his audience the otherwise invisible "light whiskers" that help orderly robots navigate their way around hospital corridors. You can view the speech in the online Media Library for this appendix.

connect

View "Medical Robots: From Science Fiction to Science Fact" in the online Media Library for this appendix (Video A.1).

1 Maureen Schrader lay on the operating table at Saint Barnabas Medical Center in Livingston, New Jersey. Four mechanical arms moved with precision over her abdomen. In one arm was a high-definition camera. The other three contained small surgical instruments that made a five-centimeter incision just below her ribcage. It was a tiny opening, but it was big enough to put a new kidney into Maureen's body.

2 At no point during the surgery did the surgeon actually touch Maureen. In fact, he sat several feet away peering into a monitor and holding what looked like video game controls. But the work of his hands was digitally recorded and sent to the robotic arms, which mimicked his every movement. The robot became an extension of the surgeon, and together they transplanted the kidney.

3 Robots in the operating room are now a reality, and the next operation you or a family member undergoes may well involve a robot. But surgery is just one of the areas in which robots are changing modern medicine. As a pre-med student interested in becoming a surgeon, I've long been fascinated with medical robots. After researching the topic for this speech, I'd like to introduce you to the world of medical robots. We'll take a look at three kinds of robots in particular—orderly robots, remote-presence robots, and surgical robots. Let's begin with orderly robots.

4 Orderly robots help hospital staff accomplish routine tasks. Their primary function is to transport medicine, food, and lab supplies—and to do so without a human by their side. Here is one of the most popular orderly robots—the TUG, or tug robot—which, according to its manufacturer, can be found in more than 100 hospitals in the United States alone.

5 A September 2010 story in *Discovery News* explains how the robot works. Relying on a digital map of the hospital, the robot moves from room to room picking up and dropping off supplies. It senses people and obstacles by what are called "light whiskers"—invisible beams of sonar, infrared, and laser. These light whiskers are represented by the colored lines you see in this drawing. They constantly scan the environment to avoid collisions.

6 TUG robots can also communicate with one another about the most efficient route to a location given current hallway conditions. They are highly efficient and make fewer delivery errors than people. Mark Weigel, director of food services at Bethesda Memorial Hospital in Maryland, notes that the TUG robot "never argues with patients, takes no breaks, is always polite and always on time."

7 But orderly robots are not the only robots transforming modern medicine. Remote-presence robots allow a doctor to visit with a patient even when the doctor is not in the same room. "Remote presence" means that the doctor can be present with the patient even when the doctor is in a remote location.

8 Imagine you're sitting in a hospital room when in comes this—the RP-7. A 2009 story in *U.S. News & World Report* explains that physicians can pilot these robots from a laptop located anywhere in the hospital or in the world. A screen, camera, microphone, and speaker system—like the ones you see in this photograph—allow the doctor to interview the patient. Hospital staff can even attach medical devices such as electronic stethoscopes to the robot so the doctor can review a patient's vital signs.

9 According to a 2010 article in *Hospital Management*, the RP-7 is used in more than 250 U.S. hospitals and has performed more than 100,000 clinic sessions. They are particularly useful in hospitals with a high patient-to-doctor ratio.

10 In addition to orderly robots and remote-presence robots, a third kind of robot is transforming modern medicine. Surgical robots, like the kind I mentioned at the start of my speech, are increasingly being used in operating rooms around the world. Most popular is the one you see here—the da Vinci. According to a 2010 article in the *Miami Herald*, there are more than 1,400 da Vinci robots in hospitals worldwide, and they're used in more than 200,000 operations every year.

11 How does da Vinci work? Intuitive Surgical, maker of da Vinci, explains that the surgeon controls the robot from a remote terminal. You can see the terminal in this photograph. Usually, the terminal is a few feet away, as in the photograph. But it can be as far as thousands of miles away, so a surgeon in San Francisco can operate on a patient in Miami. The surgeon controls the robot's arms utilizing an interactive 3-D imaging system. But make no mistake: Even though the robot is touching the patient, the surgeon is always in control.

12 Doctors love da Vinci because it dramatically improves the quality of surgical procedures. Dr. Jeffrey Wolf, a head-and-neck surgeon at the University of Maryland Medical Center, states that da Vinci "gives us unprecedented access with really good 3-D visualization. . . . We're now able to perform intricate surgeries in a very small space with great dexterity." Da Vinci also reduces the risk of postsurgery complications, allows for faster healing, and helps patients leave the hospital sooner.

13 In conclusion, we've seen that medical robots are playing an increasingly important role in modern medicine. Whether they're running errands for hospital employees, helping physicians connect with their patients, or acting as a surgeon's eyes and hands, medical robots have brought the future into the present.

14 So the next time you find yourself at the hospital, keep your eyes peeled for the kind of technological marvels that used to exist only in science fiction. Medical robots are now a matter of science fact.

RAMADAN

Choosing a topic based on one's personal experience can be an excellent decision, especially when the speaker supplements her or his existing knowledge with additional research—as in the following informative presentation on the Muslim holy month of Ramadan. As you read, notice how crisply the speech is organized, how the speaker relates her topic to the audience, and how she explains each aspect of Ramadan clearly and engagingly.

The speech also provides an instructive example of extemporaneous delivery, which you can see by watching the video in the online Media Library for this appendix. The speaker maintains strong eye contact with the audience and refers to her notes only as needed. Despite her nerves, she comes across as poised and confident. Her gestures are natural and spontaneous, and her voice conveys a strong sense of communication.

connect

View "Ramadan" in the online Media Library for this appendix (Video A.2).

1 This past month, more than one billion people around the world skipped lunch every day. They ate no food of any kind and drank no liquid of any kind from sunup to sunset. They did this every day during the month, and they do the same thing every year. I myself did it. Why? Last month was a time for tending to the mind, the body, and the spirit. Last month was the Muslim holy month of Ramadan.

2 I'm sure most of you have heard of Ramadan, but you may not know a lot about it. Ramadan refers to the ninth month in the Islamic calendar, when Muslims fast from sunrise to sunset. But Ramadan is much more than a time of fasting. As Tariq Ramadan, author of *Western Muslims and the Future of Islam,* explains, Ramadan is a time when "believers strengthen their faith and spirituality while developing their sense of social justice."

3 As a practicing Muslim, I have observed Ramadan my entire life. My parents moved to the United States from Pakistan shortly before I was born, and I remember going to the mosque as a child and breaking my fast at the end of the day with my family and friends. Nowadays, I get together with other students here on campus.

4 The goal of my speech today is to inform you about Ramadan—specifically its history and practices. In the end, I hope you'll have a better understanding of this sacred time for Muslims in the United States and around the globe. Let's begin by exploring the history of Ramadan.

5 Ramadan can be traced back 1,400 years to the Middle East and the beginnings of the Quran. As explained in Karen Armstrong's *Islam: A Short History,* in 610 A.D. the Prophet Mohammed embarked on a spiritual journey through the desert in what is now Saudi Arabia. At one point in this journey, Muslims believe, Allah spoke to Mohammed through the archangel Gabriel—the same Gabriel of the Jewish and Christian scriptures.

6 This is when the Prophet Mohammed received the first verses of the Quran. Gabriel told Mohammed to remember the revelation by observing a holy time every year. In the years after this journey, the Prophet Mohammed and his followers made the ninth month of the Muslim year the month of Ramadan.

7 The word "Ramadan" literally means "scorcher" in Arabic, because it was in the intense heat of the summer that the Prophet Mohammed encountered Gabriel. But unlike the Western calendar, the Islamic calendar follows the cycles of the moon and contains only 354 days. As a result, Ramadan always begins approximately ten days before it began the previous year. So, for example, this year Ramadan came on August 11th. Next year, it will come on August 1st.

8 Now let's take a look at what Muslims do during this holy month. The practices of Ramadan center on fasting, prayer, and charity.

9 Fasting is one of the five pillars of Islam, and it becomes especially important during Ramadan. The Ramadan fast, known as the *Sawm,* begins at sunrise and ends at sunset. Seyyed Nasr, author of *Islam: Religion, History, and Civilization,* explains that "the fast is required of all Muslims, male and female, from the age of adolescence until one no longer possesses the physical strength to undertake it." The only exceptions are for the sick, the elderly, travelers, and pregnant women.

10 At the end of daylight hours, Muslims break the fast with *Iftar*—the evening meal, during which families, friends, and communities gather. As Donna Bowen and Evelyn Early explain in their book *Everyday Life in the Muslim Middle East, Iftar* usually begins with eating a date, which is what the Prophet Mohammed is said to have done. After eating a date and drinking water, my family would eat the *Iftar* dinner my mother cooked for us. We would always marvel that even though she was fasting and couldn't taste what she was cooking, she still somehow got the spices just right.

11 Prayer is also central to Ramadan. Muslims traditionally pray five times a day, but during Ramadan prayer is encouraged even more. Ramadan prayers are often tied to oral readings of the Quran—a practice known as *Tarawih.* The goal is to read and recite the entire Quran over the course of the month.

12 In addition to fasting and prayer, charity plays a key role in Ramadan. *Iftars* are often organized and funded by the wealthy as a way of feeding the poor and the needy. Also, many Muslims increase their charitable giving during the month. At the end of Ramadan, my family donates to charity and we also exchange gifts like Christians do on Christmas.

13 If you think about it, the main purpose of Ramadan is the same as most religious holidays—spiritual development. Christians and Jews gather regularly to commemorate their histories, to enact certain rituals, and to feel closer to God. Muslims do the same thing during Ramadan.

14 Today, we've explored the history of Ramadan and its practices—fasting, prayer, and charity. I'd like to leave you with the traditional greeting that Muslims utter during this holy month: "Ramadan Kareem," which means "Ramadan is generous." Less than a year from now, when the next Ramadan comes around, I hope you'll have a better understanding of why it is so sacred for one billion people around the world.

THE DANGERS OF CELL PHONES

It is widely known that using cell phones while driving can be dangerous. But what about simply holding a cell phone up to your ear? In recent years, researchers have begun to study the health risks of prolonged cell-phone use. The following persuasive speech examines those risks and their implications. Rather than taking the unrealistic position of urging her classmates to give up their cell phones entirely, the speaker asks them to make one simple—but important—change in the way they use their phones.

connect

View "The Dangers of Cell Phones" in the online Media Library for this appendix (Video A.3).

The speech is organized in Monroe's motivated sequence. As you read, notice how the speaker builds her case as she moves through each step of the sequence. Also pay attention to her delivery and to her use of the methods of persuasion

discussed in Chapter 17. How does she establish credibility and goodwill, both at the beginning of the speech and as it proceeds? Does she present strong evidence in support of her arguments? Is her reasoning clear and convincing? How does she appeal to the emotions of her audience? You can view the speech in the online Media Library for this appendix.

1 It's your constant companion. It's in your pocket, in your bag, in your hands, or against your head. You use it at home, in class, at the gym, before you go to sleep at night and first thing when you wake up in the morning. I'm talking, of course, about your cell phone. According to my class survey, everyone in this room has a cell phone, and all of us use it dozens of times every day.

2 But what if your constant companion is dangerous? What if it's hazardous to your health? Evidence is piling up that long-term use of cell phones can lead to tissue damage, tumors, and even brain cancer. Given that there are well over 4 billion people worldwide using cell phones, we're looking at a problem of potentially staggering magnitude. According to Devra Davis, epidemiologist and author of the 2010 book *Disconnect: The Truth About Cell Phone Radiation,* we may be watching "an epidemic in slow motion."

3 I'd never thought much about the possible perils of cell phones before I saw a *CBS News* report on the subject earlier this year. But doing extensive research for this speech made me realize that cell phones do in fact pose a danger to our health.

4 Now, don't worry, I'm not going to try to persuade you to abandon your constant companion. I still use mine on a regular basis, and I probably always will. But I do hope to persuade you to make one simple change in the way you use your cell phone—a change that will protect your health and could even make the difference between a long life and premature death. But first, let's look more closely at the health risks posed by cell phones.

5 Those risks stem from the fact that cell phones emit small amounts of radiation that, over time, can damage tissue. Every time you use your cell phone, you expose yourself to that radiation. The amount is minuscule in comparison to that given off by x-ray machines—about one one-billionth of the intensity. However, Ronald Herberman of the University of Pittsburgh Cancer Institute explains that the problem with cell phone radiation is not how much is emitted at a single time, but how much we are exposed to with repeated use day after day, year after year.

6 It's this long-term use of cell phones that has led researchers to warn about their danger. In one study, for example, the World Health Organization tracked 10,000 cell phone users over the course of 10 years. As reported in the *New York Times* on November 13, 2010, the data in this study indicated that subjects who used a cell phone 10 or more years doubled the risk of developing brain tumors.

7 Other studies have reached the same conclusion. Perhaps most important is a study in the *Journal of Occupational and Environmental Medicine* that surveyed all the previous research on cell phone use. It found "a consistent pattern of increased risk" for developing brain tumors among people who used cell phones for more than 10 years.

8 Alan Marks is one of those people. A 58-year-old real estate developer and father of three, he talked on his cell phone an hour a day for 23 years. Two years ago, doctors found a golf-ball-sized tumor in his brain. "There's no question what caused it," he says. "It was my cell phone."

9 And Alan Marks isn't the only person to conclude that he's sick because of his cell phone. Ann Gittleman's 2010 book *Zapped*, which deals at length with the health problems of cell phones, catalogues people who developed blinding headaches, dizziness, circulatory problems, nausea, and cancer from the kind of radiation emitted by cell phones.

10 Still not convinced about the potential dangers posed by your constant companion? Take a look, then, inside the thick manual that comes with your phone. You'll see that all cell phone manufacturers warn against keeping the phone right next to your body. Apple, for example, recommends keeping the iPhone five-eighths of an inch away from your body. Makers of the BlackBerry recommend that you keep their phone a full inch away. Cell phone manufacturers don't publicize this information widely, but they clearly recognize that their products are potentially hazardous.

11 So what's the solution? As I said earlier, it's not to stop using cell phones altogether. I still use mine on a regular basis, and I can't imagine being without it—and I'm sure you can't imagine being without yours. You can, however, take seriously the risks of cell phones and find a way to minimize those risks. Time and again, experts point out that the single most effective way to reduce the risk is not to press your cell phone against your head while using it. Since the phone emits radiation, the closer you put it to your head, the more radiation you expose yourself to.

12 At the very least, you should hold the phone one-half an inch to one full inch away from your ear. But ideally, you should get in the habit of not putting it up to your head at all. I now use my earbuds almost every time I use my phone. Another option is to use your speakerphone.

13 As with breaking any habit, changing the way you talk on your cell phone may be slightly inconvenient at first but will soon become second nature. You'll be able to enjoy all the benefits of your constant companion without suffering the fate of Alan Marks. If Marks had known the dangers of prolonged cell phone use, he would have done things a lot differently. "I wouldn't have held it to my head," he says. "I would have used the headset. I would have used the speakerphone. . . . And I would not have had the problems I had."

14 So please get in the habit of keeping your cell phone away from your ear when talking, and encourage your friends and family to do the same. Start today, with your next phone call, and continue every day in the future.

15 We can avoid the slow-motion epidemic that doctors and scientists are warning us about—as long as we remember to keep this away from this.

PHONY PHARMACEUTICALS

According to the U.S. Food and Drug Administration, the market for counterfeit prescription drugs is close to $75 billion a year. One expert, cited in the following speech, states that criminals "can make more money in counterfeit drugs than they can in heroin." This is an arresting fact, one of many that the speaker presents in documenting the problem of phony pharmaceuticals.

The speaker does not stop with the problem, however. As is necessary in a persuasive speech on a question of policy, she goes on to present a plan for solving the problem. She outlines the plan in four distinct steps that, taken together, advance a practical course of action. The speech as a whole is concise and uncluttered; there are

connect

View "Phony Pharmaceuticals" in the online Media Library for this appendix (Video A.4).

few wasted words and the ideas progress cleanly and briskly. As you can see from the video in the online Media Library for this appendix, the speaker's persuasiveness was further strengthened by her energetic delivery and inventive visual aids.

1 Take a look at these two pills. Do you notice a difference between them? How about these two? Do you see a difference here? How about these?

2 To the naked eye, these pills are indistinguishable. But at a chemical level, they are very, very different. In each case, the pill on the left is real; it will help you get better. The pill on the right is counterfeit; it will not help you get better. In some cases, it may even kill you.

3 Katherine Eban, author of *Dangerous Doses: How Counterfeiters Are Contaminating America's Drug Supply,* explains that phony pharmaceuticals are drugs that have been diluted, drugs in which the active ingredient has been replaced with something else, or drugs that have been relabeled to appear stronger than they truly are. Taking a phony pharmaceutical means that you do not receive the medicine you need to get better, and the results can be deadly.

4 I first became aware of this issue after my younger sister received a phony drug for her asthma last summer. Fortunately, the error was discovered before it caused her any lasting harm. But I've been concerned about the issue ever since, and I did a great deal of research on it for this speech. As a result, I am convinced that we need to take action now to combat the problem of phony pharmaceuticals. Later in my speech, I'll share with you my plan for curbing the spread of these dangerous drugs. But let's start by taking a closer look at the problem.

5 Phony pharmaceuticals are dangerous because of the health risks they pose. According to Graham Jackson, editor of the *International Journal of Clinical Practice*, counterfeit drugs include ingredients such as boric acid, leaded road paint, floor polish, shoe polish, talcum powder, and cement powder. But that's not all. There's also brick dust, chalk, nickel, and arsenic. Ingesting too much boric acid or floor polish can make you sick; leaded road paint and arsenic can kill you.

6 In one highly publicized case, 81 people in the United States died in 2008 because they took a counterfeit version of the blood thinner heparin. As reported by *CNN*, the phony heparin was originally manufactured outside the United States using a cheap sulfate that proved deadly. After slipping past all regulatory checks, it ended up in the United States, with tragic results.

7 The U.S. government's Bureau of International Information Programs estimates that 700,000 people around the world will die this year from phony pharmaceuticals—almost three times the number of people who live here in Madison. In fact, Roger Bate, of the American Enterprise Institute, reports that "trafficking in counterfeit drugs has become one of the world's fastest-growing criminal enterprises."

8 Phony pharmaceuticals are so widespread that they have become big business. The FDA estimates that they will bring in close to $75 billion in revenue this year alone—up from $40 billion only a few years ago. Tom Kubic, head of the Pharmaceutical Security Institute, told *USA Today* in September 2010 that criminals "can make more money in counterfeit drugs than they can in heroin."

9 Given the rewards of the counterfeit drug trade, the problem will only get worse in the coming years unless we take steps to bring it under control. The solution I propose is similar to House Resolution 2726, which is under consideration by the U.S. Congress. There are four steps to this solution.

10 First, criminal penalties for drug counterfeiters should be increased from three years in prison, which is the current limit, to no limit at all. If a drug peddler kills someone with phony pharmaceuticals, the punishment should fit the crime.

11 Second, the Food and Drug Administration should have the authority to recall prescription drugs. Right now, the FDA can encourage drug manufacturers to issue a recall, but it has no power to issue a recall on its own. To get phony pharmaceuticals off the street, recall authority needs to rest with a central agency that will act quickly and uniformly.

12 Third, the FDA should be given the resources for spot-checking the chemical makeup of prescription medication. We have health inspectors for food, why not have inspectors for prescription drugs?

13 Fourth, legitimate drug manufacturers should be required to implement track-and-trace technology. As explained in the *New York Times*, this technology stamps each bottle and pill with a unique code tied to a secure, centralized database. The code allows pharmacies and distributors to determine whether drugs are legitimate or phony, plus the route the drugs took to get to store shelves.

14 Representative Steve Israel of New York, sponsor of House Resolution 2726, says these four steps will "ensure that the domestic drug supply chain is secure for every American." It "will crack down on counterfeiting and increase the penalties for the outlaws who are compromising our health." The time has come for Congress to pass this vital legislation.

15 In conclusion, phony pharmaceuticals are pervasive and dangerous. By implementing the solution I have outlined, we will be able to control this public-health menace.

16 You have the right to know that the medication you're taking is real. You have the right to know that your next trip to the drugstore will be a safe one. And you have the right to know that what you see is what you get.

THE WONDERFUL WORLD OF DR. SEUSS

The aim of a commemorative speech is to pay tribute to a person, a group of people, an institution, or an idea. The following talk commemorates Theodor Seuss Geisel, author of the Dr. Seuss books. Unlike an informative presentation, which would provide biographical details about Geisel's life, this speech focuses on his activist spirit, focused determination, and creative genius. The speaker says enough to illustrate these traits, but his ultimate purpose is to inspire the audience rather than to inform it.

By blending his own words with memorable passages from Dr. Seuss, the speaker captures both the linguistic whimsy for which Seuss was so beloved and the serious lessons he sought to teach children and adults alike. As you can see from the video in the online Media Library for this appendix, the speaker's delivery strikes the right tone for his subject.

connect

View "The Wonderful World of Dr. Seuss" in the online Media Library for this appendix (Video A.5).

1 His words echoed through our childhoods: "I do so like green eggs and ham! Thank you! Thank you, Sam-I-Am!" His characters played in our imaginations: Horton the elephant, Yertle the turtle, the Cat in the Hat, the Lorax. And his books connected us to a whimsical world of color and creativity. He is the great doctor, whom you know as Seuss.

2 At the time of his death in 1991, Dr. Seuss had published 44 children's books. Perhaps more than any other author, he captured our childlike wonder and inspired the imagination of generations. Today, let us return to some of his stories—not to remember them, but to honor the man behind them—Theodor Seuss Geisel, whose activist spirit, focused determination, and creative genius made him the one and only Dr. Seuss.

3 From working on student newspapers to creating advertisements to crafting humorous essays, Geisel possessed an activist spirit long before he became famous as Dr. Seuss. During World War II, he illustrated training videos to help inspire the troops in the field. He also drew political cartoons that featured the same rhythmic cadence that readers have long admired—a cadence much like the march of soldiers overseas.

4 Eventually, Geisel would bring the same cadence and spirit to his books. *The Lorax*—my personal favorite—was so controversial because of its negative portrayal of the logging industry that some towns tried to ban it. But Geisel knew he needed to make a statement for the environment:

"I repeat," cried the Lorax,
"I speak for the trees!" . . .
"which you seem to be chopping as fast as you please!"

5 Coupled with Geisel's activist spirit was a focused determination. His first published work, *And to Think That I Saw It on Mulberry Street*, was rejected by publishers more than twenty times. But Geisel pressed on, and the book appeared in 1937 to critical acclaim.

6 Determination was also central in the creation of *The Cat in the Hat.* Geisel's publisher challenged him to create a story that would introduce young readers to more than 200 new vocabulary words. Geisel met the challenge, and he put the words together in the story of a boy, a girl, a fish, a cat, a hat, Thing 1, and Thing 2:

We looked!
Then we saw him step in on the mat!
We looked!
And we saw him!
The Cat in the Hat!

7 Ultimately, what stands out most about Geisel is his creative genius. With pleasing rhyme schemes, memorable characters, and instantly recognizable art, he created not just brilliant books but new realities.

8 He created the Grinch, the green menace who stole Christmas. He created Horton, the elephant who helped hatch an egg. And he created Yertle, the turtle king who took a long fall. Geisel's creative genius turned story time into a time of imagination, play, and possibility:

And today the great Yertle, that Marvelous he,
Is King of the Mud. That is all he can see.
And the turtles, of course . . . all the turtles are free
As turtles and, maybe, all creatures should be.

9 From Seuss's activist spirit, focused determination, and creative genius came the words, characters, and books that shaped our youth. No less important, it was Seuss who gave us a sense of optimism and possibility when facing the world. As he told us in *Oh, the Places You'll Go*:

You have brains in your head.
You have feet in your shoes.
You can steer yourself any direction you choose.

ELIE WIESEL

Few people are more universally admired than Elie Wiesel. A survivor of the Nazi death camps during World War II, he went on to become a prolific author, an esteemed teacher, and a powerful voice for marginalized people the world over. When Wiesel received the 1986 Nobel Peace Prize, he was described as "a messenger to mankind" on behalf of "peace, atonement, and human dignity."

The following commemorative speech praises Wiesel as an eloquent, fearless, and selfless leader. It provides sufficient information to make clear why Wiesel is commendable without getting bogged down in biographical details. The language is vivid and uplifting. Of special note is the repetition of "A-7713," Wiesel's prisoner number at Auschwitz. The speaker uses that number to dramatic effect in the introduction and then again in the conclusion to provide artistic unity.

In addition to reading this speech, you can view it in the online Media Library for this appendix.

connect

View "Elie Wiesel" in the online Media Library for this appendix (Video A.6).

1 A-7713. His new name, the graffiti stamped on his skin. A-7713, a concentration camp tattoo. At age fifteen, A-7713 was taken from his home by the Nazis and sent to Auschwitz, one of the twentieth century's most potent symbols of evil. Here A-7713 witnessed the deaths of thousands of human beings, including his mother and younger sister.

2 Somehow, A-7713 survived, and when World War II ended, he put his pain and grief to work making sure the world did not forget the Holocaust and making sure another Holocaust did not take place.

3 Today, the world knows A-7713 as Elie Wiesel, noted speaker and lecturer, author of more than 40 books, and recipient of the Presidential Medal of Freedom, the Congressional Gold Medal, and the Nobel Peace Prize, among others. Elie Wiesel is an eloquent, fearless, selfless leader who took the evils of Auschwitz as motivation to improve the world.

4 An eloquent leader, Elie Wiesel uses the power of language to confront the problems of humanity. Through compelling prose and brutal honesty, he explains that we cannot root out evil unless we recognize it and battle it wherever it exists. In his classic book, *Night*, he says of Auschwitz: "Never shall I forget that night, the first night in camp, which turned my life into one long night, seven times cursed and seven times sealed. Never shall I forget that smoke. Never shall I forget the little faces of the children, whose bodies I saw turned into wreaths of smoke beneath a silent blue sky." Haunting words that remind us of the reality of evil.

5 A fearless leader no less than an eloquent one, Elie Wiesel has spent 40 years battling the evils that continue to plague our planet. To the Miskito Indians of Nicaragua, displaced from their homeland, he brought inspiring words of strength and compassion. To men and women facing apartheid in South Africa, he brought a powerful denunciation of racial segregation and violence. To Cambodian refugees suffering from starvation and disease, he brought food and the promise of a new beginning. And to those of us who follow his work, he continues to provide inspiration.

6 A selfless leader as much as an eloquent and fearless one, Elie Wiesel has consistently put the needs of others before his own. With every award, his modesty stands side by side with his achievements. As he stated in his Nobel Prize acceptance speech, "Neutrality helps the oppressor, never the victim. Silence encourages the tormentor, never the tormented. . . . Wherever men and women are persecuted because of their race, religion, or political views, that place must—at that moment—become the center of the universe."

7 Today, at more than 80 years of age, Elie Wiesel continues to fight against the night. Through all his trials and all his triumphs, the tattoo remains: A-7713, a constant reminder of evil, injustice, and indifference. In battling these forces, Elie Wiesel has shown the kind of moral leadership too often lacking in today's world.

8 There is no better way to end than to quote his own words: "There may be times when we are powerless to prevent injustice, but there must never be a time when we fail to protest. . . . What these victims need above all is to know that they are not alone, that we are not forgetting them, that while their freedom depends on ours, the quality of our freedom depends on theirs."

Notes

Chapter 1 Speaking in Public

[1]Pericles, quoted in Richard Whately, *Elements of Rhetoric,* 7th ed. (London: John W. Parker, 1846), p. 10.

[2]*It Takes More Than a Major: Employer Priorities for College Learning and Student Success* (Washington, D.C.: Hart Research Associates, 2013); American Management Association, *AMA 2012 Critical Skills Survey* (New York: American Management Association, 2013).

[3]Dave McGinn, "Me? Public Speaking?" *Globe and Mail,* December 1, 2009, p. L1.

[4]Quoted in Emily Driscoll, "Um, Like, Whatever: College Grads Lack Verbal Skills," Foxbusiness.com, March 4, 2011. April 6, 2011.

[5]George A. Kennedy, *Comparative Rhetoric: An Historical and Cross-Cultural Introduction* (New York: Oxford University Press, 1998).

[6]Geoffrey Brewer, "Snakes Top List of Americans' Fears," Gallup News Service, February 2001; Alex Blyth, "How to Get the Most Out of Public Speaking Training," *Training Magazine* (June 14, 2006), p. 7.

[7]A. M. Ruscio, T. A. Brown, W. T. Chiu, J. Sareen, M. B. Steain, and R. C. Kessler, "Social Fears and Social Phobia in the USA: Results from the National Comorbidity Survey Replication," *Psychological Medicine* (January 2008), pp. 15–28.

[8]Cicero, *De Oratore,* trans. E. W. Sutton (Cambridge, MA: Harvard University Press, 1942), p. xxvi.

[9]Digby Jones, "Public Speaking Tests the Nerves of Most Directors," *Birmingham Post,* August 25, 2003.

[10]Elayne Synder, *Speak for Yourself—With Confidence* (New York: New American Library, 1983), p. 113.

[11]Sharon Aschaiek, "Conquer Your Fear of Public Speaking," *Toronto Sun,* March 16, 2005.

[12]A number of studies have shown that taking a public speaking course is effective in reducing stage fright. For an excellent review of the research, consult Graham D. Bodie, "A Racing Heart, Rattling Knees, and Ruminative Thoughts: Defining, Explaining, and Treating Public Speaking Anxiety," *Communication Education,* 59 (2010), pp. 70–105.

[13]Lilly Walters, *Secrets of Successful Speakers* (New York: McGraw-Hill, 1993), pp. 32–36.

[14]See Steven Ungerleider, *Mental Training for Peak Performance,* rev. ed. (Emmaus, PA: Rodale Books, 2005).

[15]Joe Ayres, Tim Hopf, Michael T. Hazel, Debbie M. A. Sonandre, and Tanichya K. Wongprasert, "Visualization and Performance Visualization: Applications, Evidence, and Speculation," in John A. Daly et al. (eds.), *Avoiding Communication: Shyness, Reticence, and Communication Apprehension,* 3rd ed. (Cresskill, NJ: Hampton Press, 2009), pp. 375–394.

[16]Dick Cavett, quoted in Steve Allen, *How to Make a Speech* (New York: McGraw-Hill, 1986), p. 10.

[17]For more detail on the ideas in this paragraph, see Michael T. Motley, *Overcoming Your Fear of Public Speaking: A Proven Method* (Boston, MA: Houghton Mifflin, 1998).

[18]Chris R. Sawyer and Ralph R. Behnke, "Reduction in Public Speaking State Anxiety During Performance as a Function of Sensitization Processes," *Communication Quarterly,* 50 (2002), pp. 110–121.

[19]For more detail on the dimensions of critical thinking, see M. Neil Browne and Stuart M. Keeley, *Asking the Right Questions: A Guide to Critical Thinking,* 9th ed. (Upper Saddle River, NJ: Pearson Education, 2012).

[20]For other models of the speech communication process, see Em Griffin, Andrew Ledbetter, and Glenn Sparks, *A First Look at Communication Theory,* 9th ed. (New York: McGraw-Hill, 2015); Stephen W. Littlejohn and Karen A. Foss, *Theories of Human Communication,* 8th ed. (Long Grove, IL: Waveland Press, 2011).

[21]Herman Melville, *Redburn: His First Voyage* (New York: Harper and Brothers, 1850), p. 214.

[22]William B. Gudykunst and Young Yun Kim, *Communicating with Strangers: An Approach to Intercultural Communication,* 4th ed. (New York: McGraw-Hill, 2003), p. 4.

[23]For more detail on gestures and other aspects of intercultural communication, see Judith N. Martin and Thomas K. Nakayama, *Intercultural Communication in Contexts,* 6th ed. (New York: McGraw-Hill, 2013); Larry A. Samovar, Richard E. Porter, Edwin R. McDaniel, and Carolyn S. Roy, *Communication Between Cultures,* 8th ed. (Boston, MA: Wadsworth, 2013).

[24]Adapted from Roger E. Axtell (ed.), *Do's and Taboos Around the World,* 3rd ed. (New York: John Wiley and Sons, 1993), p. 41.

[25]Myron W. Lustig and Jolene Koester, *Intercultural Competence: Interpersonal Communication Across Cultures,* 6th ed. (Boston, MA: Allyn and Bacon, 2013), pp. 137–139.

[26]For more on multiculturalism and communication, see Shang Liu, Zala Volčič, and Cindy Gallois, *Introducing Intercultural Communication: Global Cultures and Contexts* (Thousand Oaks, CA: Sage, 2011).

Chapter 2 Ethics and Public Speaking

[1]Richard L. Johannesen, Kathleen S. Valde, and Karen E. Whedbee, *Ethics in Human Communication,* 6th ed. (Prospect Heights, IL: Waveland Press, 2008), p. 14.

[2]Johannesen, Valde, and Whedbee, *Ethics in Human Communication,* p. 13.

[3]See, for example, Vincent Ryan Ruggiero, *Thinking Critically About Ethical Issues,* 9th ed. (New York: McGraw-Hill, 2015).

[4]Haig A. Bosmajian, *The Language of Oppression* (Lanham, MD: University Press of America, 1983), p. 5.

[5]See Steven J. Heyman, *Free Speech and Human Dignity* (New Haven, CT: Yale University Press, 2008).

[6]Thomas L. Tedford and Dale A. Herbeck, *Freedom of Speech in the United States,* 7th ed. (State College, PA: Strata Publishing, 2013), pp. 196–203.

[7]Kenneth Blanchard and Norman Vincent Peale, *The Power of Ethical Management* (New York: Ballantine Books, 1988), p. 64.

[8]For two excellent guides to ethical decision making, see Peter Singer, *Practical Ethics,* 3rd ed. (New York: Cambridge University Press, 2011); Ronald A. Howard and Clinton D. Korver, *Ethics for the Real World* (Boston, MA: Harvard Business Press, 2008).

[9]*MLA Handbook for Writers of Research Papers,* 7th ed. (New York: Modern Language Association of America, 2009), p. 52.

[10]Michele Mandel, "Felled TDSB Director Chris Spence's Mistakes Were Not Innocent," *Toronto Sun,* January 11, 2013; Kristin Rushowy and Louise Brown, "Chris Spence Breaks Silence on Plagiarism Scandal," *Toronto Star,* July 25, 2013. Also see Kristin Rushowy, "TDSB's Chris Spence Resigns Amid Growing Plagiarism Scandal," *Toronto Star,* January 10, 2013; Oliver Moore and Simona Chiose, "DSB Director Resigns Over Plagiarism, PhD Dissertation Includes Unattributed Passages," *Globe and Mail,* January 10, 2013; Megan O'Toole, "Publisher to Investigate 'Troubling' Plagiarism Allegations Against TDSB Director Chris Spence," *National Post,* January 20, 2013.

[11]Bruce Perry, *Malcolm: The Life of the Man Who Changed Black America* (Tarrytown, NY: Station Hill, 1991), p. 380.

[12]The credo can be accessed at http://www.natcom.org/Tertiary.aspx?id=2119&terms=credo on ethical.

[13]See http://www.natcom.org/Tertiary.aspx?id=2119&terms=credo on ethical.

Chapter 3 Listening

[1]Larry Barker and Kittie Watson, *Listen Up: What You've Never Heard About the Other Half of Every Conversation* (New York: St. Martin's, 2001), p. 5.

[2]Michael P. Nichols, *The Lost Art of Listening,* 2nd ed. (New York: Guilford, 2009).

[3]See Lyman K. Steil and Richard K. Bommelje, *Listening Leaders: The Ten Golden Rules to Listen, Lead, and Succeed* (Edina, MN: Beaver's Pond Press, 2004).

[4]Judi Brownell, *Listening: Attitudes, Principles, and Skills,* 5th ed. (Boston, MA: Allyn and Bacon, 2013), p. 8.

[5]Jan Flynn, Tuula-Ritta Valikoski, and Jennie Grau, "Listening in the Business Context: Reviewing the State of Research," *International Journal of Listening,* 22 (2008), pp. 141–151; Laura A. Janusik, "Listening Pedagogy: Where Do We Go From Here?" in Andrew D. Wolvin (ed.), *Listening and Human Communication in the 21st Century* (West Sussex: Blackwell, 2010), pp. 193–194.

[6]See, for example, Melissa L. Beall, Jennifer Gill-Rosier, Jeanine Tate, and Amy Matten, "State of the Context: Listening in Education," *International Journal of Listening,* 22 (2008), pp. 123–132; Graham D. Bodie and Margaret Fitch-Hauser, "Quantitative Research in Listening: Explication and Overview," in Wolvin, *Listening and Human Communication in the 21st Century,* pp. 46–93.

[7]Andrew W. Wolvin and Carolyn Gwynn Coakley, *Listening,* 5th ed. (Dubuque, IA: Brown and Benchmark, 1995), pp. 223–396.

[8]Brownell, *Listening: Attitudes, Principles, and Skills,* p. 81.

[9]Louis Nizer, *My Life in Court,* rpnt. ed. (Whitefish, MT: 2010), pp. 297–298.

[10]Adapted from Lyman K. Steil, Larry L. Barker, and Kittie W. Watson, *Effective Listening* (Reading, MA: Addison-Wesley, 1983).

[11]Two excellent guides to the premises and methods of active listening are Bernard T. Ferrari, *Power Listening: Mastering the Most Critical Business Skill of All* (New York: Penguin, 2012), and Tim Hast, *Powerful Listening. Powerful Influence* (North Charleston, NC: CreateSpace Independent Publishing, 2013).

[12]George H. Putnam, *Abraham Lincoln* (New York: Putnam, 1909), pp. 44–45.

[13]M. Scott Peck, *The Road Less Traveled: A New Psychology of Love, Traditional Values, and Spiritual Growth,* 25th anniversary ed. (New York: Touchstone Books, 2003), p. 127.

[14]Jack Hayes, "Fifty Years of Meteorological Advances," *Vital Speeches,* 77 (2011), pp. 27–30.

[15]See Ralph G. Nichols and Leonard A. Stevens, *Are You Listening?* (New York: McGraw-Hill, 1957), pp. 113–114. This classic work still has much of value to say about its subject.

[16]On some of the other challenges involved in note taking, see Dung C. Bui, Joel Myerson, and Sandra Hale, "Note-Taking with Computers: Exploring Alternative Strategies for Improved Recall," *Journal of Educational Psychology,* 105 (2013), pp. 299–309; Annie Piolat, Thierry Olive, and Ronald T. Kellogg, "Cognitive Effort During Note Taking," *Applied Cognitive Psychology,* 19 (2005), pp. 291–312.

[17]See, for example, Tamas Makany, Jonathan Kemp, and Itiel E. Dror, "Optimizing the Use of Note-Taking as an External Cognitive Aid for Increasing Learning," *British Journal of Educational Technology,* 40 (2009), pp. 619–635.

Chapter 6 Analyzing the Audience

[1]Seeing the speech classroom as a real audience is also important because it engages students in a form of rhetorical activity that is vital to participatory democracy. See Rosa A. Eberly, "Rhetoric and the Anti-Logos Doughball: Teaching Deliberating Bodies the Practices of Participatory Democracy," *Rhetoric and Public Affairs,* 5 (2002), 296.

[2]Saul Alinsky, *Rules for Radicals* (New York: Random House, 1971), p. 81.

[3]For a broader discussion of gender issues in communication, see Julia T. Wood, *Gendered Lives: Communication, Gender, and Culture,* 11th ed. (Boston, MA: Wadsworth, 2015).

[4]Diana L. Eck, *A New Religious America* (New York: HarperCollins, 2001), p. 4.

[5]Research shows that speakers are usually more persuasive when they attempt to refute opposing arguments rather than ignoring them. See Richard M. Perloff, *The Dynamics of Persuasion: Communication and Attitudes in the 21st Century,* 5th ed. (New York: Routledge, 2014), p. 265.

Chapter 7 Gathering Materials

[1]For more detail on Internet research, see Randolph Hock, *The Extreme Searcher's Internet Handbook: A Guide for the Serious Searcher,* 4th ed. (Medford, NJ: CyberAge Books, 2013).

[2]See, for example, Imogen Casebourne, Chris Davies, Michelle Fernandes, and Naomi Norman, *Assessing the Accuracy and Quality of Wikipedia Entries Compared to Popular Online Encyclopedias: A Comparative Preliminary Study Across Disciplines in English, Spanish, and Arabic* (Brighton, UK: Epic, 2012); N. J. Reavley et al., "Quality of Information Sources About Mental Disorders: A Comparison of Wikipedia with Centrally Controlled Web and Printed Sources," *Psychological Medicine,* 42 (2012), pp. 1753–1762; Don Fallis, "Toward an Epistemology of Wikipedia," *Journal of the American Society for Information Science and Technology,* 59 (2008), pp. 1662–1674.

[3]These criteria are adapted from Sheridan Libraries, "Evaluating Information Found on the Internet," *Johns Hopkins University.* Web. April 20, 2014.

[4]For more information on various interview types and situations, see Charles J. Stewart and William B. Cash Jr., *Interviewing: Principles and Practices,* 14th ed. (New York: McGraw-Hill, 2014).

[5]For an interesting study that confirms the extent to which the process of researching and developing speeches can affect the beliefs and attitudes of student speakers, see Barbara Mae Gayle, "Transformations in a Civil Discourse Public Speaking Class: Speakers' and Listeners' Attitude Change," *Communication Education,* 53 (2004), 174–184.

Chapter 8 Supporting Your Ideas

[1]See, for example, Kathryn Greene, Shelly Campo, and Smita C. Banerjee, "Comparing Normative, Anecdotal, and Statistical Risk Evidence to Discourage Tanning Bed Use," *Communication Quarterly,* 58 (2010), pp. 111–132.

[2]I would like to thank *21st Century* and *China Daily* for permission to include this excerpt from Sun Yan's speech in the online Media Library for *The Art of Public Speaking.*

[3]Elliot Aronson, *The Social Animal,* 11th ed. (New York: Worth, 2011), pp. 92–93.

[4]This point was made by James A. Winans in his classic *Speech-Making* (New York: Appleton-Century-Crofts, 1922), p. 141.

[5]Over the years, there has been much debate over whether statistics or examples have more impact on listeners. For a recent study that addresses this subject, see Bing Han and Edward L. Fink, "How Do Statistical and Narrative Evidence Affect Persuasion? The Role of Evidentiary Features," *Argumentation and Advocacy,* 49 (2012), 39–58.

[6]One implication of Han and Fink, "How Do Statistical and Narrative Evidence Affect Persuasion," is that multiple statistics tend to be more persuasive than single statistics.

[7]Joel Best, *Stat-Spotting: A Guide to Identifying Dubious Data* (Berkeley, CA: University of California Press, 2008), provides a fascinating look at the use and misuse of statistics. For a more technical approach, see Neil J. Salkind, *Statistics for People Who (Think They) Hate Statistics,* 5th ed. (Thousand Oaks, CA: Sage, 2014).

[8]Bob Papper, "TV Salaries Fall, Radio Stagnant," Radio Television Digital News Association (RTDNA). Web. April 23, 2014.

[9]Mike Allen et al., "Testing the Persuasiveness of Evidence: Combining Narrative and Statistical Forms," *Communication Research Reports,* 17 (2000), pp. 331–336.

[10]For research confirming the importance of citing sources when presenting evidence, see Rodney A. Reynolds and J. Lynn Reynolds, "Evidence," in James Price Dillard and Michael Pfau (eds.), *The Persuasion Handbook: Developments in Theory and Practice* (Thousand Oaks, CA: Sage, 2002), pp. 429–430.

[11]Richard M. Perloff, *The Dynamics of Persuasion: Communication and Attitudes in the 21st Century,* 5th ed. (New York: Routledge, 2014), pp. 267–269.

Chapter 9 Organizing the Body of the Speech

[1]Ernest C. Thompson, "An Experimental Investigation of the Relative Effectiveness of Organizational Structure in Oral Communication," *Southern Speech Journal,* 26 (1960), pp. 59–69.

[2]Harry Sharp Jr., and Thomas McClung, "Effects of Organization on the Speaker's Ethos," *Speech Monographs,* 33 (1966), pp. 182–183.

[3]See, for example, B. Scott Titsworth and Joseph P. Mazer, "Clarity in Teaching and Learning: Conundrums, Consequences, and Opportunities," in Deanna L. Fassett and John T. Warren (eds.), *Sage Handbook of Communication and Instruction* (Thousand Oaks, CA: Sage, 2010), pp. 241–261; Amber L. Finn and Paul Schrodt, "Students' Perceived Understanding Mediates the Effects of Teacher Clarity and Nonverbal Immediacy on Learner Environment," *Communication Education,* 61 (2012), 111–130.

Chapter 10 Beginning and Ending the Speech

[1]Shaun Donovan, "We All Work for Terrell," *Vital Speeches of the Day,* 79 (2013), pp. 381–382.

[2]Robert M. Gates, "About the Institution You Will Someday Lead," *Vital Speeches of the Day,* 77 (2011), pp. 138–142.

[3]Dorothy Sarnoff, *Speech Can Change Your Life* (Garden City, NY: Doubleday, 1970), p. 189.

[4]Sarnoff, *Speech Can Change Your Life,* p. 190.

Chapter 11 Outlining the Speech

[1]Robert T. Oliver, *History of Public Speaking in America* (Boston, MA: Allyn and Bacon, 1965), p. 143.

[2]Oliver, *History of Public Speaking,* p. 145.

Chapter 12 Using Language

[1]For a valuable collection of essays on language, meaning, and culture, see Susan D. Blum (ed.), *Making Sense of Language*, 2nd ed. (New York: Oxford University Press, 2013).

[2]Dorothy Sarnoff, *Speech Can Change Your Life* (New York: Doubleday, 1970), p. 71.

[3]Annmarie Mungo, "A Child Is Born," *Winning Orations, 1980* (Mankato, MN: Interstate Oratorical Association, 1980), pp. 49–50.

[4]See Joseph M. Williams and Joseph Bizup, *Style: Lessons in Clarity and Grace,* 11th ed. (New York: Longman, 2013), for more on the principles of verbal clarity.

[5]James Geary, *I Is an Other: The Secret Life of Metaphor and How It Shapes the Way We See the World* (New York: Harper, 2011), provides a highly readable exploration of the role of metaphor in human expression.

[6]Edward Bliss Jr. (ed.), *In Search of Light: The Broadcasts of Edward R. Murrow, 1938–1961* (New York: Knopf, 1967), p. 276.

[7]Rosalie Maggio, *Talking About People: A Guide to Fair and Accurate Language* (Phoenix, AZ: Oryx Press, 1997), p. 26.

Chapter 13 Delivering the Speech

[1]Irving Bartlett, *Wendell Phillips: Boston Brahmin* (Boston, MA: Beacon Press, 1961), p. 192.

[2]A. Craig Baird, *Rhetoric: A Philosophical Inquiry* (New York: Ronald Press, 1965), p. 207.

[3]Daniel J. O'Keefe, *Persuasion: Theory and Research,* 2nd ed. (Thousand Oaks, CA: Sage, 2002), p. 185.

[4]Dorothy Sarnoff, *Speech Can Change Your Life* (Garden City, NY: Doubleday, 1970), p. 73.

[5]See William Labov, *Dialect Diversity in America: The Politics of Language Change* (Charlottesville, VA: University of Virginia Press, 2012), for a provocative examination of regional dialects in the United States.

[6]For more detail on all aspects of voice production, consult Kenneth C. Crannell, *Voice and Articulation,* 5th ed. (Boston, MA: Wadsworth, 2012).

[7]Mark L. Knapp, Judith A. Hall, and Terrence G. Horgan, *Nonverbal Communication in Human Interaction,* 8th ed. (Boston, MA: Wadsworth, 2014), pp. 17–18.

[8]Richard M. Perloff, *The Dynamics of Persuasion: Communication and Attitudes in the 21st Century,* 5th ed. (New York: Routledge, 2014), pp. 253–259.

[9]For more on delivery, plus other aspects of public speaking, see Carmine Gallo, *Talk Like TED: The 9 Public Speaking Secrets of the World's Top Minds* (New York: St. Martin's, 2014); Garr Reynolds, *The Naked Presenter* (Berkeley, CA: New Riders, 2011).

[10]Thomas F. Calcagni, *Tough Questions—Good Answers: Taking Control of Any Interview* (Sterling, VA: Capital Books, 2008), provides many practical tips on managing question-and-answer sessions.

[11]Adapted from Timothy J. Koegel, *The Exceptional Presenter Goes Virtual* (Austin, TX: Greenleaf Book Group, 2010), p. 117.

[12]Koegel, *The Exceptional Presenter Goes Virtual,* p. 100.

[13]Cynthia Clay, *Great Webinars: How to Create Interactive Learning That Is Captivating, Informative, and Fun* (San Francisco, CA: Pfeiffer, 2012), p. 5.

Chapter 14 Using Visual Aids

[1]For a review of research on these subjects, see Richard E. Mayer, "Instruction Based on Visualizations," in Richard E. Mayer and Patricia A. Alexander (eds.), *Handbook of Research on Learning and Instruction* (New York: Routledge, 2011), pp. 427–445.

[2]See Stephen Few, *Now You See It: Simple Visualization Techniques for Quantitative Analysis* (Oakland, CA: Analytics Press, 2009), for a revealing look at the art of statistical graphics.

[3]Garr Reynolds, *Presentation Zen: Simple Ideas on Presentation and Delivery,* 2nd ed. (Berkeley, CA: New Riders, 2012), p. 11.

[4]See, for example, Eunmo Sung and Richard E. Mayer, "When Graphics Improve Liking but Not Learning from Online Lessons," *Computers in Human Behavior,* 28 (2012), pp. 1618–1625.

[5]Garr Reynolds, *Presentation Zen Design: A Simple Visual Approach to Presenting in Today's World*, 2nd ed. (Berkeley, CA: New Riders, 2014), provides a wealth of insight about designing high-impact visual aids.

[6]Bert E. Bradley, *Fundamentals of Speech Communication: The Credibility of Ideas*, 6th ed. (Dubuque, IA: William C. Brown, 1991), p. 280.

[7]For a fascinating look at the principles of information graphics in general, consult Albert Cairo, *The Functional Art: An Introduction to Information Graphics and Visualization* (Berkeley, CA: New Riders, 2013).

Chapter 15 Speaking to Inform

[1]John R. Johnson and Nancy Szczupakiewicz, "The Public Speaking Course: Is It Preparing Students with Work-Related Public Speaking Skills?" *Communication Education*, 36 (1987), pp. 131–137; Andrew D. Wolvin and Diana Corley, "The Technical Speech Communication Course: A View from the Field," *Association for Communication Administration Bulletin*, 49 (1984), pp. 83–91.

[2]Richard E. Mayer, Sherry Fennell, Lindsay Farmer, and Julie Campbell, "A Personalization Effect in Multimedia Learning: Students Learn Better When Words Are in Conversational Style Rather Than Formal Style," *Journal of Educational Psychology*, 96 (2004), pp. 389–395.

[3]Joseph Conrad, "Youth: A Narrative," in Samuel Hynes (ed.), *Collected Stories of Joseph Conrad* (Hopewell, NJ: Ecco Press, 1991), p. 166.

[4]James Humes, *Roles Speakers Play* (New York: Harper and Row, 1976), p. 25.

Chapter 16 Speaking to Persuade

[1]There are many competing definitions of persuasion. Mine is drawn from Gerald R. Miller, "On Being Persuaded: Some Basic Distinctions," in James Price Dillard and Lijiang Shen (eds.), *The SAGE Handbook of Persuasion: Developments in Theory and Practice*, 2nd ed. (Thousand Oaks, CA: Sage, 2013), pp. 70–82.

[2]Amanda Bennett, "Economics + Meeting = A Zillion Causes and Effects," *Wall Street Journal*, January 10, 1995, B1.

[3]See Richard L. Johannesen, Kathleen S. Valde, and Karen E. Whedbee, *Ethics in Human Communication*, 6th ed. (Prospect Heights, IL: Waveland Press, 2008), for a full look at communication ethics.

[4]Adapted from Herbert W. Simons and Jean G. Jones, *Persuasion in Society*, 2nd ed. (New York: Routledge, 2011), p. 46.

[5]This view of the interaction between speaker and listener reflects cognitive processing models of persuasion and attitude change in general and the elaboration likelihood model in particular. For a concise explanation of the latter, see Em Griffin, Andrew Ledbetter, and Glenn Sparks, *A First Look at Communication Theory*, 9th ed. (New York: McGraw-Hill, 2015), pp. 188–199.

[6]There is a great deal of research confirming the need for persuasive speakers to answer potential objections to their arguments. See John A. Banas and Stephen A. Rains, "A Meta-Analysis of Research on Inoculation Theory," *Communication Monographs*, 77 (2010), pp. 282–311.

[7]For an insightful look at the research on courtroom persuasion, see John C. Reinard, "Persuasion in the Legal Setting," in Dillard and Shen, *SAGE Handbook of Persuasion*, pp. 331–353.

[8]Richard M. Perloff, *The Dynamics of Persuasion: Communication and Attitudes in the 21st Century*, 5th ed. (New York: Routledge, 2014), pp. 351–352.

[9]Daniel J. O'Keefe, *Persuasion: Theory and Research*, 2nd ed. (Thousand Oaks, CA: Sage, 2002), pp. 218–219.

[10]See, for example, Amber Marie Reinhart, Heather M. Marshall, Thomas Hugh Feeley, and Frank Tutzauer, "The Persuasive Effects of Message Framing in Organ Donation: The Mediating Role of Psychological Reactance," *Communication Monographs*, 74 (2007), pp. 229–255.

Chapter 17 Methods of Persuasion

[1]James C. McCroskey, *An Introduction to Rhetorical Communication*, 9th ed. (Boston, MA: Allyn and Bacon, 2006), pp. 84–96.

[2]Rachel A. Smith and Edward L. Fink, "Compliance Dynamics within a Simulated Friendship Network I: The Effects of Agency, Tactic, and Node Centrality," *Human Communication Research*, 36 (2010), pp. 232–260.

[3]Richard M. Perloff, *The Dynamics of Persuasion: Communication and Attitudes in the 21st Century*, 5th ed. (New York: Routledge, 2014), pp. 281–283.

[4]See John A. Banas and Stephen A. Rains, "A Meta-Analysis of Research on Inoculation Theory," *Communication Monographs*, 77 (2010), pp. 282–311.

[5]John C. Reinard, "The Empirical Study of the Persuasive Effects of Evidence: The Status after Fifty Years of Research," *Human Communication Research*, 15 (1988), pp. 37–38.

[6]See, for example, Michael T. Stephenson, "Examining Adolescents' Responses to Antimarijuana PSAs," *Human Communication Research*, 29 (2003), pp. 343–369.

[7]Rodney A. Reynolds and J. Lynn Reynolds, "Evidence," in James Price Dillard and Michael Pfau (eds.), *The Persuasion Handbook: Developments in Theory and Practice* (Thousand Oaks, CA: Sage, 2002), pp. 429–430.

[8]Daniel J. O'Keefe, *Persuasion: Theory and Research*, 2nd ed. (Thousand Oaks, CA: Sage, 2002), pp. 216–218.

[9]Adapted from James C. Humes, *A Speaker's Treasury of Anecdotes about the Famous* (New York: Harper and Row, 1978), p. 131.

[10]In classical systems of logic, reasoning from particular facts to a general conclusion was known as induction. Contemporary logicians, however, have redefined induction as any instance of reasoning in which the conclusion follows from its premises with probability, regardless of whether the reasoning moves from specific instances to a general conclusion or from a general premise to a specific conclusion. In this scheme, reasoning from specific instances is one kind of inductive argument—as are causal reasoning and analogical reasoning. See, for example, Nancy M. Cavender and Howard Kahane, *Logic and Contemporary Rhetoric: The Use of Reason in Everyday Life*, 12th ed. (Boston, MA: Wadsworth, 2014).

[11]Lionel Ruby, *The Art of Making Sense* (Philadelphia: Lippincott, 1954), p. 261.

[12]In classical systems of logic, reasoning from a general premise to a specific conclusion was known as deduction. But just as contemporary logicians have redefined induction (see note 10 above), they have redefined deduction as any instance of reasoning in which the conclusion follows from its premises with certainty. Some deductive arguments move from general premises to a specific conclusion, but others move from specific premises to a general conclusion. Many speech textbooks confuse reasoning from principle, which is one form of deduction, with deductive reasoning in general.

[13]For more on fallacies and argumentation in general, see Douglas Walton, *Methods of Argumentation* (New York: Cambridge University Press, 2013).

[14]H. E. Butler (trans.), *The Institutio Oratoria of Quintilian* (Cambridge, MA: Harvard University Press, 1961), IV, p. 141.

[15]George Campbell, *The Philosophy of Rhetoric*, ed. Lloyd F. Bitzer (Carbondale, IL: Southern Illinois University Press, 1988), p. 77.

[16]Research on fear appeals, for example, has demonstrated that messages devoted exclusively to arousing fear in the audience are usually less effective than messages that combine fear appeals with reasonable explanations of how to eliminate or cope with the source of fear. For an excellent review of that research, see Paul A. Mongeau, "Fear Appeals," in James Price Dillard and Lijiang Shen (eds.), *The SAGE Handbook of Persuasion: Developments in Theory and Practice*, 2nd ed. (Thousand Oaks, CA: Sage, 2013), pp. 184–199.

Chapter 18 Speaking on Special Occasions

[1]James C. Humes, *Roles Speakers Play* (New York: Harper and Row, 1976), p. 8.

[2]For both speeches, see "President Obama Welcomes the Teacher of the Year," April 24, 2012 (http://www.whitehouse.gov/blog/2012/04/24/president-obama-welcomes-teacher-year), May 13, 2014.

[3]Humes, *Roles Speakers Play,* pp. 33–34, 36.

Chapter 19 Speaking in Small Groups

[1]Gloria J. Galanes and Katherine Adams, *Effective Group Discussion: Theory and Practice,* 14th ed. (New York: McGraw-Hill, 2013), pp. 233–244.

[2]See Kyle R. Andrews, Franklin J. Boster, and Christopher J. Carpenter, "Persuading in the Small Group Context," in James Price Dillard and Lijiang Shen (eds.), *The SAGE Handbook of Persuasion: Developments in Theory and Practice,* 2nd ed. (Thousand Oaks, CA: Sage, 2013), pp. 354–370, for a review of scholarship on this subject.

[3]For more on the many dimensions of group leadership, see John W. Gastil, *The Group in Society* (Thousand Oaks, CA: Sage 2010), pp. 139–166.

[4]Consult Scott A. Myers and Carolyn Anderson, *Fundamentals of Small Group Communication* (Thousand Oaks, CA: Sage, 2008), pp. 199–215, for more detail on dealing with conflict in small groups.

[5]Charles Pavitt and Kelly K. Johnson, "Scheidel and Crowell Revisited: A Descriptive Study of Group Proposal Sequencing," *Communication Monographs,* 69 (2002), pp. 19–32.

[6]For research on this subject, see Michele H. Jackson and Marshall Scott Poole, "Idea-Generation in Naturally Occurring Contexts: Complex Appropriation of Simple Group Procedure," *Human Communication Research,* 29 (2003), pp. 560–591.

[7]For more on small-group oral presentations, see Katherine Adams and Gloria J. Galanes, *Communicating in Groups: Applications and Skills,* 9th ed. (New York: McGraw-Hill, 2015).

Photo Credits

About the Author

Courtesy of Dr. Stephen Lucas

Contents

Page v: © Shaw Thew/Corbis; p. vi: © Chris Jackson/Pool/Reuters/Corbis Images; p. vii: © Michael Buckner/WireImage/Getty Images; p. viii: © The McGraw-Hill Companies, Inc./Mannic Media, photographer; p. ix: © J. Countess/Getty Images; p. x: © Earl Mcgehee/WireImage/Getty Images; p. xi: © Emmanuel Dunand/AFP/Getty Images; p. xii: © Michael Tran/FilmMagic/Getty Images.

Design Elements

Page 17: © Image Source/Getty Images RF; 1.1(left): © Veer RF; 1.1(right): © Ryan McVay/Getty Images RF; p. 25(microphone): © Andreas Kermann/E+/Getty Images RF; p. 41: © Ingram Publishing RF; p. 63(woman with braid): © The McGraw-Hill Companies, Inc; p. 83: © UpperCut Images/Getty Images; p. 110: © Wavebreak-media LTD/Getty Images RF; p. 129: © Thinkstock/JupiterImages RF; p. 174: © Image Source/Corbis RF; p. 198: © Image Source/Corbis RF; p. 215(bottom): © Stockbyte/Getty Images RF; p. 231: © Dave and Les Jacobs/Blend Images LLC RF; p. 253: © Stockbyte/Getty Images RF; p. 265(female speaker): © Photodisc/Getty Images RF; p. 272: © The McGraw-Hill Companies, Inc./Andrew Resek, photographer; 14.6: © Nick Ledger/JAI/Corbis; p. 295: © Stockbyte/Getty Images RF; p. 323: © Corbis RF; p. 348: © Monty Rakusen/cultura/Corbis RF.

Chapter 1

Opener: © Shawn Thew/Corbis; p. 7: © Dave and Les Jacobs/Blend Images/Alamy RF; p. 11: © Eyad Al Baba/Anadolu Agency/Getty Images; p. 14: © Christopher Polk/Getty Images; p. 19: © Purestock/Getty Images RF; p. 23: © Sam Panthaky/AFP/Getty Images.

Chapter 2

Opener: © Gregorio Borgia/AP Images; p. 33: © Pier Marco Tacca/Getty Images; p. 35: © Jeff Malet Photography/Newscom; p. 39: © Hero Images/Getty Images RF; p. 43: © Alan Diaz/AP Images.

Chapter 3

Opener: © John Fedele/age fotostock RF; p. 51: © 68/Ocean/Corbis RF; p. 55: © Wavebreak Media ltd/Alamy RF; p. 59: © Toby Talbot/AP Images.

Chapter 4

Opener: © The McGraw-Hill Companies, Inc./Mannic Media, photographer; p. 65: © The McGraw-Hill Companies, Inc./Mannic Media, photographer; p. 68: © Mark M. Murray/The Republican/Landov.

Chapter 5

Opener: © Chris Jackson/Pool/Reuters/Corbis Images; p. 79: © ersler/iStock/360/Getty Images RF; p. 85: © David & Micha Sheldon/age fotostock; p. 91: © Fancy/Corbis/age fotostock RF.

Chapter 6

Opener: © Wendy Maeda/The Boston Globe/Getty Images; p. 101: © Michael Buckner/WireImage/Getty Images; p. 104: © Wolfgang Kumm/dpa/Corbis; p. 109: © Charlie Neibergall/AP Images; p. 115: © Janine Wiedel/Photolibrary/Alamy.

Chapter 7

Opener: © Fred de Noyelle/Godong/Corbis; p. 122: © Greg Hinsdale/Corbis RF; p. 125: © Tess Freeman/The Register Guard/AP Images; p. 131: © Tim Pannell/Corbis; p.137: © Noah Berger/Reuters/Corbis.

Chapter 8

Opener: © Win McNamee/Getty Images; p. 145: © Kevin Wolf/Volkswagen America/AP Images; p. 149: © Mario Cruz/epa/Corbis; p. 157: © The McGraw-Hill Companies, Inc.

Chapter 9

Opener: © Gordon Chibroski/Portland Press Herald/Getty Images; p. 169: © Linda Davidson/The Washington Post/Getty Images; p. 171: © sdbower/iStock 360/Getty Images RF; p. 173: © Chris Rout/Alamy Images; p. 180: © Jean-Christophe Bott /epa/Corbis.

Chapter 10

Opener: © J. Countess/Getty Images; p. 187: © Anthony Harvey/Getty Images; p. 191: © Hill Street

Studios/Blend Images/age fotostock RF; p. 193: © Joe Scarnici/J/P Haitian Relief Organization/Getty Images; p. 197: © Jessica Rinaldi/Reuters/Corbis.

Chapter 11

Opener: © Ellis Bronte/Kalium/age fotostock RF; p. 207: © Image Source/Getty Images RF; p. 215(top): © Eric Gay/AP Images.

Chapter 12

Opener: © Andy Rain/epa/Corbis; p. 223: © Pierre Andrieu/AFP/Getty Images; p. 227: © Ronald Foster Sharif /Demotix/Corbis; p. 229: © Goh Seng Chong/Bloomberg/Getty Images; p. 233: © John Coletti/JAI/Corbis.

Chapter 13

Opener: © Alfredo Estrella/AFP/Getty Images; p. 243: © Bill Clark/Getty Images; p. 245: © Xu Suhui/Xinhua Press/Corbis; p. 249: © The Augusta Chronicle/ZUMA Press/Corbis; p. 251: © Yan Sheng/CNImaging/Newscom; p. 255: © Art Widak/Demotix/Corbis; p. 257: © Dave and Les Jacobs/Alamy RF.

Chapter 14

Opener: © Earl Mcgehee/WireImage/Getty Images; p. 267: © Andrew Gunners/Photodisc/Getty Images RF; p. 271: © BSIP/UIG/Getty Images; p. 277: © Carlos Alvarez/Getty Images.

Chapter 15

Opener: © Emmanuel Dunand/AFP/Getty Images; p. 287: © Per-Andre Hoffmann/Getty Images; p. 291: © Bob Daemmrich/Corbis; p. 293: © Kevin Ma/Zuma/Newscom; p. 298: © Yuriko Nakao/Bloomberg/Getty Images.

Chapter 16

Opener: © Kevork Djansezian/Getty Images; p. 309: © Kevin Wolf/AP Images; p. 313: © Imaginechina/Corbis; p. 317: © Chip Somodevilla/Getty Images; p. 321: © David Paul Morris/Bloomberg/Getty Images.

Chapter 17

Opener: © Rich Pedroncelli/AP Images; p. 335: © Mohd Zakir/Hindustan Times/Getty Images; p. 339: © Seth Perlman/AP Images; p. 341: © Gary W. Green/Orlando Sentinel/AP Images; p. 345: © AmmentorpDK/iStock/360/Getty Images RF; p. 349: © Elaine Thompson/AP Images; p. 351: © Punit Paranjpe/AFP/Getty Images.

Chapter 18

Opener: © Scott Schild/The Post-Standard/Landov; p. 363: © Michael Tran/FilmMagic/Getty Images; p. 368: © Brendan Hoffman/Smithsonian Magazine/Getty Images.

Chapter 19

Opener: © Hero Images/Getty Images RF; p. 373: © Hero Images/Getty Images RF; p. 379: © Troy House/Corbis; p. 382: © John Fedele/Blend Images/Getty Images RF.

Appendix

Page A-1: © Adam Blasberg/Getty Images RF.

Online Supplements

McGraw Hill Education connect®

Connect Online Access for The Art of Public Speaking, 12th Edition

McGraw-Hill Connect is a digital teaching and learning environment that improves performance over a variety of critical outcomes. With Connect, instructors can deliver assignments, quizzes and tests easily online. Students can practice important skills at their own pace and on their own schedule.

HOW TO REGISTER

Using a Print Book?
To register and activate your Connect account, simply follow these easy steps:

1. **Go to the Connect course web address provided by your instructor or visit the Connect link set up on your instructor's course within your campus learning management system.**
2. **Click on the link to register.**
3. **When prompted, enter the Connect code found on the inside back cover of your book and click Submit. Complete the brief registration form that follows to begin using Connect.**

Using an eBook?
To register and activate your Connect account, simply follow these easy steps:

1. **Upon purchase of your eBook, you will be granted automatic access to Connect.**
2. **Go to the Connect course web address provided by your instructor or visit the Connect link set up on your instructor's course within your campus learning management system.**
3. **Sign in using the same email address and password you used to register on the eBookstore. Complete your registration and begin using Connect.**

**Note: Access Code is for one use only. If you did not purchase this book new, the access code included in this book is no longer valid.*

Need help? Visit mhhe.com/support

Digital Products

The following Digital Products, Access Code(s), and instructions are listed below.

Note: The Access Code can only be used once.

Access Code: JKFG-ME4Q-AT3R-ETGU-E8TD

Connect Online Access for The Art of Public Speaking, 12th Edition

Instructions:

Print Books:
1: Go to Connect section web address provided by your Instructor. Click "Register Now." 2: Follow instructions to either register a new account or sign-in. 3: Type in your access code which appears above.

eBooks: (The purchase of this eBook has licensed your account for the product above.)
1: Go to Connect section web address provided by your Instructor. Click "Register Now." 2: Follow instructions to sign-in using the same username and password you used to access the eBookstore site.

URL: http://www.mcgrawhillconnect.com/class/instructorname_section_name

McGraw Hill Education create™

ISBN-13: 978-1-308-50639-5
ISBN-10: 1-308-50639-2

9 781308 506395 90000

SCI 685188